"No one in the world has studied facial expressions as deeply as Paul Ekman. In *Emotions Revealed* he presents—clearly, vividly, and in the most accessible way—his fascinating observations about the overt or covert expressions of emotions we all encounter hundreds of times daily, but so often misunderstand or fail to see. There has not been a book on this subject of such range and insight since Darwin's famous *Expression of the Emotions* more than a century ago." —OLIVER SACKS, author of *Uncle Tungsten*

"*Emotions Revealed* showcases Paul Ekman's forty years of academic research and great common sense, providing a fascinating and enormously helpful picture of our emotional lives." —JOHN CLEESE

"Ever since Darwin, no one has contributed more to our understanding of how humans go about communicating emotions than Paul Ekman. In this masterful overview, he reviews how emotions are communicated, and the implications for topics ranging from mental health and interpersonal relationships to law enforcement and violence. A fascinating and important book." —ROBERT M. SAPOLSKY, professor, Stanford University, and author of *Why Zebras Don't Get Ulcers*

"Paul Ekman is the master of emotional expression, and this is a masterful account of his field. He even suggests how we can use findings about emotional expressions to guide and improve our lives." —JOSEPH LEDOUX, professor, New York University, and author of *Synaptic Self* and *The Emotional Brain*

"What a pleasure to have Paul Ekman, a pioneer of detailed facial analysis, help us to see what others feel." —FRANS DE WAAL, professor, Emory University, and author of *The Ape and the Sushi Master*

W9-AQV-279

ALSO BY PAUL EKMAN

Telling Lies

Face of Man

Why Kids Lie

Emotions
Revealed

Emotions
Revealed

RECOGNIZING FACES AND FEELINGS TO IMPROVE
COMMUNICATION AND EMOTIONAL LIFE

Paul Ekman

AN OWL BOOK

HENRY HOLT AND COMPANY . NEW YORK

Henry Holt and Company, LLC
Publishers since 1866
115 West 18th Street
New York, New York 10011

Henry Holt® is a registered trademark of Henry Holt and Company, LLC.

Library of Congress Cataloging-in-Publication Data
Ekman, Paul.
    Emotions revealed : recognizing faces and feelings to improve communication and
emotional life / Paul Ekman.—1st ed.
        p. cm.
    Includes index.
    ISBN 0-8050-7516-X (pbk.)
        1. Expression. 2. Emotions. 3. Interpersonal communication. I. Title.
BF591 .E35 2003
152.4—dc21   2002029036

Henry Holt books are available for special promotions and premiums.
For details contact: Director, Special Markets.

First Owl Books Edition 2004

Designed by Debbie Glasserman

Printed in the United States of America

10 9 8 7 6 5 4 3 2 1

To Bert Boothe, Steve Foote, Lynne Huffman, Steve Hyman, Marty Katz, Steve Koslow, Jack Maser, Molly Oliveri, Betty Pickett, Eli Rubinstein, Stan Schneider, Joy Schulterbrandt, Hussain Tuma, and Lou Wienckowski from the National Institute of Mental Health

and

Robert Semer and Leo Siegel

Contents

Acknowledgments xiii

Preface to the Paperback Edition xv

Introduction xvii

1. Emotions Across Cultures 1

2. When Do We Become Emotional? 17

3. Changing What We Become Emotional About 38

4. Behaving Emotionally 52

5. Sadness and Agony 82

6. Anger 110

7. Surprise and Fear 148

8. Disgust and Contempt 172

9. Enjoyable Emotions 190

CONCLUSION: Living with Emotion 213

AFTERWORD 219

APPENDIX: Reading Faces—The Test 225

NOTES 247

ILLUSTRATION CREDITS 263

INDEX 265

Acknowledgments

Some of the people at the National Institute of Mental Health to whom this book is dedicated took an interest in my career back when I was a beginning graduate student in 1955. The others joined in over the years. It has been an amazing span—1955 to 2002—of encouragement, advice, and, in the early years, considerable faith. I would not have become a research psychologist, a university professor, and would not have learned what I write about without their help. The writing of this book was supported by Senior Scientist Award K05MH06092.

I also dedicate this book to my two maternal uncles, Leo Siegel and the late Robert Semer. When I was eighteen, untried, and for the first time on my own in the world, they enabled me to continue my education. Sine qua non.

Wally Friesen and I worked together for twenty-five years. Nearly all of the research that I write about we did together. I am grateful for his help and friendship. David Littschwager provided very useful advise on the photographic setup I used for the pictures of Eve that appear in chapters 5 through 9. My daughter Eve had the patience and the talent to make the faces that appear in this book and the thousands more that I shot. Wanda Matsubayashi, who has been my assistant for more than twenty-five years, organized the text and the references. David Rogers did the Photoshop image manipulations and was of great help in getting the permissions for the commercial photographs.

Psychologists Richard Lazarus and Philip Shaver gave me helpful feedback on an early draft of the first half of this book. Phil also provided detailed, insightful line editing and useful challenges to my thinking. Philosopher Helena Cronin encouraged and challenged much of my thinking. Psychiatrist Bob Rynearson and psychologists Nancy Etcoff and Beryl Schiff gave me useful suggestions on an early draft. Among the many students who gave me feedback, Jenny Beers and Gretchen Lovas were especially generous with their time. My friends Bill Williams and Paul Kaufman gave me useful suggestions and criticisms.

Toby Mundy, now publisher of Atlantic Press London, in an earlier incarnation encouraged me to broaden the scope of my endeavor and tackle the issues I consider in chapters 2 through 4. Claudia Sorsby provided criticism, suggestion, and editorial help in an earlier draft, and my editor at Times Books, Robin Dennis, was very helpful in pushing me to consider issues I sometimes neglected and contributed some fine line editing. My agent Robert Lescher has been a wonderful source of encouragement and advice.

Preface
to the Paperback
Edition

I am particularly delighted that this paperback edition of *Emotions Revealed* affords me the opportunity to share new ideas, insights, and research findings that can help readers lead a better emotional life. In the nearly two years since I finished the original manuscript, and the year since it appeared in the hardback edition, I have received letters from psychotherapists, criminal investigators, portrait artists, lawyers, parents with disturbed children, couples with problems in their marriage, people in business, and others. I share some of the thoughts their letters have inspired here in the preface, to provide an overall guide to what you will learn in the book, and expand a bit on them in a new afterword.

My goal in writing *Emotions Revealed* was to help people improve four essential skills, and thus I have included suggestions and exercises in the book that I hope you will find both helpful and provocative. Those four skills are:

First, becoming more consciously aware of when you are becoming emotional, even before you speak or act. This is the hardest skill to acquire; the book explains why this is so difficult in chapter 2, and provides exercises to help you increase awareness of your emotions in chapter 3 and in sections of chapters 5 through 8, which deal with specific emotions. Developing this skill allows you to have some choice about when you are emotional.

Second, choosing how you behave when you are emotional, so you achieve your goals without damaging other people. The purpose of emotional episodes is to help us quickly achieve our objectives, whether to draw people to comfort us, scare off a perpetrator, or some other of thousands of goals. The best emotional episodes do no harm to and cause no problems for those with whom we are engaged. This is not an easy skill to develop, but with practice it can become part of your life. (The information and exercises on this topic are discussed in chapters 4 through 8.)

Third, becoming more sensitive to how others are feeling. Since emotions are at the core of every important relationship we have, we must be sensitive to how others are feeling. If you would like to go beyond what you read and learn in the book, two new CDs that can help you develop this skill rapidly are now available at my Web site, www.emotionsrevealed.com.

Fourth, carefully using the information you acquire about how others are feeling. Sometimes that means asking the person about the emotion you have spotted, acknowledging how he or she is feeling, or re-calibrating your own reactions in light of what you have recognized. Your response will depend on who the other person is and the history of your relationship with that person. How this varies within a family, in the workplace, and in friendship is explained in the last sections of chapters 5 through 8.

At the end of this edition of *Emotions Revealed*, you will find a new afterword that provides my newest ideas about developing some of these skills.

Introduction

Emotions determine the quality of our lives. They occur in every relationship we care about—in the workplace, in our friendships, in dealings with family members, and in our most intimate relationships. They can save our lives, but they can also cause real damage. They may lead us to act in ways that we think are realistic and appropriate, but our emotions can also lead us to act in ways we regret terribly afterward.

If your boss were to criticize the report you thought she would praise, would you react with fear and become submissive rather than defend your work? Would that protect you from further harm, or might you have misunderstood what she was up to? Could you hide what you were feeling and "act professional"? Why would your boss smile when she started to talk? Could she be relishing the prospect of chewing you out, or could that be the smile of embarrassment? Could her smile have been meant to reassure you? Are all smiles the same?

If you were to confront your spouse with the discovery of a big purchase that he had not discussed with you, would you know if it was fear or disgust he showed, or if he was pulling the face he shows when he is waiting out what he calls "your overly emotional behavior"? Do you feel emotions the same way he does, the same way other people do? Do you get angry or afraid or sad about matters that don't seem to bother others, and is there anything you can do about that?

Would you get angry if you were to hear your sixteen-year-old daughter coming home two hours after her curfew? What would trigger the anger: Would it be the fear you felt each time you checked the clock and realized that she hadn't called to say she would be late, or the sleep you lost waiting for her to come home? The next morning when you talked to her about it, would you control your anger so well that she would think you really didn't care about the curfew, or would she see your stifled anger and become defensive? Could you know from the look on her face if she was embarrassed, guilty, or a bit defiant?

I have written this book to provide answers to such questions. My goal is to help readers better understand and improve their emotional life. It still amazes me that up until very recently we—both scientists and laymen—knew so little about emotion, given its importance in our lives. But it is in the nature of emotion itself that we would not fully know how emotions influence us and how to recognize their signs in ourselves and others, all matters I explain in this book.

Emotions can, and often do, begin very quickly, so quickly, in fact, that our conscious self does not participate in or even witness what in our mind triggers an emotion at any particular moment. That speed can save our lives in an emergency, but it can also ruin our lives when we overreact. We don't have much control over what we become emotional about, but it is possible, though not easy, to make some changes in what triggers our emotions and how we behave when we are emotional.

I have been studying emotion for more than forty years, focusing primarily on the expression and more recently on the physiology of emotion. I have examined psychiatric patients, normal individuals, adults, and some children, in this country and many other countries, when they overreact, underreact, react inappropriately, lie, and tell the truth. Chapter 1, "Emotions Across Cultures," describes this research, the platform from which I speak.

In chapter 2, I ask the question: Why do we become emotional when we do? If we are to change what we become emotional about, we must know the answer to that question. What triggers each of our emotions? Can we remove a particular trigger? If our spouse tells us we are taking the long route to get to our destination, annoyance or even anger may boil up within us at being directed and having our driving acumen criticized. Why couldn't we accept the information without getting emotional? Why does it get to us? Can we change so that such minor matters don't make us emotional? These issues are discussed in chapter 2, "When Do We Become Emotional?"

In chapter 3 I explain how and when we can change what we become emotional about. The first step is to identify the hot emotional triggers that lead us to act in ways we subsequently regret. We also need to be able to identify whether a particular trigger is going to resist change or be more easily weakened. We won't always succeed, but we can, through understanding how emotional triggers become established, have a better chance of changing what we become emotional about.

In chapter 4, I explain how our emotional responses—our expressions, actions, and thoughts—are organized. Can we manage irritation so it doesn't appear in our voice or show on our face? Why does it sometimes feel as though our emotions are a runaway train, and as though we have no control over them? We don't have a chance unless we can become more aware of when we are acting emotionally; very often we are not aware until someone objects to what we have done, or until we reflect later. Chapter 4 explains how we can become more attentive to our emotions as we have them so there is a possibility of behaving emotionally in constructive ways.

To reduce destructive emotional episodes and enhance constructive emotional episodes, we need to know the story of each emotion, what each emotion is about. By learning the triggers for each emotion, the ones we share with others and those that are uniquely our own, we may be able to lessen their impact, or at least learn why some of the emotion triggers are so powerful that they resist any attempt to lessen their control over our lives. Each emotion also generates a unique pattern of sensations in our body. By becoming better acquainted with those sensations, we may become aware early enough in our emotional response that we have some chance to choose, if we like, whether to go along or interfere with the emotion.

Each emotion also has unique signals, the most identifiable being in the face and the voice. There's still much research to do on the vocal emotional signals, but the photographs provided in the chapters on each emotion show the most subtle, easy-to-miss facial expressions that signal when an emotion is just beginning or when it is being suppressed. With the ability to identify emotions early on, we may be better able to deal with people in a variety of situations and to manage our own emotional responses to their feelings.

Separate chapters describe sadness and anguish (chapter 5), anger (chapter 6), surprise and fear (chapter 7), disgust and contempt (chapter 8), and the many kinds of enjoyment (chapter 9), with sections covering:

- the most common specific triggers for the emotion
- the function of the emotion, how it serves us, and how it can get us into trouble
- how the emotion is involved in mental disorders
- exercises that will improve the reader's awareness of the bodily sensations involved in the emotion, increasing the possibility that readers will be able to choose how they act when they are emotional
- photographs of the subtlest sign of the emotion in others, so readers will be more aware of how others are feeling
- an explanation of how to use this information about how others are feeling in your relationships in the workplace, in your family, and in friendships

The appendix provides a test you can take before reading the book to find out how well you are able to recognize subtle facial expressions. You might want to take that test again when you finish the book to see if you have improved.

You might wonder why one of the emotions you are curious about doesn't appear in this book. I have chosen to describe the emotions we know are universal, experienced by all human beings. Embarrassment, guilt, shame, and envy are probably universal, but I have focused instead on the emotions that have clear universal expressions. I discuss love in the chapter on enjoyable emotions; violence, hate, and jealousy in the chapter on anger.

Science is still delving into the ways each of us experiences the emotions—why some of us have more intense emotional experiences, or tend to become emotional quickly—and I conclude the book with what we are learning, what we might learn, and how you can use this information in your own life.

It is hard to overestimate the importance of emotions in our lives. My mentor, the late Silvan Tomkins, said emotions are what motivate our lives. We organize our lives to maximize the experience of positive emotions and minimize the experience of negative emotions. We do not always succeed, but that is what we try to do. He claimed that emotion motivates all the important choices we make. Writing in 1962, a time when emotions were completely neglected in the behavioral sciences, Silvan overstated the matter, for surely there can be other motives. But emotions are important, very important in our lives.

Emotions can override what most psychologists have rather simplemindedly considered the more powerful fundamental motives that drive our lives: hunger, sex, and the will to survive. People will not eat if they think the only food available is disgusting. They may even die, although other people might consider that same food palatable. Emotion triumphs over the hunger drive! The sex drive is notoriously vulnerable to the interference of emotions. A person may never attempt sexual contact because of the interference of fear or disgust, or may never be able to complete a sexual act. Emotion triumphs over the sex drive! And despair can overwhelm even the will to live, motivating a suicide. Emotions triumph over the will to live!

Put simply, people want to be happy, and most of us don't want to experience fear, anger, disgust, sadness, or anguish unless it is in the safe confines of a theater or between the covers of a novel. Yet, as I will explain later, we couldn't live without those emotions; the issue is how to live better with them.

Emotions
Revealed

1 Emotions Across Cultures

I have included in this book all that I have learned about emotion during the past forty years that I believe can be helpful in improving one's own emotional life. Most of what I have written is supported by my own scientific experiments or the research of other emotion scientists, but not everything. My own research specialty was to develop expertise in reading and measuring facial expressions of emotions. So equipped, I have been able to see—on the faces of strangers, friends, and family members—subtleties that nearly everyone else misses, and by that means I have learned a great deal more than I have yet had the time to prove through experiments. When what I write is based just on my observations, I note that by phrases such as "I have observed," "I believe," "it seems to me. . . ." And when I write based on scientific experiments I cite in endnotes the specific research supporting what I say.

Much of what I have written in this book was influenced by my cross-cultural studies of facial expression. The evidence changed forever my view of psychology in general and of emotion in particular. Those findings, in places as varied as Papua New Guinea, the United States, Japan, Brazil, Argentina, Indonesia, and the former Soviet Union, led me to develop my ideas about the nature of emotion.

At the start of my research in the late 1950s, I wasn't even interested in facial expression. It was the movements of the hands that drew my interest. My method of classifying hand movements distinguished neurotic from psychotically depressed patients, and indicated how much the patients improved from treatment.[1] In the early 1960s there wasn't even a tool for directly and precisely measuring the complex, often rapidly changing facial movements shown by the depressed patients. I had no idea where to begin, and so I didn't. Twenty-five years later, after I had developed a tool for measuring facial movement, I returned to those patient films and unearthed important findings, which I describe in chapter 5.

I don't think I would have shifted my research focus to facial expression and emotion in 1965 if it hadn't been for two strokes of luck. Through serendipity the Advanced Research Projects Agency (ARPA) of the Department of Defense gave me a grant to do cross-cultural studies of nonverbal behavior. I had not sought the grant, but because of a scandal—a research project being used to camouflage counter-insurgency activity—a major ARPA project was canceled and the money budgeted for it had to be spent during that fiscal year on overseas research, and on something noncontroversial. By accident I happened to walk into the office of the man who had to spend the funds. He was married to a woman from Thailand and was impressed by differences in their nonverbal communication. He wanted me to find out what was universal and what was culturally variable. I was reluctant at first, but I couldn't walk away from the challenge.

I began the project believing that expression and gesture were socially learned and culturally variable, and so did the initial group of people I asked for advice—Margaret Mead, Gregory Bateson, Edward Hall, Ray Birdwhistell, and Charles Osgood. I recalled that Charles Darwin had made the opposite claim, but I was so convinced that he was wrong that I didn't bother to read his book.

The second stroke of luck was meeting Silvan Tomkins. He had just written two books about emotion in which he claimed that facial expressions were innate and universal to our species, but he had no evidence to back up his claims. I don't think I would ever have read his books or met him if we hadn't both submitted articles on nonverbal behavior to the same journal at the same time—Silvan's a study of the face, mine a study of body movement.[2]

I was very impressed with the depth and breadth of Silvan's thinking, but I thought he was probably wrong in his belief, like

Darwin's, that expressions were innate and therefore universal. I was delighted that there were two sides to the argument, that it wasn't just Darwin, who had written a hundred years earlier, who opposed Mead, Bateson, Birdwhistell, and Hall. It wasn't a dead issue. There was a real argument between famous scientists, elder statesmen; and I, at the age of thirty, had the chance, and the funding, to try to settle it once and for all: Are expressions universal, or are they, like language, specific to each culture? Irresistible! I really didn't care who proved to be correct, although I didn't think it would be Silvan.*

In my first study I showed photographs to people in five cultures—Chile, Argentina, Brazil, Japan, and the United States—and asked them to judge what emotion was shown in each facial expression. The majority in every culture agreed, suggesting that expressions might really be universal.[3] Carrol Izard, another psychologist who had been advised by Silvan, and was working in other cultures, did nearly the same experiment and got the same results.[4] Tomkins had not told either of us about the other, something that we initially resented when we found out we were not doing this work alone, but it was better for science that two independent researchers found the same thing. It seemed that Darwin was right.

There was a problem: How could we have found that people from many different cultures agreed about what emotion was shown in an expression when so many smart people thought just the opposite? It wasn't just the travelers who claimed that the expressions of the Japanese or the Chinese or some other cultural group had very different meanings. Birdwhistell, a respected anthropologist who specialized in the study of expression and gesture (a protégé of Margaret Mead), had written that he abandoned Darwin's ideas when he found that in many cultures people smiled when they were unhappy.[5] Birdwhistell's claim fit the view that dominated cultural anthropology and most of

*I found just the opposite of what I thought I would discover. That's ideal. Behavioral science findings are more credible when they counter rather than confirm the scientist's expectations. In most fields of science it is just the opposite; findings are more trusted if they were predicted ahead of time. That is because the possibility of bias or error is checked by the tradition of scientists repeating one another's experiments to see if they will get the same results. Unfortunately, that tradition doesn't exist in the behavioral sciences. Experiments are rarely repeated, either by the scientist who originally did the work or by others. Without that safeguard, behavioral scientists are more vulnerable to finding unwittingly only what they want to find.

psychology—anything socially important, such as emotional expressions, must be the product of learning, and therefore different in each culture.

I reconciled our findings that expressions are universal with Birdwhistell's observation of how they differ from one culture to another by coming up with the idea of *display rules*. These, I proposed, are socially learned, often culturally different, rules about the management of expression, about who can show which emotion to whom and when they can do so. It is why in most public sporting contests the loser doesn't show the sadness and disappointment he or she feels. Display rules are embodied in the parent's admonition—"Get that smirk off your face." These rules may dictate that we diminish, exaggerate, hide completely, or mask the expression of emotion we are feeling.[6]

I tested this formulation in a series of studies that showed that when *alone* Japanese and Americans displayed the same facial expressions in response to seeing films of surgery and accidents, but when a scientist sat with them as they watched the films, the Japanese more than the Americans masked negative expressions with a smile. In private, innate expressions; in public, managed expressions.[7] Since it is the public behavior that anthropologists and most travelers observe, I had my explanation and evidence of its operation. In contrast, symbolic gestures—such as the head nod yes, the head shake no, and the A-OK gesture—are indeed culture-specific.[8] Here Birdwhistell, Mead, and most other behavioral scientists were right, though they were wrong about the facial expressions of emotion.

There was a loophole, and if I could see it, so might Birdwhistell and Mead, who I knew would search for any way to dismiss my findings. All the people I (and Izard) had studied might have learned the meaning of Western facial expressions by watching Charlie Chaplin and John Wayne on the movie screen and television tube. Learning from the media or having contact with people from other cultures could explain why people from different cultures had agreed about the emotions shown in my photographs of Caucasians. I needed a visually isolated culture where the people had seen no movies, no television, no magazines, and few, if any, outsiders. If they thought the same emotions were shown in my set of facial expression photographs as the people in Chile, Argentina, Brazil, Japan, and the United States, I would have it nailed.

My entry to a Stone Age culture was Carleton Gajdusek, a neurologist who had been working for more than a decade in such isolated places in the highlands of Papua New Guinea. He was trying to find the cause of a strange disease, kuru, which was killing about half the people in one of these cultures. The people believed it was due to sorcery. When I arrived on the scene, Gajdusek already knew that it was due to a slow virus, a virus that incubates for many years before any symptoms become apparent (AIDS is such a virus). He didn't yet know how it was transmitted. (It turned out to be cannibalism. These people didn't eat their enemies, who would be more likely to be in good health if they died in combat. They ate only their friends who died of some kind of disease, many of them from kuru. They didn't cook them before eating, so diseases were readily passed on. Gajdusek some years later won the Nobel Prize for the discovery of slow viruses.)

Fortunately, Gajdusek had realized that Stone Age cultures would soon disappear, so he took more than one hundred thousand feet of motion picture films of the daily lives of the people in each of two cultures. He had never looked at the films; it would have taken nearly six weeks to look just once at his films of these people. That's when I came along.

Delighted that someone had a scientific reason for wanting to examine his films, he lent me copies, and my colleague Wally Friesen and I spent six months carefully examining them. The films contained two very convincing proofs of the universality of facial expressions of emotion. First, we never saw an unfamiliar expression. If facial expressions are completely learned, then these isolated people should have shown novel expressions, ones we had never seen before. There were none.

It was still possible that these familiar expressions might be signals of very different emotions. But while the films didn't always reveal what happened before or after an expression, when they did, they confirmed our interpretations. If expressions signal different emotions in each culture, then total outsiders, with no familiarity with the culture, should not have been able to interpret the expressions correctly.

I tried to think how Birdwhistell and Mead would dispute this claim. I imagined they would say, "It doesn't matter that there aren't any new expressions; the ones you did see really had different meanings. You got them right because you were tipped off by the social context in which they occurred. You never saw an expression removed from what was happening before, afterward, or at the same time. If you had, you wouldn't have known what the expressions meant." To close this loophole, we brought Silvan from the East Coast to spend a week at my lab.

Before he came we edited the films so he would see only the expression itself, removed from its social context, just close-up shots of a face. Silvan had no trouble at all. Every one of his interpretations fit the social context he hadn't seen. What's more, he knew exactly how he got the information. Wally and I could sense what emotional message was conveyed by each expression, but our judgments were intuitively based; we usually could not specify exactly what in the face carried the message unless it was a smile. Silvan walked up to the movie screen and pointed out exactly which specific muscular movements signaled the emotion.

We also asked him for his overall impression of these two cultures. One group he said seemed quite friendly. The other was explosive in their anger, highly suspicious if not paranoid in character, and homosexual. It was the Anga that he was describing. His account fit what we had been told by Gajdusek, who had worked with them. They had repeatedly attacked Australian officials who tried to maintain a government station there. They were known by their neighbors for their fierce suspiciousness. And the men led homosexual lives until the time of marriage. A few years later the ethologist Irenäus Eibl-Eibesfeldt literally had to run for his life when he attempted to work with them.

After that meeting I decided to devote myself to the study of facial expression. I would go to New Guinea and try to get evidence to support what I then knew to be true—that at least some facial expressions of emotion are universal. And I would work to develop an objective way to measure facial behavior so that any scientist could objectively derive from facial movement what Silvan could see so keenly.

Late in 1967 I went to the South East Highlands to do research on the Fore people, who lived in small scattered villages at an elevation of seven thousand feet. I did not know the Fore language, but with the help of a few boys who had learned Pidgin from a missionary school, I could go from English to Pidgin to Fore and back again. I brought with me pictures of facial expressions, mostly the pictures I had been given by Silvan for my studies of literate cultures. (Below on page 9 are three examples.) I also brought photographs of some Fore people I had selected from the motion picture film, thinking they might have trouble interpreting the expressions shown by Caucasians. I even worried that they might not be able to understand photographs at all, never having seen any before. Some anthropologists had earlier claimed that people who hadn't seen photographs had to learn how to interpret them. The Fore had no such problem, though; they immediately understood the photographs, and it didn't seem to make much of a difference what nationality the person was, Fore or American. The problem was what I asked them to do.

They had no written language, so I couldn't ask them to pick a word from a list that fit the emotion shown. If I were to read them a list of emotion words, I would have to worry about whether they remembered the list, and whether the order in which the words were read influenced their choice. Instead I asked them to make up a story about each facial expression. "Tell me what is happening now, what happened before to make this person show this expression, and what is going to happen next." It was like pulling teeth. I am not certain whether it was the translation process, or the fact that they had no idea what it was I wanted to hear or why I wanted them to do this. Perhaps making up stories about strangers was just something the Fore didn't do.

I did get my stories, but it took each person a lot of time to give me each story. They and I were exhausted after each session. Nevertheless, I had no shortage of volunteers, even though I suspect the word was out that what I was asking wasn't easy to do. There was a powerful incentive to look at my photographs: I gave each person either a bar of soap or a pack of cigarettes for helping me. They had no soap, so it was highly valued. They grew their own tobacco, which they smoked in pipes, but they seemed to like my cigarettes better.

Most of their stories fit the emotion each photograph supposedly depicted. For example, when looking at a picture depicting what people in literate cultures judged as sadness, the New Guineans most often said that the person's child had died. But the storytelling procedure was awkward, and proving that the different stories fit a particular emotion would not be an easy task. I knew I had to do it differently, but I didn't know how.

I also filmed spontaneous expressions and was able to catch the look of joy when people from another nearby village met their friends. I arranged situations to provoke emotions. I recorded two men playing their musical instruments, and then I filmed their surprise and delight when for the first time they heard their voices and music come out of a tape recorder. I even stabbed a boy with a rubber knife I had brought with me, as my movie camera recorded his response and the reactions of his friends. They thought it was a good joke. (I had the good sense not to try this trick with one of the men.) Such film clips could not serve as my evidence, for those committed to the view that expressions differ in each culture could always argue I had selected only those few occasions when universal expressions were shown.

I left New Guinea after a few months—not a hard decision because I was hungry for conversation, something I couldn't have with any of these people, and for food, since I had made the mistake of thinking I would enjoy eating the local cuisine. Yams and something resembling the part of the asparagus we discard grew pretty tiresome. It was an adventure, the most exciting one of my life, but I was still worried that I had not been able to get definitive evidence. I knew this culture would not stay isolated much longer, and there were not many others like it still left in the world.

Back home I came across a technique that psychologist John Dashiel had used in the 1930s to study how well young children could interpret facial expressions. They were too young to read, so he couldn't give them a list of words from which to choose. Instead of asking them to make up a story—as I had done in New Guinea—Dashiel cleverly read them a story and showed them a set of pictures. All they had to do was pick the one that fit the story. I knew that would work for me. I went over the stories the New Guineans had made up, picking the story that had been given most often for each type of emotional expression. They were pretty simple: "His/her friends have come and s/he is happy; s/he is angry and about to fight; his/her child has died and s/he feels very sad; s/he is looking at something s/he dislikes, or s/he is looking at something that smells bad; he/she is just now looking at something new and unexpected."

There was a problem with the most frequent story for fear, about the danger posed by a wild pig. I had to change it to reduce the chance that it would be relevant to surprise or anger. It went like this: "S/he is sitting in her/his house all alone, and there is no one else in the village. There is no knife, axe, or bow and arrow in the house. A wild pig is standing in the door of the house, and the man (woman) is looking at the pig and is very afraid of it. The pig has been standing in the doorway for a few minutes and the person is looking at it very afraid, and the pig won't move away from the door and s/he is afraid the pig will bite him/her."

I made up sets of three pictures, which would be shown while one of the stories was read (an example appears below). The subject would only have to point to the picture. I made up many sets of pictures, I didn't want any picture to appear more than once, so the person's choice wouldn't be made by exclusion: "Oh, that was the one where the child died, and that was the one where I said she was about to fight, so this one must be the one about the pig."

I returned to New Guinea late in 1968 with my stories and pictures and a team of colleagues to help gather the data.[9] (This time I also brought canned food.) Our return was heralded, I suppose, because apart from Gajdusek and his filmmaker, Richard Sorenson (who was of great help to me in the prior year), very few outsiders ever visited, and even fewer returned. We did travel to some villages, but once the word got out that what we were asking was very easy to do, people from villages far away started coming to us. They liked the task and were again delighted with the soap and cigarettes.

I took special care to ensure that no one in our group would unwittingly tip off the subjects as to which picture was the correct one. The sets of pictures were mounted onto transparent pages, with a code number written on the back of each picture that could be seen from the backside of the page. We did not know, and made a point of not finding out, which codes went with each expression. Instead a page would be turned toward the subject, arranged so that the person writing down the answers would not be able to see the front of the page. The story would be read, the subject would point to the picture, and one of us would write down the code number for the picture the subject had chosen.*

In the space of just a few weeks we saw more than three hundred people, about 3 percent of this culture, and more than enough to analyze statistically. The results were very clear-cut for happiness, anger, disgust, and sadness. Fear and surprise were not distinguished from each other—when people heard the fear story, they just as often picked a surprise as a fear expression, and the same was true when they heard the surprise story. But fear and surprise were distinguished from anger, disgust, sadness, and happiness. To this day I do not know why fear and surprise were not distinguished from each other. It could have been a problem with the stories, or it could have been that these two emotions are so often intermingled in these people's lives that they aren't distinguished. In literate cultures fear and surprise are distinguished from each other.[10]

All except twenty-three of our subjects had seen no movies, television, or photographs; they neither spoke nor understood English

---

*Despite the care we took, one of those committed to the view that expressions are learned and not innate was to claim fifteen years later that we might have in some way tipped off our subjects about which picture to choose. He didn't know how, he just thought we must have, for he could not give up his commitment to the belief that expressions are culture-specific.

or Pidgin, had not lived in any Western settlement or government town, and had never worked for a Caucasian. The twenty-three exceptions had all seen movies, spoke English, and had attended a missionary school for more than a year. There were no differences between the majority of the subjects who had little contact with the outside world and the few who had, nor were there any differences between males and females.

We did one more experiment, which was not as easy for our subjects. One of the Pidgin speakers read them one of the stories and asked them to show what their face would look like if they were the person in the story. I videotaped nine men doing this, none of whom had participated in the first study. The unedited videotapes were shown to college students in America. If the expressions were culture-specific, then these college students would not be able to interpret correctly the expressions. But the Americans correctly identified the emotion except for the fear and surprise poses, where they were equally likely to call the pose fear or surprise, just like the New Guineans. Here are four examples of the New Guineans' poses of emotion.

ENJOYMENT   SADNESS

ANGER   DISGUST

I announced our findings at the annual anthropology national conference in 1969. Many were unhappy with what we had found. They were firmly convinced that human behavior is all nurture and no nature; expressions must be different in each culture, despite my evidence. The fact that I had actually found cultural differences in the *management* of facial expressions in my Japanese American study was not good enough.

The best way to dispel their doubts would be to repeat the entire study in another preliterate, isolated culture. Ideally, someone else should do it, preferably someone who wanted to prove me wrong. If such a person found what I found, that would enormously strengthen our case. Because of another stroke of luck, the anthropologist Karl Heider did just that.

Heider had recently come back from spending a few years studying the Dani, another isolated group in what is now called West Irian, part of Indonesia.[11] Heider told me there must be something wrong with my research because the Dani didn't even have words for emotions. I offered to give him all of my research materials and teach him how to run the experiment the next time he went back to the Dani. His results perfectly replicated my findings, even down to the failure to distinguish between fear and surprise.[12]

Nevertheless, not all anthropologists are convinced, even today. And there are a few psychologists, primarily those concerned with language, who complain that our work in literate cultures, where we asked people to identify the emotion word that fit the expressions, does not support universals since the words for each emotion don't have perfect translations. How emotions are represented in language is, of course, the product of culture rather than evolution. But in studies of now more than twenty literate Western and Eastern cultures, the judgment made by the majority in each culture about what emotion is shown in an expression is the same. Despite the translation problems, there has never been an instance in which the majority in two cultures ascribes a different emotion to the same expression. Never. And, of course, our findings are not limited to studies in which people had to label a photograph with a single word. In New Guinea we used stories about an emotional event. We also had them pose emotions. And in Japan we actually measured facial behavior itself, showing that when people were alone the same facial muscles moved when viewing an unpleasant film whether the person was Japanese or American.

Another critic disparaged our research in New Guinea because we used stories describing a social situation instead of single words.[13] This critic presumed that emotions are words, which, of course, they are not. Words are representations of emotions, not the emotions themselves. Emotion is a process, a particular kind of automatic appraisal influenced by our evolutionary and personal past, in which we sense that something important to our welfare is occurring, and a set of physiological changes and emotional behaviors begins to deal with the situation. Words are one way to deal with our emotions, and we do use words when emotional, but we cannot reduce emotion to words.

No one knows exactly what message we get automatically when we see someone's facial expression. I suspect that words like anger or fear are not the usual messages conveyed when we are in the situation. We use those words when we talk about emotions. More often the message we get is much like what we had in our stories, not an abstract word but some sense of what that person is going to do next or what made the person feel the emotion.

Another quite different type of evidence also supports Darwin's claim that facial expressions are universal, a product of our evolution. If expressions do not need to be learned, then those who are born congenitally blind should manifest similar expressions to those of sighted individuals. A number of studies have been done over the past sixty years, and repeatedly that is what has been found, especially for spontaneous facial expressions.[14]

Our cross-cultural findings provided the impetus to seek answers to a host of other questions about facial expressions: How many expressions can people make? Do expressions provide accurate or misleading information? Is every movement of the face a sign of an emotion? Can people lie with their faces as well as with their words? There was so much to do, so much to find out. Now there are answers to all of these questions, and more.

I discovered how many expressions a face can make—more than ten thousand!—and identified the ones that appear to be most central to the emotions. More than twenty years ago Wally Friesen and I wrote the first atlas of the face, a systematic description in words, photographs, and films of how to measure facial movement in anatomical terms. As part of this work I had to learn how to make every muscle movement on my own face. Sometimes, to verify that the movement I was making was due to a specific muscle, I put a needle through the skin of my face to electrically stimulate and contract the muscle producing an expression. In 1978 our tool for measuring the face—the Facial Action Coding System (FACS)—was published and is now being used by hundreds of scientists around the world to measure facial movements, and computer scientists are busily working on how to make this measurement automatic and speedy.[15]

I have since used the Facial Action Coding System to study thousands of photographs and tens of thousands of filmed or videotaped facial expressions, measuring each muscular movement in each expression. I have learned about emotion by measuring the expressions of psychiatric patients and the expressions of patients with coronary heart disease. I have studied normal people, when they appear on news shows such as CNN and in experiments in my laboratory in which I provoked emotions.

In the last twenty years I collaborated with other investigators to learn what is happening inside the body and in the brain when an emotional expression occurs on the face. Just as there are different expressions for anger, fear, disgust, and sadness, there appear to be different profiles of physiological changes in the bodily organs that generate unique feelings for each emotion. Science is just now determining the patterns of brain activity that underlie each emotion.[16]

Using the Facial Action Coding System we have identified the facial signs that betray a lie. What I have termed *micro expressions*, very fast facial movements lasting less than one-fifth of a second, are one important source of *leakage*, revealing an emotion a person is trying to conceal. A false expression can be betrayed in a number of ways: it is usually very slightly asymmetrical, and it lacks smoothness in the way it flows on and off the face. My work on lying has brought me into contact with judges, police, lawyers, the FBI, CIA, ATF, and similar agencies in some friendly countries. I have taught all these people how to determine more accurately whether someone is truthful or lying. This work has also given me the chance to study the facial expressions and emotions of spies, assassins, embezzlers, murderers, foreign national leaders, and others whom a professor would not ordinarily encounter.[17]

When I was more than halfway through writing this book, I had the opportunity to spend five days discussing destructive emotions with His Holiness, the Dalai Lama. There were six other participants—scientists and philosophers—who presented their ideas and joined in the discussion.[18] Learning about their work and listening to the discussions provided me with new ideas that I have incorporated into this book. For the first time I learned about the Tibetan Buddhist view of emotion, a very different perspective from that which we hold in the West. I was amazed to find that the ideas I had been writing about in chapters 2 and 3 were compatible with the Buddhist view, in part, and the Buddhist view suggested extensions and refinements of my ideas that led me to rewrite these chapters extensively. Most of all, I learned from His Holiness, the Dalai Lama, on many different levels, from the experiential to the intellectual, and I believe the book has benefited from my learning.[19] This is not a book about a Buddhist view of emotion, but I do occasionally mention points of overlap, and times when that meeting sparked particular insights.

One of the most active new areas of research is on brain mechanisms of emotion.[20] What I write is informed by that work, but we don't yet know enough about the brain to answer many of the questions I discuss in this book. We do know a lot about emotional *behavior*, enough to provide answers to some of the most central questions about the role of emotions in our everyday life. What I write in the next chapters is primarily based on my own research on emotional behavior, having examined in fine detail what I see people do in many different emotional situations in many different cultures, and, learning from that, what I think people need to know in order to understand their emotions better.

Although my research and the findings of others provide the basis for what I describe in this book, I have reached beyond what has been proven scientifically to include also what I believe to be true but is not yet proven. I have addressed some of the issues about which I think people who seek to improve their emotional life want to know. Preparing this book has given me new understandings of emotions, and I hope it will do the same for you.

2 When Do We Become Emotional?

Much of the time, for some people all of the time, our emotions serve us well, by mobilizing us to deal with what is most important in life and providing us with many different kinds of enjoyment. But sometimes our emotions get us into trouble. That happens when our emotional reactions are inappropriate, in one of three ways: We may feel and show the right emotion but at the wrong intensity; e.g., worry was justified, but we overreacted and got terrified. Or we may feel the appropriate emotion, but we show it the wrong way; e.g., our anger was justified, but resorting to the silent treatment was counterproductive and childish. In chapter 4 I describe ways in which we can change these first two inappropriate emotional reactions—wrong intensity or wrong way of expressing the emotion. Here and in chapter 3 I consider a third type of inappropriate emotional reaction, one that is harder to change and one that is even worse than the first two. It's not that our reaction is too intense, nor that our way of expressing it is incorrect; it's that we are feeling the wrong emotion altogether. The problem isn't that we got too fearful, or that we showed it the wrong way; the problem is, as we realize afterward, that we shouldn't have become afraid at all.

Why would an inappropriate emotion be triggered? Can we erase an emotional trigger completely, so, for example, when someone cuts in front of us in line we don't get angry? Or could we change our emotional reaction so that we become amused or contemptuous instead of angry when someone cuts in line? If we can't erase or change our emotional reaction to a trigger, can we at least weaken its power so we don't react inappropriately?

These questions would not arise if we all reacted the same way when something happened, if every event triggered the same emotion in everyone. Clearly that is not the case: some people are afraid of heights, others aren't; some people mourned the death of Princess Diana as if she were their close relative, while others couldn't have cared less. Yet there are some triggers that do generate the same emotion in everyone; near-miss car accidents, for example, invariably spark a moment of fear. How does this happen? How do we each acquire our own unique set of emotional triggers and at the same time have the same emotional reaction everyone else does to other triggers? Nearly everyone feels fear if the chair they are sitting in suddenly collapses, but some people are afraid of flying in airplanes and others are not. We share some triggers, just as we share the expressions for each emotion, but there are triggers that are not only culture-specific, they are individual-specific. How do we acquire the emotion triggers that we wish we didn't have? These are the questions this chapter addresses. We need to know the answers before we can tackle the practical question dealt with in the next chapter of whether we can change what triggers our emotions.

Answering these questions is difficult because we can't look inside a person's head to find the answers, nor, as I will explain later, can we always find the answers simply by asking people why or when they get emotional. There are brain-imaging techniques such as functional Magnetic Resonance Imaging (f MRI), in which the head is placed inside a magnetic coil and pictures are produced of the active parts of the brain over two- to three-second periods. Unfortunately, that is much too long for studying how emotions begin, because they often start in less than one second. And even if f MRI had the right time resolution, it wouldn't give us much insight, since it simply identifies which brain structures are active, not what the activity is.

While the scientific evidence does not yet exist to provide final answers to these questions about how emotion triggers get established in our brain and whether we can erase them—and it may be decades before there are answers—some approximations can be made based on the careful examination of how and when people behave emotionally. The answers I can suggest, while tentative, may help us deal better with our own emotions and the emotional reactions of others.

We don't become emotional about everything; we are not in the grip of emotion all the time. Emotions come and go. We feel an emotion one moment and may not feel any emotion at another moment. Some people are much more emotional than others (see the concluding chapter), but even the most emotional people have times when they are not feeling any emotion. A few scientists claim that there is always some emotion occurring, but the emotion is too slight for us to notice it, or to affect what we do. If it is so tiny that it isn't noticeable, I think we might just as well say that those are times when there is no emotion. (Incidentally, even those who think we are always feeling some emotion acknowledge that it isn't always the same emotion. So they, too, confront the problem of explaining why we feel one emotion at one moment and another emotion at another moment.)

Given that not every minute of life is emotional, the question remains: Why do we become emotional when we do? The most common way in which emotions occur is when we sense, rightly or wrongly, that something that seriously affects our welfare, for better or worse, is happening or about to happen. This isn't the only route for becoming emotional, but it is very important, perhaps the central or core route for becoming emotional, so let's focus on it. (Later, I describe eight other paths for generating emotion.) It is a simple idea but a central one—emotions evolved to prepare us to deal quickly with the most vital events in our lives.

Recall a time when you were driving your car and suddenly another car appeared, going very fast, seeming as if it were about to hit you. Your conscious mind was focused on an interesting conversation with a friend in the passenger's seat or the program on the radio. In an instant, before you had time to think, before the conscious, self-aware part of your mind could consider the matter, danger was sensed and fear began.

As an emotion begins, it takes us over in those first milliseconds, directing what we do and say and think. Without consciously choosing to do it, you automatically turned the steering wheel to avoid the other motorist, hitting the brake with your foot. At the same time an expression of fear flashed across your face—brows raised and drawn together, eyes opened very wide, and lips stretched back toward your ears. Your heart began to pump more rapidly, you began to sweat, and the blood rushed to the large muscles of your legs. Note that you would have made that facial expression even if there were no one sitting in the car, just as your heart would begin to pump more rapidly even if you did not engage in a sudden physical exertion requiring increased blood circulation. These responses occur because over the course of our evolution it has been useful for others to know when we sense danger, and it has similarly been useful to be prepared to run when afraid.

Emotions prepare us to deal with important events without our having to think about what to do. You would not have survived that near-miss car accident if part of you weren't continually monitoring the world for signs of danger. Nor would you have survived if you had had to think consciously about what you should do to cope with the danger once it was apparent. Emotions do this without your knowing it is happening, and much of the time that's good for you, as it would be in a near-miss car accident.

Once the danger passed, you would still feel the fear churning away inside. It would take ten to fifteen seconds for those sensations to subside, and there would not be much you could do to cut that short. Emotions produce changes in parts of our brain that mobilize us to deal with what has set off the emotion, as well as changes in our autonomic nervous system, which regulates our heart rate, breathing, sweating, and many other bodily changes, preparing us for different actions. Emotions also send out signals, changes in our expressions, face, voice, and bodily posture. We don't choose these changes; they simply happen.

When the emotion is strong and it starts abruptly, as in the car example, our memory of the emotion episode after it is over won't be very accurate. You can't know what your brain did, what processes were involved in recognizing the danger posed by the other car. You would know that you turned the wheel and hit the brake, but you probably would not realize that an expression flashed across your face. You would have felt some of the sensations in your body, but it would be hard for you to find words to describe those sensations. If we wanted to know how it was that you were even able to sense the danger when you had been focused on your conversation or the music on the car radio, you would not be able to tell us. You are unable to witness or direct the processes that saved your life. This wonderful feature of our emotions—that they can and usually do begin without our awareness of the processes involved—can also work against us, causing inappropriate emotional reactions. More about that later.

If the process were slower, we might be aware of what was happening inside our brain; indeed, we might all know the answers to the questions posed in this chapter. But we wouldn't survive near-miss car accidents; we wouldn't be able to act quickly enough. In that first instant, the decision or evaluation that brings forth the emotion is extraordinarily fast and outside of awareness. We must have *automatic* appraising mechanisms that are continually scanning the world around us, detecting when something important to our welfare, to our survival, is happening.

When we get to the point where we can actually observe the operation of automatic appraising in the brain, I expect we will find many mechanisms, not one; so from now on I will use the plural form when referring to automatic-appraising mechanisms, which I will abbreviate as *autoappraisers.**

Nearly everyone who does research on emotion today agrees with what I have described so far: first, that emotions are reactions to matters that seem to be very important to our welfare, and second, that emotions often begin so quickly that we are not aware of the processes in our mind that set them off.[1] Research on the brain is consistent with what I have so far suggested. We can make very complex evaluations very quickly, in milliseconds, without being aware of the evaluative process.

We can now rephrase the first set of questions about how there

---

*When I first wrote, thirty years ago, about the autoappraisers, I did not specify what senses might be involved. Presumably it can be any of them: sight, hearing, touch, smell, taste. I suspect that the visual is especially important, but that may reflect my own bias. I have always been most sensitive to what I see; hence, my interest in emotion began with a fascination with facial expression. For now we should presume that every sensory organ provides input to the autoappraisers.

can be both universal and individual-specific emotion triggers. What are the autoappraisers sensitive to, and how did they become sensitive to those triggers? How do emotion triggers become established? The answers will tell us why we have an emotion when we do. It will also help us answer the question of why we sometimes have emotions that don't seem at all appropriate to us while at other moments our emotions are perfectly tuned to what is happening, and may even save our lives.

The answers will also tell us whether it is possible to change what produces an emotion. For example, is there something we could do so we would no longer experience fear when an airplane hits an air pocket? (Airline pilots tell me they have achieved that, because they are almost always warned ahead of time by their equipment when rough weather is about to be encountered. But what if there were no warning; would they then feel fear? I couldn't get any of the pilots to tell me, but the flight attendants say yes, they do feel momentary fear.) What would we need to do so that we no longer felt the impulse to return anger with anger, for example? Is that an impossible goal? Perhaps all we can do is change the sensitivity of the autoappraisers to certain triggers. Maybe even that is more than we can achieve. We will get to that.

We can infer something about what events our autoappraisers are sensitive to by examining when emotions happen. Most of what we know has not come from actually observing when people experience one or another emotion. Instead, it comes from their answers to questionnaires about when they remember feeling one or another emotion. Philosopher Peter Goldie in his insightful book calls this kind of information post-rationalizing.[2] This is not to dismiss such information. The answers people give on such questionnaires, like the explanations we give ourselves after an emotional episode to account for why we did what we did, may be incomplete and perhaps stereotyped because they go through the filters of what people are aware of and remember. On questionnaires there is the additional issue of what people are willing to tell others. But the answers can still teach us quite a bit.

My former student, psychologist Jerry Boucher, asked such questions of people in Malaysia and in the United States in the 1970s.[3]

Some years later my colleague psychologist Klaus Scherer, and his collaborators,[4] did similar research on students in eight Western cultures. They both found evidence of universals—the same kinds of triggers were reported to evoke the same emotions across very different cultures. They both also found evidence of cultural differences in the specific events that call forth an emotion. For example, in every culture loss of something important was the trigger for sadness, but exactly what that loss was reported to be varied from one culture to another.

One of the Malaysians in Boucher's study told a story about a person who had just heard the call to prayers for a major Muslim religious holiday. "This has made him feel sad when he thinks of his wife and children in the village, to celebrate the [holiday]. He is now in the thick jungle to defend his country. He is on duty as a soldier, and he could not celebrate [the religious holiday] with his wife and children [who are home in their village]." A European in Scherer's study said, "I was thinking about something which triggered off a memory of a school friend who was killed in a road accident. He was a brilliant scholar and a wonderful personality. His life wasted and for what?" Loss is the theme in both stories, but different kinds of loss.

My own interviews with people within my own culture document many differences among Americans in what makes them sad, angry, afraid, disgusted, and so forth. It is not that there is no overlap. Some things make nearly everyone feel the same emotion—a menacing person, carrying a club, who suddenly appears on a dark street, almost always triggers fear. But my wife is afraid of mice, and they don't frighten me at all. I get annoyed when the service at a restaurant is slow, and she couldn't care less. So, here again is the problem: How did the autoappraisers become sensitive both to emotional triggers that are found in everyone, the universals, and to triggers that call forth different emotions across individuals even within a culture?

Puzzling about this, it seemed clear that the autoappraisers must be on the alert for two kinds of triggers. They must be scanning for events that everyone encounters, events that are important to the welfare or survival of all human beings. For each emotion there might be a few such events that are stored in the brains of every human being. It might be a schema, an abstract outline, or the bare bones of a scene, such as the threat of harm for fear, or some important loss for sadness. Another equally likely possibility is that what is stored is not at all abstract, but is a specific event, such as for fear, the loss of support or something coming at us so quickly that it is likely to hit us. For sadness, the universal trigger might be the loss of a loved one, of a person to whom one is strongly attached. There is no scientific basis yet for choosing between these two possibilities, but it does not make a difference for how we lead our emotional lives.

Over the course of our lives we encounter many specific events that we learn to interpret in such a way as to frighten, anger, disgust, sadden, surprise, or please us, and these are added to the universal antecedent events, expanding on what the autoappraisers are alert to. These learned events may closely or distantly resemble the originally stored events. They are elaborations of or additions to the universal antecedent events. They are not the same for all people but vary with what we each experience. When I studied members of a Stone Age culture in New Guinea in the late 1960s, I found they were afraid of being attacked by a wild pig. In urban America, people are more afraid of being attacked by a mugger, but both cases represent a threat of harm.[5]

In an earlier book[6] my coresearcher Wally Friesen and I described the scenes we thought were universal for seven emotions. Psychologist Richard Lazarus later made a similar proposal.[7] He used the phrase *core relational themes* to reflect his view that emotions are primarily about how we deal with other people, a point with which I very much agree (although impersonal events such as a sunset or an earthquake can also trigger emotions). The word *theme* is a good one because we can then talk about the universal themes and the *variations* on those themes that develop in each person's experiences.

When we encounter a theme, such as the sensations we experience when a chair unexpectedly falls out from under us, it triggers an emotion with very little evaluation. It may take a bit longer for the autoappraisers to evaluate any of the variations on each theme, the ones we learn in the course of growing up. The further removed the variation is from the theme, the longer it may take, until we get to the point where *reflective appraising* occurs.[8] In reflective appraising, we are consciously aware of our evaluative processes; we are thinking about and considering what is happening. Suppose someone heard that there was going to be a cutback in the workforce at her place of employment. She would think about whether she is likely to be hit, and as she thinks about this potential threat, she might become afraid. She can't afford to lose that job; she needs the money it provides to support her. The event is related to the theme of loss of support—as I suggest that is one of the themes for fear—but it is far enough removed from the theme that the appraising would not be automatic but reflective. Her conscious mind is in on the process.

It is obvious how the idiosyncratic variations, each person's own emotional triggers, are acquired. They are learned, reflecting what each of us experiences (mugger or wild pig). But how are the universal themes acquired? How do they get stored in our brain so that the autoappraisers are sensitive to them? Are they also learned, or are they inherited, the product of our evolution? It is worth taking the time to consider this carefully, because the answer to this question—how the universal themes are acquired—has implications for how readily they can be modified or erased. Regrettably, there is no evidence about how the universal themes are acquired. I will spell out two alternatives and explain why I think only one is likely to be true.

The first explanation argues that it is not just the variations that are learned; the themes for each emotion are also learned. Since the same themes have been found to occur in many different cultures, they must be based on experiences that everyone, or nearly everyone has, through what is called *species-constant learning*.

Let's take anger as an example. Every human being will experience being thwarted when someone interferes with what he or she very much wants to do or is in the midst of doing. And everyone will learn that by moving toward and threatening or attacking the source of the interference, they will sometimes succeed in removing it. All this explanation assumes about what is built into human nature by genetic inheritance is the desire to pursue goals, the capacity to threaten or attack, and the ability to learn from success in removing obstacles. If we grant that desire, capacity, and ability do exist, we can expect that people will learn that it will often be useful to try removing an obstacle by threatening or attacking the source of the obstacle. Such activity requires an increase in heart rate, with blood going to the hands in anticipation of their use to attack the obstacle—all known components of the anger emotional response.[9]

If the universal themes are learned, then it should be possible to unlearn them. If we learn the anger theme, then perhaps we can unlearn it. I started out my own research believing this was the case; I thought that every aspect of emotion, including what triggers emotions, was socially learned. My own findings on the universality of facial expressions and the findings of others changed my mind. Learning is not the only source of what transpires during emotion. Species-constant learning cannot explain why facial expressions in congenitally blind children are similar to expressions shown by sighted children. Nor can it explain which muscles are deployed in particular expressions; for example, why, in enjoyment, the lips go up rather than down and the muscle around the eyes contract; and why this happens worldwide, though it may not be seen when people try to mask their expressions. Species-constant learning also cannot account easily for our recent findings that anger, fear, sadness, and disgust are marked by different changes in heart rate, sweating, skin temperature, and blood flow (all of these findings are described in chapter 4). I was forced by these findings to the conclusion that our evolutionary heritage makes a major contribution to the shaping of our emotional responses. If that is so, it seems likely that evolution would also play a major role in determining the universal themes that trigger emotions. The themes are given, not acquired; it is only the variations and elaborations of the themes that are learned.[10]

Clearly, natural selection has shaped many aspects of our lives. Consider the feature of having an opposable thumb. This feature is not found in most other animals, so how did humans come to have it? Presumably, far back in our history those of our predecessors who happened, by genetic variation, to be born with this useful feature were more successful in having and caring for progeny, and in dealing with prey and predators. So they would have contributed more offspring to succeeding generations, until over time virtually everyone had this feature. Having an opposable thumb was *selected*, and now it is part of our genetic heritage.

By similar reasoning, I suggest that those who responded to interference with vigorous attempts to remove that interference and who had a clear signal of their intention were more likely to win competitions, whether it be for food or mates. They would be likely to have more offspring, and, over time, everyone would have this anger theme.

The difference between the two explanations of universal themes—species-constant learning and evolution—is their account of *when* specific things happen. The evolutionary explanation points to our ancestral past as the time when these themes (and other aspects of emotions that I will be describing in other chapters) were developed. Species-constant learning grants that some parts of the anger theme (wanting to pursue goals) were laid in place over the course of evolution, but other parts of the anger theme (removing obstacles to those goals by threats or attack) are learned in each person's life. It is just that everyone learns the same things, and therefore they are universal.

It seems to me very unlikely that natural selection would not operate on something as important and central to our lives as what triggers our emotions. We are born prepared, with an unfolding sensitivity to the events that were relevant to the survival of our species in its ancestral environment as hunters and gatherers. The themes for which the autoappraisers are constantly scanning our environment, typically without our knowing it, were selected over the course of our evolution.

Evidence consistent with this view comes from a brilliant series of studies by the Swedish psychologist Arne Ohman.[11] He reasoned that over most of our evolutionary history, snakes and spiders have been dangerous. Those of our ancestors who learned quickly that they were dangerous and avoided them would have been more likely to survive, have children, and be able to care for them than those who were slow to learn to be afraid of snakes and spiders. If indeed we are prepared by our evolution to become afraid of what has been dangerous in our past environment, then people today, he predicted, would learn more quickly to be afraid of snakes and spiders than of flowers, mushrooms, or geometric objects. That is exactly what he found.

Ohman presented an electric shock (what is technically called an *unconditioned stimulus,* since it produces emotional arousal without any learning having to take place) with either a fear-relevant (snake or spider) or fear-irrelevant (mushroom, flower, or geometric object) stimulus. After just one pairing of the shock with one of the fear-relevant stimuli, people showed fear when the snake or spider was shown without the shock, while it took more pairings of the shock and the flower, mushroom, or geometric object for fear to be aroused by these fear-irrelevant stimuli alone. People also stayed afraid of the snake or spider, while fear faded over time in response to the flower, mushroom, or geometric object.*

Of course we are afraid of snakes and spiders in our current environment, so is it really evolution that explains Ohman's results? If this counterargument were true, then people should respond to other dangerous objects in our current environment, such as guns and electrical outlets, just as they do to spiders and snakes. But that is not what Ohman found. It took just as long to condition fear to guns and electrical outlets as it took to condition fear to flowers, mushrooms, and geometric objects. Guns and electrical outlets have not been around long enough for natural selection to have developed them into universal triggers.[12]

In his extraordinarily prescient book *The Expression of the Emotions in Man and Animals,* Charles Darwin described an experiment with a snake he performed more than a hundred years ago that fits quite nicely with Ohman's recent work. "I put my face close to the thick glass-plate in front of a puff-adder in the Zoological Gardens, with the firm determination of not starting back if the snake struck at me; but, as soon as the blow was struck, my resolution went for nothing, and I jumped a yard or two backwards with astonishing rapidity. My will and reason were powerless against the imagination of a danger which had never been experienced."[13] Darwin's experience shows how rational thought cannot prevent a fearful response to an innate fear theme, an issue to which I will return shortly.

It is not certain whether any such emotion themes operate as active triggers prior to experience linking them to an emotional outcome. Remember that in Ohman's research some experience was required for the snake and spider to become fear triggers; they were not frightening on initial exposure. It took only one association with

---

*E. O. Wilson has discussed the fear of snakes in terms that are very consistent with what I have presented. Although he does not apply his framework specifically to emotion, it is very consistent with what I am suggesting about the emotion data base. (See *Consilience*, Random House, 1998, especially pages 136–40.)

an unpleasant outcome for these to become fear triggers, but it still took that one. Perhaps this is not always so, for Darwin wrote that he was afraid of snakes without any prior direct experience with them. From a practical viewpoint it doesn't matter whether some learning is required to establish an emotion theme, or whether some themes don't require experience for us to be sensitive to their occurrence. In either case we benefit from the experience of our species on this planet, quickly responding to triggers that have been relevant to our survival.

I am convinced that one of the most distinctive features of emotion is that the events that trigger emotions are influenced not just by our individual experience, but also by our ancestral past.[14] Emotions, in the felicitous phrase of Richard Lazarus, reflect the "wisdom of the ages," both in the emotion themes and the emotion responses. The autoappraisers are scanning for what has been important to survival not just in our own individual lives, but also in the lives of our hunter-gatherer ancestors.

Sometimes we respond emotionally to matters that were important to us earlier in our lives but that are no longer relevant. The variations on each theme that add and provide detail to what is identified through automatic appraising begin to be learned very early in life—some in infancy, others in childhood. We may find ourselves responding inappropriately to things that angered, frightened, or disgusted us earlier, reactions that we now deem inappropriate to our adult life. There is a greater likelihood that we will make mistakes in our early learning of emotional triggers simply because our learning mechanisms are less well developed. Yet what we learn early in life may have greater potency, greater resistance to unlearning, than what we learn later in life. (This assumption is common to many forms of psychotherapy and is supported by some research.)

Our autoappraisers are powerful, scanning continuously, out of our conscious awareness, watching out for the themes and variations of the events that have been relevant to our survival. To use a computer metaphor, the automatic appraising mechanisms are searching our environment for anything that resembles what is stored in our *emotion alert database,* which is written in part by our biology, through natural selection, and in part by our individual experience.[15]

Remember that what is written by natural selection may not be triggers themselves, but preparations that allow some triggers to become quickly established in the database. Many psychologists have focused on a related but different set of issues, how the automatic appraisers evaluate a new event to determine, in my terms, whether it fits an item already in the emotional appraisal database. I have some doubts about the validity of what they have suggested, as it is based on what people tell them, and none of us is aware of what our mind is doing at the moment it is doing it in the automatic appraisal process. This research has provided good models to account for how people explain what makes them emotional. In any case, their suggestions are not directly relevant to the theory I suggest in the rest of this chapter about what we become emotional about.

This database is open, not closed; information gets added to it all the time.[16] Throughout life we encounter new events that may be interpreted by automatic appraising as similar to a theme or variation stored in the database, and when that happens an emotion is triggered. Psychologist Nico Frijda importantly emphasized that what I am calling the variations are not just the result of prior direct experience, but often are new stimuli we encounter that seem relevant to matters we care about, what he called our *concerns*.[17]

Since we don't need to divert our conscious attention to watch for the events that have become emotional triggers, we can use our conscious processes to do other things. (It is a sign of mental disorder, as I will explain later, if our conscious mind is preoccupied with the possibility that emotional events may be about to occur.) Once we have learned to drive a car, we do so automatically, free to focus our awareness on a conversation, listen to the radio, think about some upcoming event, and so forth. When we make a left turn, we don't have to stop listening to the radio to go to the correct lane after the turn. And yet, if danger occurs, we will still do the right thing. This is one of the great strengths of emotions, why they are functional.

Unfortunately, what we respond to may not always be appropriate to our current environment. If we visit a country where they drive on the other side of the road, our automatic processing can kill us, for we can easily do the wrong thing when we come to a traffic circle or make a turn. We can't have a conversation or listen to the radio. We must consciously guard against the automatic decisions that we would otherwise make. Sometimes we may find that emotionally we are living in another "country," another environment than the one to which our automatic appraising mechanisms are sensitive. Then our emotional reactions may be inappropriate to what is happening.

That would not be much of a problem if it were not for the fact that our emotional appraising mechanisms operate incredibly quickly. If they were slower, they wouldn't be as useful, but there would be time for us to become conscious of what was making us become emotional. Our conscious evaluations could allow us to interrupt the process when we think it inappropriate or not useful to us, before an emotion begins. Nature did not give us that choice. If on odds it had been more often useful to have slow- rather than fast-appraising mechanisms, more useful over the history of our species, then we would not have such rapid, out-of-awareness, automatic-appraising mechanisms.

While emotions are most often triggered by automatic appraisers, that is not the only way in which they can begin. Let's turn now to consider eight more pathways that generate emotion. Some of them provide more opportunity to control whether or not we are going to become emotional.

Sometimes emotions begin following *reflective appraising*, in which we consider consciously what is occurring, while still not certain what it means. As the situation unfolds or our understanding of it proceeds, something clicks; it fits something in our emotion alert database and the automatic appraising mechanisms take over. Reflective appraising deals with ambiguous situations, situations to which the automatic-appraising mechanisms are not already tuned. Suppose you meet someone who begins to tell you about her life, and it isn't clear why she is telling you or what her point is. You think about what she is saying, trying to figure out what, if anything, it means to you. At some point you may realize that she is threatening your job, at which time the automatic-appraisal mechanisms take over and you begin to feel fear, or anger, or another relevant emotion.

There is a price we pay for reflective appraisal—time. The

automatic-appraisal mechanisms save us those moments or minutes. Often, our automatic appraisals can, and do, save us from disaster by shaving those moments or minutes required by reflective appraising.

On the positive side, there is an opportunity for us to influence what transpires when emotions begin as a result of reflective appraisal.* To do so we need to be well acquainted with our own emotional hot triggers—the specific variations on the universal themes that are most prominent in our lives for each emotion. Reading about the themes and common variations in chapters 5 through 9 may help you figure out your own personal hot triggers and those of the people around you. If we know our hot triggers, then we can make a deliberate effort not to allow them to bias our interpretation of what is transpiring.

Suppose a trigger for your sadness/anguish reaction is the subtlest hint that a woman is going to abandon you because she has discovered your closely guarded secret, your (learned) feelings of fundamental worthlessness. When time is available, you can use reflective appraising to guard against the judgment that you are being abandoned. It won't come easily, but with practice it may be possible to decrease the chance that you will snap into sadness/anguish when you were not really being abandoned. Reflective appraisal gives your conscious mind more of a role. You have the opportunity to learn how deliberately to guard against the likelihood of misinterpreting what is happening.

We can also become emotional when remembering a past emotional scene. We may choose to remember the scene, reworking it in our mind, going over it to figure out what happened, or why it happened, or how we might have acted differently. Or, the memory may not be a choice; it may be unbidden, popping into our mind. Regardless of how the memory begins, whether by choice or unbidden, it may include from the start not just the scene and the script of what transpired emotionally, but an emotional reaction. We may

*After speaking with His Holiness, the Dalai Lama about what he terms *destructive emotions* and the attempts made through Buddhist practices to become free of them, I had the impression that what he and others have achieved is substituting reflective for automatic appraising. With many years of practice it seems possible to have the choice, most of the time, not to become emotional, or, when emotional, to act and speak in a way that will not be harmful to others. In the coming years I hope to be able to do research to learn more about how this is achieved, and whether there are other means to accomplish it in a shorter time.

replay the emotions we felt in the original scene, or we may now feel a different emotion. For example, a person might be disgusted with herself for having been afraid in the original scene, feeling now only the disgust and none of the fear that was originally experienced. It can also happen that initially we remember the emotional events, but do not again experience those or other emotions. Or the emotions may begin as the scene unfolds in our mind.

Robert Levenson and I have used a memory task to produce emotions in the laboratory in order to study the expressions and physiological reactions that mark each emotion. We thought it would be hard for people to reexperience past emotional scenes when they knew they were being videotaped and had wires attached to different parts of their body to measure their heart rate, respiration, blood pressure, sweating, and skin temperature. It was just the opposite. Most people seem eager for an opportunity to replay and reexperience a past emotional scene. Give them the chance to do so, and it happens almost immediately, for some, if not all, emotions.

We asked people to remember their own personal version of one of the events that has been found to be universal for each emotion. For example, to call forth sadness we asked people to remember a time in their life when someone to whom they were attached had died. We asked them to visualize a moment when they had felt the most intense sadness and then to try to experience again the emotion they had felt when the death first happened.

Almost before these short instructions were over, their physiology, their subjective feelings, and, in some people, even the facial expressions of emotions changed. This should be no surprise, as everyone has had the experience of remembering an important event and feeling an emotion. What was not known before our research is whether the changes that occur when emotions are remembered actually resemble the changes that occur when emotions begin by other means, and indeed they do. Memories about emotional events, those that we choose to call to mind, which do not immediately cause us to reexperience the originally felt emotions, provide an opportunity to learn how to reconstrue what is happening in our life so that we have a chance to change what is making us emotional.

Imagination is still another way in which we can bring about an emotional reaction. If we use our imagination to create scenes that we know make us emotional, we may be able to cool off a trigger. We can, in our own minds, rehearse and try out other ways of interpreting what is occurring, so that it doesn't fit our usual hot triggers.

Talking about past emotional experiences can also trigger emotions. We might tell the very person with whom we had an emotional reaction about how we felt and why we think we felt that way or we may tell a friend or a psychotherapist. Sometimes the simple act of talking about an emotional episode will cause us to reexperience the emotion all over again, just as it happens in our experiments when we ask people to try to do so.[18]

Reexperiencing the feelings we had in a past emotional episode can have benefits. It may give us a chance to bring matters to a different end; it may bring forth support or understanding from the person with whom we are talking. Of course, sometimes reexperiencing emotions gets us into trouble. You might have thought you could talk dispassionately with your spouse about a misunderstanding that happened a few days earlier, only to find that you became angry again, just as angry or even angrier than you were originally. That can happen even if you had hoped it wouldn't; for most of the time we don't have control over when we will become emotional. And if we do become emotional, our face probably will show it to others, and our spouse may get angry because we have gotten angry again.

Let's suppose you are talking to a friend about how terrible you felt when the vet told you that your dearly loved dog would not survive his illness. Telling the story causes you to reexperience and show grief, and as your friend listens, she also begins to look very sad. That is not uncommon, even though it is not your friend's dog, not your friend's loss. All of us can feel the emotions that others feel, feeling emotions empathetically. This is the sixth way emotions can begin—by witnessing someone else's emotional reaction.

It doesn't always happen; it won't happen if we don't care about the person, if we don't in some way identify with the person. And sometimes we witness someone's emotions and feel an entirely different emotion. For example, we may be contemptuous of them for getting so angry or afraid, or afraid of the anger they show.

It need not be our friend whose misfortune sets off our empathic emotional reaction. It could be a perfect stranger, and that stranger may not even be in our presence. We may see that person on the television screen, or in a movie, or read about the person in the newspaper or a book. Although there is no doubt that we can become emotional by reading about a stranger, it is amazing that something that came so late in the history of our species—written language—can generate emotions. I imagine that written language is converted into sensations, pictures, sounds, smells, or even tastes, in our mind, and once this happens, these images are treated like any other event by the automatic-appraisal mechanisms to arouse emotions. If we could block the production of those images, I believe emotions would not be evoked through language alone.

We may be told by others what to be afraid of, to get angry about, to enjoy, and so forth. This symbolic pathway will usually involve a caregiver in our early life, and its impact will be strengthened if the emotion we are instructed about is highly charged. We may also observe what significant people in our lives become emotional about, and unwittingly adopt their emotion variations as our own. A child whose mother is afraid of crowds may also develop such a fear.

Most of those who have written about emotions have discussed norm violations, the emotions we feel when we ourselves or someone else has violated an important social norm.[19] We may be angry, disgusted, contemptuous, ashamed, guilty, surprised, perhaps even amused and pleased. It depends on who violated the norm and what the norm was about. Norms, of course, are not universal; they may not even be shared entirely within a national group or culture. Consider, for example, the difference between young and older generations in America today about the propriety and significance of oral sex. We learn norms about what people should do early in life and throughout our life.

Here is the last way in which emotions can begin—a novel, unexpected way. I discovered it when my colleague Wally Friesen and I were developing our technique for measuring facial movements. To learn how the facial muscles change the visible appearance of the face, we videotaped ourselves as we systematically made different combinations of facial movements. We started with single muscle actions and worked our way up to combinations of six different muscles acting at once. It wasn't always easy to make these movements, but over many months of practice we learned how to do so, and we made and recorded ten thousand different combinations of facial muscle actions. By studying the videotapes afterward, we learned how to recognize from each expression which muscles had produced it. (That knowledge became the basis for our measurement system, the Facial Action Coding System,[20] FACS, which I discussed in chapter 1.)

I found that when I made certain expressions, I was flooded with strong emotional sensations. It wasn't just any expression, only the ones I had already identified as universal to all human beings. When I asked Friesen if this was happening to him also, he reported that he, too, was feeling emotions when he made some of the expressions, and they often felt very unpleasant.

A few years later Bob Levenson spent a year in my laboratory. It seemed perfectly appropriate to him, being in San Francisco and on a sabbatical, to spend his time helping us test our crazy idea that simply making an expression would produce changes in people's autonomic nervous systems. Over the next ten years, we did four experiments, including one in a non-Western culture, the Minangkabau of Western Sumatra. When people followed our instructions about which muscles to move, their physiology changed and most reported feeling the emotion. Again, it wasn't just any facial movement that produced this change. They had to make the muscular movements that our earlier research had found were universal expressions of emotion.[21]

In another study focusing just on smiles, Richard Davidson, a psychologist who studies the brain and emotion, and I found that making a smile produced many of the changes in the brain that occur with enjoyment. It wasn't just any kind of smile; only the smile that I had earlier found truly signified enjoyment (see chapter 9).[22]

In this research we asked people to make certain facial movements, but I believe we could also have obtained the same results if people had made the voice sound for each emotion. It is much harder for most people to produce the vocal sounds of emotion deliberately than to make the facial expression. But we did find one woman who could do so, and, indeed, she produced the same results with the voice or the face.

Generating emotional experience, changing your physiology by deliberately assuming the appearance of an emotion, is probably not the most common way people experience emotion. But it may occur more often than we initially think. Edgar Allan Poe knew about it, writing in the *Purloined Letter*:

> When I wish to find out how wise or how stupid or how good or how wicked is anyone, or what are his thoughts at the moment, I fashion the expression of my face, as accurately as possible, in accordance with the expression of his, and then wait to see what thoughts or sentiments arise in my mind or heart, as if to match or correspond with the expression.

I have described nine paths for accessing or turning on our emotions. The most common one is through the operation of the autoappraisers, the automatic-appraising mechanisms. A second path begins in reflective appraisal that then clicks on the autoappraisers. Memory of a past emotional experience is a third path, and imagination is a fourth path. Talking about a past emotional event is a fifth path. Empathy is the sixth path. Others instructing us about what to be emotional about is the seventh path. Violation of social norms is an eighth path. Last is voluntarily assuming the appearance of emotion.

The next chapter builds on what we have learned about how emotions are triggered, considering why and when it is so hard to change what we become emotional about. It includes suggestions about what we can do to become more aware of when emotions begin through automatic appraisal, for that is when we most often get into trouble and regret afterward how we have behaved.

3
Changing What
We Become
Emotional About

Walking near the edge of a cliff can be frightening, despite the knowledge that a clearly visible fence would prevent a person's fall. It matters little that the path is not slippery and the fence is not fragile; the heart still beats faster and the palms still become sweaty. The knowledge that there is nothing to fear does not erase the fear. Even though most people can control their actions, keeping themselves on the path, they may be able to steal only a quick glance at the beautiful view. The danger is felt even though it does not objectively exist.[1]

The cliff walk shows that our knowledge cannot always override the autoappraisers' evaluations that generate emotional responses. After our emotional responses have been triggered, we may consciously realize that we need not be emotional, and yet the emotion may persist. I propose that this usually happens when the trigger is an evolved emotional theme or a learned trigger that is very similar to the theme. When the learned trigger is more distantly related to the theme, our conscious knowledge may be better able to interrupt the emotional experience. Put in other terms, if our concerns are only distantly related to a theme, we may be able to override them by choice.

There is another, more serious way in which emotions override what we know. Emotions can prevent us from having access to all that we know, to information that would be at our fingertips if we were not emotional but that during the emotion is inaccessible to us.

When we are gripped by an inappropriate emotion, we interpret what is happening in a way that fits with how we are feeling and ignore our knowledge that doesn't fit.

Emotions change how we see the world and how we interpret the actions of others. We do not seek to challenge why we are feeling a particular emotion; instead, we seek to confirm it. We evaluate what is happening in a way that is consistent with the emotion we are feeling, thus justifying and maintaining the emotion. In many situations this may help focus our attention and guide our decisions about how to respond to the problems at hand and understand what is at stake. But it can cause problems, for when we are gripped by an emotion we discount or ignore knowledge we already have that could disconfirm the emotion we are feeling, just as we ignore or discount new information coming to us from our environment that doesn't fit our emotion. In other words, the same mechanism that guides and focuses our attention can distort our ability to deal with both new information and knowledge already stored in our brain.*

Suppose someone is furious about having been insulted in public. During his or her fury it will not be easy to consider whether what was said was actually meant as an insult. Past knowledge about that person and about the nature of insults will be only selectively available; only that part of the knowledge that supports the fury will be remembered, not that which would contradict it. If the insulting person explains or apologizes, the furious person may not immediately incorporate this information (the fact of an apology) in his behavior.

For a while we are in a *refractory* state, during which time our thinking cannot incorporate information that does not fit, maintain, or justify the emotion we are feeling. This refractory state may be of more benefit than harm if it is brief, lasting for only a second or two. In that short window it focuses our attention on the problem at hand, using the most relevant knowledge that can guide our initial actions, as well as preparations for further actions. Difficulties can arise or inappropriate emotional behavior may occur when the refractory period lasts much longer, for minutes or perhaps even

---

*What I am suggesting here is very similar to psychologist Jerry Fodor's account of how information can become encapsulated, by which he meant that information that might not fit with a way of interpreting the world, information the person has stored and knows, becomes inaccessible for a time.

hours. A too-long refractory period biases the way we see the world and ourselves.[2]

In a near-miss car accident, we do not remain in a state of fear once we avoid the other car. We realize very quickly that the danger is past, and we wait for our breathing and heart rate to return to normal, which happens in five to fifteen seconds. But suppose the fear is about something that cannot be so instantly or dramatically disproven. Suppose a person is afraid that the ache he is feeling in his lower back is a symptom of liver cancer. During the refractory period he will reject contradictory information, forgetting that yesterday he helped move his friend's furniture and that this is why his back hurts.

Consider a common family situation: In the morning, before they both go to work, Jim tells his wife, Helen, that he is sorry but that something has come up and he can't pick up their daughter after school. Helen, he says, will have to do so. Helen replies with an edge in her voice and a look of anger on her face, as she has become annoyed, "Why didn't you give me more notice? I have a meeting with one of my supervisees scheduled at that time!" Helen didn't think consciously about her response; she didn't choose to become annoyed. It happened because the autoappraisers interpreted her husband's message as interfering with her goals (a likely theme for anger), without considering her.

Sensing that she is annoyed by her voice and facial expression, Jim challenges her right to be angry. He now gets annoyed with Helen, as anger often brings forth anger. "Why are you getting angry about it? I couldn't tell you ahead of time, because my boss just called a few minutes ago and told me there is an emergency meeting in my section and I must be there." Helen now knows that Jim wasn't being inconsiderate, and there is no reason to be angry about an unavoidable, unintended frustration, but if she is still in a refractory period, it will be a struggle. Her annoyance wants to justify itself. She might be tempted to get in the last word, "You should have told me that in the first place!" but she could restrain herself and not act on her anger.

If Helen can incorporate the new information Jim supplies, it will change her perception of why he did what he did. She can then discard her interpretation that he was inconsiderate and her annoyance will vanish. There are many reasons, though, why the refractory period might be long, causing Helen to hold on to her anger and not yield ground once Jim provided information that should have turned it off. Maybe she didn't have enough sleep the night before. Perhaps she is under a lot of pressure at work, has not been able to deal with it, and is taking out those frustrations on Jim. Maybe they have been arguing for months about a serious issue, such as whether to have another child, and Helen has been harboring angry feelings about Jim's seemingly selfish attitude. Helen might have the type of personality in which anger plays a dominant role. (I describe my research on people who have a hostile personality trait in chapter 6.) Or Helen might be *importing* into this situation a script from another part of her life, a script that is highly emotionally charged, which she replays again and again.

A script has a cast of characters, the person who is importing it and other pivotal people, plus a plotline of what happened in the past. Not everyone imports from their past into current situations emotional scripts that don't really match. The conventional wisdom in psychoanalytic theories of personality is that scripts are imported when people have unresolved feelings, feelings that were never fully or satisfactorily expressed, or if expressed did not lead to a desired outcome. Scripts distort current reality, causing inappropriate emotional reactions and lengthening the refractory period.

Suppose Helen was the younger child, and her brother Bill was a bully, always dominating her. If Helen was seared by that experience, if her parents took Bill's side and thought she was exaggerating, she might often import the "I am being dominated" script into situations that, even in the slightest way, seem similar. One of Helen's most important concerns is not to be dominated, and this causes her to sense domination even when it may not be present. Helen doesn't want to import this script. She is a smart woman, and she has learned from feedback from those with whom she is intimate that she is prone to just this kind of misinterpretation and overreaction. But during the refractory period she can't do much about it. She is not even aware that she is in a refractory period. It is only afterward, upon reflection, that Helen realizes she acted inappropriately and regrets how she behaved. She would like to get the "he is trying to dominate me" trigger out of her emotion alert database. Her life would be better if she could derail this trigger; she wouldn't be prone to long periods of anger, and she wouldn't distort other people's motives to fit her emotions.

Many people would like to have just that kind of control over when they have an emotional reaction. One of the reasons people seek the help of psychotherapists is that they don't want to continue to become emotional about some of the things that make them emotional. But none of us wants completely and irrevocably to turn off *all* our emotions. Life would be dull, less juicy, less interesting, and probably less safe if we had the power to do that.

Fear does protect us; our lives are saved because we are able to respond to threats of harm protectively, without thought. Disgust reactions make us cautious about indulging in activities that literally or figuratively might be toxic. Sadness and despair over loss may bring help from others. Even anger—the emotion most people would like to turn off—is useful to us. It warns others, and us as well, when things are thwarting us. That warning may bring about change, although it may also bring about counteranger. Anger motivates us to try to change the world, to bring about social justice, to fight for human rights.

Would we really want to eliminate those motivations? Without excitement, sensory pleasure, pride in our achievements and the achievements of our offspring, amusement in the many odd and unexpected things that happen in life, would life be worth living? Emotion is not like an appendix, a vestigial apparatus we don't need and should remove. Emotions are at the core of our life. They make life livable.

Rather than turning off our emotions completely, most of us would like the ability to turn off our emotional reactions to specific triggers selectively. We would like to use a delete key to erase a specific trigger or set of triggers, a script or concern, stored in our emotion alert database. Unfortunately, there is no definitive, solid evidence about whether this can be done.

One of the foremost students of the brain and emotion, psychologist Joseph LeDoux, recently wrote: "Conditioned fear learning is particularly resilient, and in fact may represent an indelible form of learning.[3] . . . The indelibility of learned fear has an upside and a downside. It is obviously very useful for our brain to be able to retain records of those stimuli and situations that have been associated with danger in the past. But these potent memories, which are typically formed in traumatic circumstances, can also find their way into everyday life, intruding into situations in which they are not especially useful. . . ."[4]

I fortunately had the opportunity to talk with LeDoux about this while I was writing this chapter, and to push him a bit on exactly what he meant and how certain he was about it. First, I should be clear that LeDoux is referring *only* to learned triggers, what I have called the variations. The themes, which are the product of our evolution, both LeDoux and I believe are indelible, such as the findings about rats who were born in a laboratory and never had any experience with a cat, yet showed fear when they first saw a cat. It is an inborn theme, a fear trigger that doesn't require learning. The power of a theme to trigger an emotion can be weakened but not totally removed. But can we unlearn the variations, the triggers we acquire in the course of our lives?

Without going into the technical details of LeDoux's brain research, we do need to know that when an emotional trigger becomes established, when we learn to be afraid of something, new connections are established among a group of cells in our brain, forming what LeDoux calls a *cell assembly*.[5] Those cell assemblies, which contain the memory of that learned trigger, seem to be permanent physiological records of what we have learned. They make up what I called the emotion alert database. However, we can learn to interrupt the connection between those cell assemblies and our emotional behavior. The trigger still sets off the established cell assembly, but the connection between the cell assembly and our emotional behavior can be broken, at least for a time. We are afraid, but we don't act as if we are afraid. We also can learn to break the connection between the trigger and those cell assemblies so the emotion is not triggered, but the cell assembly remains, the database is not erased, and its potential to be reconnected to the trigger and the response remains within us. Under some circumstances, when we are under stress of one kind or another, the trigger will again become active, connecting to the cell assembly, and the emotional response springs forth once again.

While all of LeDoux's research has been on fear, he thinks there is no reason to believe it would be any different for anger or anguish. This fits my personal experience, and what I have observed in others, so I will assume that his findings generalize to the other emotions, perhaps even to emotions that feel good.*

Our nervous system doesn't make it easy to change what makes us emotional, to unlearn either the connection between an emotional cell assembly and a response, or between a trigger and an emotional cell assembly. The emotion alert database is an open system, in that new variations continually get added to it, but it is not a system that allows data to be easily removed once entered. Our emotion system was built to keep triggers in, not get them out, mobilizing our emotional responses without thought. We are biologically constructed in a way that does not allow us to interrupt them readily.

Let's return to my example of the near-miss car accident once again to see how LeDoux's findings help us understand what happens when we try to change what we become emotional about. Every driver has had the experience, when sitting in the passenger seat, of having her foot involuntarily shoot out toward a nonexistent brake pedal when it seems that another car is veering toward her. Hitting the brake pedal is a learned response to the fear of being hit by another car. Not only is the response—hitting the brake pedal—learned, but so, too, is the trigger. Cars were not part of the environment of our ancestors; a car veering toward us is not a built-in theme but a learned variation. We learn it quickly because it is very close to one of the likely fear themes—something that moves quickly into our sight, approaching us as if it is about to hit us.

While most of us will, when sitting in the passenger seat, involuntarily press down on a nonexistent brake pedal when we sense

*Not everything that makes us emotional is a result of conditioning, however. Frijda points out that some emotional stimuli have "little to do with having experienced aversive or pleasurable consequences accompanying a particular stimulus." Emotions result "from inferred consequences or causes. . . . Losing one's job, receiving criticism, perceiving signs of being neglected or slighted, being praised, and seeing norm violations [actions that contradict our dearly held values] are all quite indirectly or remotely connected to the actual aversive or pleasurable conditions that they somehow signal and that give them emotional life." I view these as all instances of variations that resemble the universal themes, even though some of them are distantly related.

danger, driving instructors learn not to do so. They may learn to interrupt the response, in which case they will still feel afraid, but they won't physically respond. (I suspect there would still be a trace of fear on their face or in the sound of their voice.) Or they may learn to break the connection between the trigger—that car lurching toward them—and the cell assembly in the brain that was established for this fear trigger.* Perhaps they finely tune the connection between the trigger and the cell assembly so that fear is aroused and the protective brake pedal response is activated only when the danger is very likely to occur. But if they have had a bad night's sleep, or are still mulling over an unfinished argument with their spouse that morning, that foot will shoot out once again, just as it would for any of us who are not driving instructors, who have not learned to interrupt this trigger. The links between the trigger, the cellular connections, and the response have not been erased, only weakened.

My focus in the rest of this chapter is on weakening emotional triggers, whether they are ones established directly through conditioning or indirectly through a connection to one of the emotional themes. In the next chapter I explain how we can weaken the connection between an emotional event and our emotional responses. It is not easy to do either one. Let me explain how this might work in the context of another example.

Suppose a boy, let's call him Tim, was teased by a father whose teases, while ostensibly made as jests, had a cruel edge, mocking Tim's inadequate performances. Quite early, probably before age five, the script of a powerful person disparaging him through teasing entered Tim's emotion alert database. As he grew up, Tim responded with nearly immediate anger to teasing, even when it was not intended meanly. This delighted his father, who further taunted him for losing his temper over a joke. Some twenty years later, Tim still reacts with anger at the first sign that someone is teasing him. That doesn't mean that Tim always acts on his anger, but Tim would be better off if he didn't have to struggle with his impulse to strike back whenever someone jokes with him.

Six quite different factors are likely to determine how successful

---

*We could find out which one they do by measuring their physiology when this happens, but it doesn't really matter for my point here.

anyone can be in reducing the heat, the salience, and the power of an emotion trigger, and the length of the refractory period, the period when we are only able to use information that supports the emotion we are feeling. The first factor is *closeness to the evolved theme.* The closer the learned trigger is to the unlearned theme, the harder it will be to decrease its power. Road rage is an example of an event that closely resembles a theme, not a learned variation. This is illustrated in the following puzzle. When my department chairman drives to the university each day, he encounters a place where two lines of traffic have to merge. There is an unwritten rule that cars in each lane take turns, but sometimes people sneak in ahead of their turn right in front of him. My chairman gets furious, even though it really doesn't matter; the difference in terms of when he arrives at the university is only a few seconds. Yet at work, when someone on the faculty writes a critique of one of his plans for the department, a matter on which he has worked very hard and which really matters to him, he rarely gets angry. Why anger over a seemingly trivial event, when he doesn't become angry about an important one?

It is because the driver's actions resemble the likely universal, evolved anger theme of being thwarted, not by words but by someone's physical actions interfering with the pursuit of a goal. The impolite driver's actions are much closer to the theme than the colleague who writes a critique. (For those who wonder why road rage seems to have become so prevalent today, I suspect that it has always occurred, but less frequently because there was less traffic. Also, the media had not named it, which focuses attention on it.)

Applying these ideas to Tim's problems, we can expect Tim would have an easier time weakening a trigger that is distant rather than close to the universal theme. Being teased and humiliated by his father's words is further away from the theme than if his father had "joked" with him by physically pinning his arms to his side so he could not move. Tim would have a better chance as an adult to weaken the trigger if the original experiences had involved words rather than physical restraint to tease and humiliate him.

A second matter to consider is how closely current instances of the triggering event *resemble the original situation* in which the trigger was first learned. It was Tim's father who so mercilessly teased him—a strong, dominant man. Teasing by a woman, a peer, or a subordinate is not as close as teasing by a man who has some authority over him, and it should be easier for Tim to weaken the trigger when he is teased by someone other than an authority figure.

A third issue is how early in a person's life the trigger was learned. Presumably, the *earlier* the trigger was learned, the harder it will be to weaken it. In part, that is because the ability to control emotional reactions to any emotion trigger is not as well developed in early life. Thus, there will be a stronger emotional reaction associated with triggers learned early in life compared to those learned in adulthood, all other things being equal. In part, it is also because of the possibility (suggested by some developmental psychologists and all psychoanalysts, and now supported by growing evidence from studies of the brain and emotion[6]) that early childhood is critical in forming personality and emotional life. What is learned then is stronger and more resistant to change. Triggers learned in such a critical period may produce a longer refractory period.

The *initial emotional charge* is the fourth key factor. The stronger the emotions that were experienced when the trigger was first learned, the harder it will be to weaken its impact. If that teasing episode was a mild or moderate one, rather than a strong one, if the feelings of humiliation, worthlessness, and resentment over loss of power were mild rather than strong, then it would be easier to cool the trigger.

The *density* of the experience is a fifth factor, contributing to the strength and indelibility of the trigger. Density refers to repeated episodes, highly charged emotionally, occurring during a short period of time, that have the effect of overwhelming the person. So, if there was a period when Tim was teased mercilessly, intensely, again and again, it would be a very difficult trigger to diminish. When there is a very strong, highly dense initial emotional charge, I expect that the refractory period in later reactions to that trigger will be long, making it difficult for people to realize in the first second or two that they are responding inappropriately. If the initial emotional charge was very strong, that alone may be sufficient to extend the refractory period for that trigger, even if it was not dense or repeated again and again.

A sixth factor is *affective style*.[7] We each differ in the speed of our emotional responses and the strength of our responses, and in how long it takes for us to recover from an emotional episode. My research over the last ten years has focused on these matters. (The conclusion describes four other aspects of affective style in addition to speed, strength, and duration.) Those individuals who generally have faster and stronger emotional responses will have a much harder time cooling off a hot trigger.

Let us now consider how Tim could go about weakening the teasing trigger. The first step is for Tim to identify what it is that is getting him so angry. He may not know that being teased by a dominant person is a very hot anger trigger. Automatic appraising operates in milliseconds, before consciousness, before he might be able to become aware of what is making him so angry. Perhaps he knows it is teasing, but he doesn't know it has to be by someone who has some power over him. He may not realize it has any connection to his childhood experience of being unmercifully teased by his father. Tim may be very defensive, not ready to accept that he is becoming angry, or not ready to face the fact that his father was cruel. The very first step is to become aware that he is feeling angry, to recognize the sensations in his own body (suggestions on how to accomplish that are in chapter 6 on anger), and to understand the effect he has on other people.

Let's suppose Tim begins to recognize that he is unduly angry at times but doesn't understand when or why it happens. Tim's next step is to start a log about his anger episodes. He should note those occasions when either he recognizes that he has become angry or others tell him so. Entered into the log should be as much information as possible about what transpired in the moments before he became angry. A friend or psychotherapist might be able to help Tim figure out from hearing about these episodes that it is teasing interpreted as humiliation that is his hot trigger. Hopefully, when he thinks about this, he may become aware of the script he is importing, those terrible scenes with his father. I am not certain whether he must know that in order to weaken this script. It might be sufficient for Tim to realize that he is overreacting to teasing, that he is treating teasing as if it is always meant to humiliate.

It might seem that the simplest solution would be for Tim now simply to avoid any situations in which he is likely to be teased.

That presumes he can get away with never showing up at the company dinners at which he is likely to be roasted, and that he can readily anticipate other situations when he might be teased. A better approach would be to try to cool the trigger.

Tim needs to consider how often he perceived teasing either when it wasn't there, or when it was not meant to humiliate. He must learn how to reappraise what motivates teasing. Such careful consideration can help, if it is done repeatedly.[8] He can do this by thinking about each teasing episode afterward, carefully considering alternative explanations for why he was teased other than the humiliation theme. Over time he can learn to do that reappraising sooner, while still in the situation. He can also learn to sense when there is the possibility of being teased, and can brace himself not to interpret it as an insult or an attempt to humiliate him. Over time teasing may become a cooler trigger. At the very least, if Tim gets as far as learning that teasing is a trigger, and that it is the intended humiliation that sets it off, he will be in a better position to control his anger when he does become angry.[9] (See more about controlling emotional responses in chapter 4.)

If what I have suggested doesn't work, if an emotion trigger continues to call forth difficult-to-control emotional responses again and again, there are other approaches to consider. Psychotherapy is one possibility, although in my experience it is often limited to making one aware of what the trigger is and what script is being imported, without always being helpful in weakening the trigger. Behavior therapy is another approach to consider, meditation training another.[10]

Suppose that Tim has identified the trigger, has spent time analyzing the kinds of situations in which he often misperceives teasing when it isn't there, and has practiced reevaluating situations so he can take teasing as a joke, not as an insult and humiliation. Let's grant further that this was made easier because earlier in his life there were only a few teasing episodes spread out over a number of months, and none of them went on for very long—low charge and low density. And let's stipulate that Tim is not burdened by a very fast and very strong anger profile. Tim now rarely has to struggle with becoming angry when someone teases him. But it could happen, and most likely it will happen when Tim is, for some other reason, in an irritable *mood*.

This is a good place to distinguish emotions from moods. All of us have both of them, but they are different, even though both involve feelings. The most obvious difference is that emotions are much shorter than moods. Moods can last a whole day, sometimes two days, while emotions can come and go in minutes, sometimes seconds. A mood resembles a slight but continuous emotional state. If it is irritability, it is like being mildly annoyed all the time, ready to become angry. If it is a blue mood, we are slightly sad, ready to become very sad. A disdainful mood involves the emotions of disgust and contempt, a euphoric or high mood involves excitement and pleasure, an apprehensive mood involves fear.

A mood activates specific emotions. When we are irritable, we are seeking an opportunity to become angry; we interpret the world in a way that permits, or even requires, us to become angry. We become angry about matters that do not typically get us angry, and when we become angry, the anger is likely to be stronger and last longer than it would if we were not in an irritable mood. Moods don't have their own signal in either the face or voice. Instead we can tell that someone is in a mood because we see the signs of the emotion that saturates that mood. Moods reduce our flexibility, as they make us less responsive to the changing nuances in our environment, biasing how we interpret and respond. Emotions do that, too, but only for moments if the refractory period is not extended; moods last for hours.

Another way moods differ from emotions is that once an emotion has begun and we have become aware of it, we can usually point to the event that caused it. Rarely do we know why we are in a mood. It just seems to happen to us. We may wake up one morning in a particular mood, or for no apparent reason in the middle of the day we notice we feel moody. While there must be autonomous, neurochemical changes that set off and maintain moods, I believe moods can also be brought about by highly dense emotional experiences. Dense anger can result in an irritable mood, just as dense joy can result in a high or euphoric mood. Then, of course, we do know why we are in a mood.

Earlier I argued that emotions are necessary for our lives, and we wouldn't want to be rid of them. I am far less convinced that moods are of any use to us.[11] Moods may be an unintended consequence of our emotion structures, not selected by evolution because they are adaptive.[12] Moods narrow our alternatives, distort our thinking, and make it more difficult for us to control what we do, and usually for no reason that makes any sense to us. One could argue that when moods are brought about by dense emotional experience, they serve the function of keeping us prepared for more of the same thing. Perhaps, but to my mind that is a small benefit compared to the troubles moods cause. If I could, I would forgo ever having any mood again and just live with my emotions. I would gladly give up euphoric moods to be rid of irritable and blue moods. But none of us has that choice.

Triggers that, through hard work, have become cool, get hot again when a person is in a mood relevant to that trigger. When Tim is in an irritable mood, teasing may once again set off his anger. It is not just a stressful situation, as LeDoux suggested, that will again link up a trigger to the emotion; a mood can also do so. Even when a trigger has been weakened, or cooled off so that it doesn't bring forth an emotion, it will become hot again when the right mood comes along.

Even when we are not made especially vulnerable by a mood, many of us will at least some of the time still have emotions triggered upon which we don't want to act. The next chapter considers the involuntary emotional responses, and how well we can control what we do when we are emotional.

4 Behaving Emotionally

Y ou are about to go in to a meeting with your boss. You don't know what it is about; you don't know the agenda; you didn't call this meeting. Your boss's secretary told you "it was very important" when she scheduled the meeting. How you react—whether you look afraid, angry, or sad; whether you keep your cool or seem too detached; what you say and how you act—could be crucial to the outcome. Would you trust how you would react emotionally, or, if need be, your ability to control your emotional behavior, or would you take a drink or down a Valium ahead of time?

It is hard not to behave emotionally when the stakes are high, which is when we are likely to feel strong emotions. Our emotions are often our best guides, directing us to do and say what is exactly right for the situation, but that isn't always so for anyone. There are times when we wish we had not acted or spoken under the influence of our emotions. But if we could, if we could turn off our emotions completely for a time, that might make matters worse, for the people around us might think we are detached, or worse, inhuman.* To experience our emotions, to care about what happens while behaving in a way that we and others do not consider to be too emotional,

---

*The recent use of botoxin injections to decrease signs of aging does so at the cost of making the face wooden, the person less animated and unemotional in appearance; and (paradoxically) less animated people are less attractive to others.

can sometimes be extremely difficult. And some people have just the opposite problem: they feel the emotions, they care, but they do not express them the way others expect, or they do not express them at all; people think they are overcontrolled.

We don't choose how we look and sound or what we are impelled to do and say when we are emotional any more than we choose when to become emotional. But we can learn to moderate emotional behavior we would regret afterward, to inhibit or subdue our expressions, to prevent or temper our actions or words. We can also learn not to be overcontrolled, appearing unemotional, if that is our problem. It would be even better still if we could learn how to choose the way we feel and choose how to express our emotions so that we could express our emotions constructively.

We can look as far back as Aristotle's description of the temperate person for a standard for what is constructive emotional behavior.[1] Our emotions must be in the right amount, proportional to the event that called them forth; they must be expressed at the right time, in a way that is appropriate to the emotional trigger and the circumstances in which it occurred; and they must be expressed in the right way, in a way that does no harm.* Admittedly, these are very abstract ideas, but they do explain the reasons we sometimes regret afterward how we have behaved.

Chapter 3 described what triggers emotions and how to weaken hot emotional triggers so they don't always make us emotional. But suppose that has failed and the emotion has already begun. Now the question is: Can we choose what we say and do? When we are in the refractory period—that period during which we don't have access to information that would change how we are feeling—we don't want to suppress our emotions. What our emotions are pushing us to do and say seems justified and necessary.

If we try to control what we do and say, it will be a struggle between our deliberate, voluntary efforts and our involuntary emotional behavior. That struggle will be greatest for those among us who experience emotions much more quickly, and much more

---

*There is an exception. When another person threatens our life or the lives of others, then in our anger we may be justified in harming the person who poses the threat if there is no other way to prevent injury. The Dalai Lama, with some hesitation, agrees on this point.

strongly, than others. Sometimes all we can do is leave the scene. Even that, for some people and in some emotional episodes, can require a great act of will. With practice, moderating our emotional behavior becomes easier, but it takes time, concentration, and understanding. Just as there are factors that determine when and how a hot trigger can be weakened, there is a set of related factors that determine when we are most likely to succeed in moderating our emotional behavior. When we fail to do so, and everyone fails sometimes, there are steps we can take to profit from that failure, decreasing the likelihood we will fail again.

Before I can address these two issues—how to moderate our emotional behavior, and, when we fail, how we can learn from those mistakes—we must consider what it is we are trying to moderate: emotional behavior itself—the signals, the actions, and the internal changes. We need also to understand how these emotional behaviors are generated and how we can influence that process. We will begin with the signals, the emotional expressions.

The emotion signals given off by other persons often determine how we interpret their words and actions. Their expression also triggers our own emotional response, and that in turn colors our interpretation of what the person is saying, what we think are that person's motives, attitudes, and intentions.

In the last chapter we met Helen, who became annoyed with her husband, Jim, when he told her he could not pick up their daughter after school that day. Helen had replied, "Why didn't you give me more notice?" Jim might not have become angry in return if it had not been for the edge in her voice or the anger written on her face. Her words alone might have been enough, though. A softer way of saying the same thing would have been, "I wish you could have given me more notice," or "What happened that you couldn't let me know before now?" That last version would have let Jim know that she recognized that there must be a reason why he was inconveniencing her. But even the softer language wouldn't have succeeded if it were said with anger in her voice or on her face.

Even if Helen had said nothing, the expression on her face might have tipped Jim off that she was annoyed, for emotions are not private. Most of our emotions have a distinctive signal that tells others how we are feeling. Thoughts, on the other hand, are totally private. No one knows if we are thinking about our mother, the show we are missing on television, or how to change our Internet stock investments unless emotions are mixed in with those thoughts, as they often are. While there is no external signal that even tells people we *are* thinking, let alone *what* we are thinking, that is not the case with emotion. Although individuals differ in how expressive they are, emotions are not invisible or silent. Others who look at us and listen to what we say could tell how we are feeling, unless we were to make a concerted effort to squelch our expressions. Even then, some trace of our emotions might leak out and could be detected.[2]

We may not always like the fact that others can know how we feel; even the most open people find times when they would prefer to keep their feelings private. Helen might not have wanted to let Jim know she was annoyed, but her face might have betrayed her even if she kept herself from saying anything. It is part of our evolutionary heritage that we signal when each emotion begins. Presumably, over the course of our history as a species, it was more useful than not for others to know what emotion we were experiencing without our having to make the choice to tell them. For Helen, a slight look of annoyance might serve to prod Jim to explain why he couldn't give her more notice: "I know this will be hard on you, honey, but I have no choice; my boss just called when you were in the shower and said there was an emergency meeting." Now knowing that Jim wasn't being inconsiderate, Helen's anger fades. But her anger might not fade if, as I mentioned in chapter 3, she were resentful about other matters, or if she imported into this situation anger based on her experience with her bullying brother.

Another remarkable feature about the emotion signal system is that it is always "on." It is ready to broadcast instantly every emotion we feel. Think what life would be like if there were a switch, if it could be in the "off" position unless we chose to switch it "on." It would make child care impossible, for one thing. If it were off, how would we know what to do and when to do it? As parents of older children, would we want to have to plead with our kids to turn their emotional signals back on? In friendships, in courting, even in the workplace, it would become a central issue: "Do you have your emotion signals switched on or off?" Who would be willing to spend time with us, other than those with whom we have the most trivial exchanges, such as the fellow who sells us the morning newspaper, if they knew we had chosen to deprive them of information about how we are feeling?

Fortunately we don't have that choice, and, while we do have the ability to dampen our emotional signals, we are rarely perfect in our attempts to inhibit them. Of course, some people are much more able than others to dampen or even eliminate any sign of the emotions they are feeling. It is not certain whether this is because these people experience emotions less intensely, or if they have a superior ability in suppressing any sign of the emotion they are experiencing. John Gottman and Robert Levenson have found that men who "stonewall," showing little about how they feel when their wives express anger, are actually, on a physiological level, experiencing their emotions very intensely.[3] Stonewalling itself can be considered an emotional signal, a signal of being overpowered, of being unable or unwilling to deal with the matter at hand. Although I have not done the work, I expect that careful examination would find that fear or anger is signaled through subtle facial or vocal expressions prior to stonewalling or during the stonewalling itself.

Emotion signals emerge almost instantly when an emotion begins. When we are sad, for example, our voices automatically become softer and lower, and the inner corners of our eyebrows are pulled up. If the emotion begins slowly, building up over a few seconds, the signal may become stronger, or there may be a series of signals in rapid sequence. The signals mark clearly when emotions begin, and, to a lesser extent, when they end. As long as an emotion is on, it will color the voice, but it is less certain whether there will be change in the facial expressions. We can tell when a person is no longer in the grip of an emotion because we hear the absence of that emotion and we no longer see the expression on the face, or because we hear and see instead the expression of the next emotion that is on.

It is important to remember that emotional signals do not tell us their source. We may know someone is angry without knowing exactly why. It could be anger at us, anger directed inward at his or her self, or anger about something the person just remembered that has nothing to do with us. Sometimes we can figure it out from our knowledge of the immediate context. Suppose you were to say to your son, "Johnny, you can't go out to the movies with your friends tonight; you have to stay home and take care of your younger brother, because the baby-sitter canceled and your father and I must go to our dinner party." If Johnny looks angry, it is probably with you for interfering with his plans, for thinking your commitments for the evening take precedence over his. Then again, Johnny might be angry with himself for caring that much, for feeling so much disappointment. Not likely, but still possible.

We have to avoid *Othello's error*.[4] Recall that in Shakespeare's play, Othello accuses his wife, Desdemona, of loving Cassio. He tells her to confess since he is going to kill her for her treachery. Desdemona asks Othello to call Cassio to testify to her innocence. Othello tells her that he has already had Cassio murdered. Desdemona realizes she will not be able to prove her innocence and that Othello will kill her.

> DESDEMONA: Alas, he is betrayed, and I undone!
> OTHELLO: Out, strumpet! Weep'st thou for him to my face?
> DESDEMONA: O, banish me, my lord, but kill me not!
> OTHELLO: Down, strumpet!

Othello's mistake was not a failure to recognize how Desdemona felt; he knew she was anguished and afraid. His error was in believing that emotions have only one source, in interpreting her anguish as due to the news of her supposed lover's death, and her fear as that of an unfaithful wife who has been caught in her betrayal. He kills her without considering that her anguish and fear could have different sources. That they were the reactions of an innocent woman who knew her intensely jealous husband was about to kill her, and that there was no way she could prove her innocence.

If we are to avoid Othello's error, we have to resist the temptation of jumping to conclusions, and strive to consider alternative reasons other than the reason we most suspect for why an emotion is shown. Fear has many sources. The fear of the guilty person about being caught looks just like the fear of the innocent person about being disbelieved.* Emotion signals provide important information about what a person is feeling and what he or she may do next, but there is almost always more than one possibility. A person filled with fear may fight rather than run or hide.

Let's begin with the facial expressions, the briefest of the emotional signals. In chapter 1 I described my research, which established that seven emotions each have a distinct, universal, facial expression: sadness, anger, surprise, fear, disgust, contempt, and happiness. I don't need to define those words, except perhaps for contempt, which, though highly recognizable, is not a very frequently used word in English. Contempt is a feeling of being better than another person, of being superior, usually morally superior, but it can also be felt toward someone who is weaker in intelligence, strength, and so forth. Contempt can be quite an enjoyable emotion.

Each of these emotion terms—sadness, anger, surprise, fear, disgust, contempt, and happiness—stands for a family of related emotions. Anger, for example, can vary in *strength,* ranging from annoyance to rage, and in *type,* such as sullen anger, resentful anger, indignant anger, and cold anger, to mention just a few. The variations in intensity within each emotion family are clearly marked on the face, but the scientific work has not yet been done to determine if the different types within each emotion family also have unique facial expressions.

It is common in science today to lump anger, fear, disgust, sadness, and contempt into one bin—negative emotion—and contrast that with positive emotion. Since surprise can be either positive or negative, it is usually ignored. There are two problems with such a simple dichotomy. First, it ignores the very important differences among the so-called negative emotions: in what triggers each of those emotions; in how they feel; in what we are impelled to say and do; in their facial and vocal signals; and in how people are likely to respond to us. The other problem is that even the so-called negative emotions aren't always experienced as unpleasant. For some people

---

*This is a serious problem in any type of lie detection. Polygraphers attempt to reduce an innocent person's fear of being wrongly judged by affirming the accuracy of the machine, but since it isn't very accurate and people increasingly know that, both the innocent and guilty person may manifest the same fear.

an angry argument is enjoyable, and many people enjoy a good cry when seeing a sad movie, to name just two examples. On the other hand, amusement, a presumably positive feeling, can be cruel, involving ridicule. I believe we must examine the specifics of each emotional episode before we can tell whether it is pleasant or unpleasant for the person feeling it.

The term *happiness* is problematic because, like unhappiness, it isn't specific enough. As we'll see in chapter 9, there are many different happy emotions. Amusement and relief, for example, are very different happy experiences, differing as much from each other as do fear and anger. The happy emotions don't have different facial expressions; they all share one type of smiling countenance. The different types of happiness may be revealed in the timing of this facial expression, but the primary signal system for happy emotions is the voice, not the face.

The voice is another emotion signal system, equal in importance to facial expression but different in interesting ways.[5] The face is always observable unless a person leaves the scene, or a culture dictates the wearing of masks or veils, which is increasingly rare. The voice, though, is an intermittent system, which usually can be turned off completely at will. We can't really hide our face completely, although the wish to do so may be part of why people often prefer to use the telephone in place of having face-to-face communication. (Of course there are other benefits to the telephone: not having to be appropriately dressed, being able to do other things secretly while listening to the other person, etc.). E-mail provides the further benefit of not even having to listen and be heard, no chance that the voice would reveal an emotion, and not allowing an immediate reply or protest. Some people try to achieve that by calling when they think the recipient is not there so they can leave a message on an answering machine, but there is always the chance the recipient may pick up.

While I do believe Silvan Tomkins was correct in saying that there is an impulse to make a sound whenever an emotion is aroused—a different sound for each emotion—people can easily suppress those sounds. Yet once someone begins to talk, it is very hard to keep signs of what is felt out of the voice.

Very few of us can convincingly simulate the sound of an emotion we are not feeling. It takes an actor's skill, and often the actor accomplishes the convincing vocal performance by creating the emotion itself, remembering a past event in his or her life. On the other hand, it is easier to put on an insincere facial expression, and my research shows such expressions fool most people who have not practiced identifying expressions.[6] The voice rarely gives false emotional messages, although it gives no messages at all if the person doesn't speak. The face more often than the voice gives false emotional messages, although it can never be totally turned off. Even when listening and not speaking, a subtle sign of an expression may leak out.

The last way in which the vocal and facial signals differ is that the voice captures our attention even when we are ignoring the person who sends out the signal, while we must be paying attention to the person to pick up facial expressions. If there were no vocal emotional signals, if it were only the face that signaled what emotion is felt, caregivers would take serious risks whenever they went out of sight of their infants. What trouble it would be always to have to make a visual check to know an infant's emotional state. As it is, a baby's cry of hunger, pain, anger, fear, or joy can catch the attention of the caregiver who is totally out of sight, and that offers caregivers the opportunity to, in computer parlance, multitask, to do other things in other places as long as the infant's voice can reach them.

Given the importance of the voice, it is regrettable that we know so little, as compared to the face, about how it signals emotions. My colleague and sometimes partner in research Klaus Scherer is the leading scientist studying the voice and emotion. His work has shown that the vocal signals of emotion are, like the face, universal.[7] Scherer has also been working to specify exactly what changes in the voice signal each emotion. There is not as much to report as there is for the face, partly because not as much work has been done. Also, it is hard to describe the sound of the different emotions in a way that can be practically used. That may require hearing the voice, just as the best way to explain the facial clues to emotion is through photographs, films, or video. For most people it is also easier to visualize from a verbal explanation of a facial sign what it will look like than it is to imagine the sound from a verbal description of a vocal sign. In the chapters to follow I will describe what has been found for the voice signals of emotion, as well as showing photographs depicting the various facial expressions for each emotion.

In addition to the facial and vocal emotion signals, there are also emotional impulses to physical action that can be recognized. I believe they are just as universal as the expressions in the face and voice, although there has not been much research about them. I will describe them briefly here because they are not as familiar to us as the facial and vocal expressions. In anger and also in some forms of enjoyment there is an impulse to move closer to the emotion trigger. In fear there is an impulse to freeze if that will avoid detection, or to get out of harm's way if it won't. There is a similar impulse in disgust, but I think it is not as strong; the point seems to be not so much trying to move away as it is getting rid of the offensive object. For example, people may turn away if the offensive object is visual; they may gag or even vomit if it is gustatory or olfactory.

In sadness, but not in anguish, there is a loss of overall muscle tone; the posture slumps in withdrawal, without action. In contempt there is an impulse to look down upon the object of contempt. In surprise and in wonderment there is fixed attention on the object of the emotion. In relief there is a relaxation of body posture; in tactile sensory pleasure there is a movement toward the source of the stimulation, and in the other sensory pleasures there is an orientation toward the source of the stimulation, although no movement may occur other than the direction of the person's glance. Watching athletes make a difficult point suggests that there may be an impulse for action, often involving the hands, in the moment when one takes pride in having achieved something. The laughter that often occurs during intense amusement produces repetitive bodily movements, together with the laughing spasms.

None of these impulses to action[8] would technically be considered signals, because they have not been elaborated over the course of our evolution specifically for the purpose of conveying information clearly. I have described them here because they can provide us with information about what emotion is occurring. They are involuntary, like the facial and vocal emotion signals, but probably much easier to inhibit. Like the facial and vocal signals, they are universal and preset, in the sense that we do not need to learn them.

Everything else that we do when we are emotional is learned, not preset, and is likely to be specific to the culture or a particular individual. These learned actions, which include physical activity and the words we speak, are the product of our continuing lifelong experience (and assessment) of what works when coping with what triggered the emotion and the events that unfold over the course of an emotional episode. It is easier and faster for us to learn actions that are consistent with our preset, automatic emotional actions. For example, for fear we would more easily learn an action pattern that involves literal or figurative withdrawal than one that involves attack. But any action pattern can become established for any emotion. Once learned, these action patterns operate automatically, just as if they were preset.

We can deliberately interfere, overriding or supplanting our reflexes and impulses with quite different actions or no action at all. The interference may also occur automatically, governed by an overlearned habit and not by deliberation. The man stonewalling may do so without thought, without conscious choice. Either way, by deliberate choice or well-established habit, interfering with emotional expressions and actions may be a struggle when the emotion is very intense. For most people it will be easier to prevent an action than totally to remove any sign of the emotion in our face or voice. I believe this is so because we have such excellent voluntary control over the bodily (skeletal) muscles, without which we could not engage in all the complex and skilled actions necessary for our survival. Indeed, we have much better control over our bodily muscles and our words than we have for our facial muscles or the settings in our vocal apparatus.

Just because something we do occurs involuntarily, governed by automatic appraisal without conscious consideration, does not mean that it is the product of our evolution and universal. Habits are learned and operate automatically, often outside of our awareness. In understanding the cascade of changes that occur during an emotional episode, we must remember that the initial second or two will typically combine both preset facial and vocal expressions and preset and learned actions, as well as other nonvisible or nonaudible changes.

So far I have described what can be observed, heard, or seen when someone becomes emotional. There is a set of internal physiological changes that also produces some visible or audible signs of what is happening. Robert Levenson and I have studied some of the changes in the autonomic nervous system (ANS) that occur during emotion, such as sweating, which we can sometimes see or smell; respiration, which we can hear; and cardiac activity and skin temperature, which are invisible. Our finding of different patterns of ANS activity for each of the emotions we have examined also supports what I earlier described as the preset actions. In both anger and fear, for example, heart rate increases, preparing the person to move. In anger blood flow increases to the hands, making them warm and preparing them to strike or otherwise engage the object of anger. In fear blood flow increases to the legs, making the hands colder and preparing the leg muscles for fleeing.[9] Perspiration increases with fear and anger, especially when they are intense. Respiration increases with fear, anger, and anguish, and there is a different kind of breathing—a sigh—in relief. (Blushing is still another quite visible sign, but I will reserve discussion of it until the conclusion of the book.)

Now let's turn from the external behaviors—the signals, the actions, the signs of changes in the ANS—to consider the internal changes that we cannot see or hear. Unfortunately, there is not much research on how thinking itself changes from one moment to the next during an emotional episode, but I have little doubt that there is a profound change in how we interpret the world around us. There is research showing that memories related to the emotion we are feeling are retrieved, even memories that may not be easily accessible when we are not feeling that particular emotion.[10] Most important, we evaluate what is happening in a way that is consistent with the emotion we are feeling, thus justifying and maintaining the emotion. Expectations are formed, judgments made, that typically serve to maintain rather than diminish the felt emotion.

Another set of internal changes that occurs when emotions begin is the attempt to regulate emotional behavior. Traditionally, we think that emotional regulation occurs after an emotion has begun, rather than with the onset of the emotion. Certainly, deliberate attempts to control emotion do occur after an emotion has begun and is registered in consciousness, but my colleague and sometime research collaborator Richard Davidson suggests that regulation also occurs simultaneously with all the other emotional changes—the signal, the changes in thinking, and the impulses to action.[11] Although this is not firmly established, I think Davidson is right, that there is an initial, involuntary stage of regulation that is set off when all the other emotional changes happen, intermixed with them. However, Davidson has not yet been very clear about what the processes are nor how they are established.[12] In the coming decade we will be learning much more about this.

The initial regulatory pattern is, I believe, based on learning, probably early social learning, and is potentially modifiable. It may include how quickly one becomes conscious of experiencing an emotion; once conscious, how readily one can recognize, or label, one's emotional state; and whether there is an immediate insertion of a brake on action, or the reverse, an indulgence of impulsive actions. Admittedly, we know little about this initial regulatory pattern, but it seems that emotions may not spring forth totally unregulated once learning begins, and learning begins early in infancy. Those regulatory patterns are likely to be so well learned that they operate involuntarily and are resistant to change. How resistant we do not know, but if they are at all changeable, that would be quite an opportunity for modifying emotional life.

Consider for a moment a person who is extremely unemotional, so restrained in his emotional reactions that he is dissatisfied with his life, who would like to become more emotionally responsive. Temperament, a genetically based emotional disposition, is one explanation for his pallid emotional life. But if emotional regulation is learned very early in life, perhaps this fellow had the types of experiences that led him to overcontrol his emotions. Perhaps he was punished, disparaged, or ignored for any sign of emotion. If his behavior is caused by learned regulation, there would be a possibility that he might be able to change his reactions. If it is based on his natural temperament, though, there isn't much chance for change. The existence of such initial regulatory patterns points to the enormous importance of the infant's and child's interactions with others in structuring the nature of that individual's subsequent emotional life, in agreement with much other research on that topic[13] and a fundamental tenet of psychoanalysis.

When we are in the grip of an emotion, a cascade of changes occurs in split seconds, without our choice or immediate awareness, in: the emotional signals in the face and voice; preset actions; learned actions; the autonomic nervous system activity that regulates our body; the regulatory patterns that continuously modify our behavior; the retrieval of relevant memories and expectations; and how we interpret what is happening within us and in the world.* These changes are involuntary; we don't choose them. Psychologist Robert Zajonc calls them *inescapable*.[14] By becoming aware of them, and we usually do at some point before an emotional episode is over, we have a chance to choose, if we wish, to try to interfere with them. Before explaining what such awareness entails and steps we can take to heighten it, we need to consider one more aspect of the emotion process—what is running the show, what is generating this cascade of inescapable emotional activity.

To have so many responses—different for each of the emotions and to some extent the same for all human beings—begin so quickly tells us something about the central brain mechanisms that are organizing and directing our emotional responses. The central mechanisms that guide our emotional responses are set into action by the automatic appraising discussed in chapter 2. Stored in these central mechanisms there must be sets of instructions guiding what we do, instructions that reflect what has been adaptive in our evolutionary past. Understanding my theory about what these central mechanisms are and how they operate is essential to what we can expect people will be able to accomplish in regulating their emotional behavior once they achieve awareness of their momentary emotional experience.

Tomkins proposed the phrase *affect program* to refer to an inherited central mechanism that directs emotional behavior. The term *program* comes from two sources: *pro,* meaning "before," and *graphein,* meaning "write," so program refers to mechanisms that store information written before, or in this case, inherited. There would have to be many programs, different programs for each emotion.

---

*There are also changes in our neurochemistry. Although these changes have many of the properties that I am discussing, I am not covering them here.

Affect programs are, like the emotion databases, a metaphor, for I do not think there is anything like a computer program sitting in the brain, nor do I mean to imply that only one area of the brain directs emotion. We know already that many areas of the brain are involved in generating emotional behavior, but until we learn more about the brain and emotion, a metaphor can serve us well in understanding our emotions.[15]

Given that affect programs control our emotional behavior, knowing more about how they work can help guide us in controlling our emotional behavior. The zoologist Ernst Mayr distinguished between open and closed programs. In a closed program nothing can be inserted by experience, while an open genetic program "allows for additional input during the life span of its owner."[16] Mayr pointed out that in creatures that have a long period of parental care, and therefore a long time for learning, there would be a selective advantage to having an open rather than a closed genetic program. (It is consistent with Mayr's thinking to suggest that all animals that manifest emotions will have open affect programs. That is an essential part of the nature of emotion.) For example, contrast humans, notable for many years of dependency, with the Maleo birds of northern Sulawesi, an island that is part of Indonesia. The mother bird buries her egg deep in warm volcanic sand and then leaves. When the baby Maleo bird climbs out of its shell and struggles up out of the sand, it is on its own. It must know immediately what it needs to know for its survival, for there is no dependency period during which it is taught by a parent. We humans are at the opposite end of the spectrum: if abandoned at birth, we die. Our affect programs are open so that we can learn what will work in the particular environment in which we are living, and store this information in a way that will allow it to guide our behavior automatically.

The evidence on universals in the emotion signals and in some of the changes in the autonomic nervous system activity suggests that although the affect programs are open to new information learned through experience, the programs do not start out as empty shells, devoid of information. Circuits are already there, unfolding over development, influenced but not totally constructed by experience.

There must be different circuits for the different responses that characterize each emotion. Evolution preset some of the instructions or circuitry in our open affect programs, generating the emotion signals, the emotion impulses to action, and the initial changes in autonomic nervous system activity, and establishing a refractory period so we interpret the world in a way consistent with the emotion we are feeling.[17]

Further, the evidence on universals in emotion signals and autonomic physiology suggests that typically the instructions for the production of these changes will develop in a similar way for everyone, unless modified by unusual experiences. While there isn't much evidence about how such experiences would modify facial expressions, the research on posttraumatic stress disorder (PTSD) suggests that the thresholds for the arousal of autonomic activity can be radically changed. For example, when asked to speak in front of a group, a task that makes some people ill at ease, women who had suffered abuse early in life were found to produce more stress-related hormones than a comparison group of more fortunate women.[18]

Affect programs contain more than just what is prewritten by our evolutionary past because it was useful to our ancestors. They also contain what we found useful in our own lives in dealing with the most important transactions we have with others—the emotional ones. The initial regulatory pattern associated with each of the emotions varies from one individual to another, depending on what they learn early in life. It, too, is entered into the affect programs; once entered it runs automatically, just as if it had been preset by evolution, and is resistant to change. Also entered into the affect programs are the behavioral patterns we learn throughout our lifetime for dealing with different emotion triggers, which may be congruent with or quite different from those that are preset. As discussed earlier, these, too, operate automatically, once learned.

I do not believe we can rewrite the preset instructions in our affect programs, but that is still to be proven. We can try to interfere with these instructions, but that is an immense struggle precisely because we can't delete or rewrite them. (An exception is that brain injuries can damage the instructions.) If we could rewrite the instructions, then we would encounter people whose emotions would be totally different from our own—with different signals, different impulses to action, different changes in their heart rate, respiration, etc. We would need translators not just for words but also for emotions.

This does not mean that the preset instructions produce identical changes in everyone. The instructions operate on different bodily systems, quite apart from differences between individuals and cultures in what they learn about managing their emotional behavior. Even with the same preset instructions there will be both individual differences and commonalities in emotional experience.

Once set into motion through automatic appraising, the instructions in the affect programs run until they have been executed; that is, they cannot be interrupted. How long the changes resulting from the instructions are noninterruptible varies with the particular emotional response system being considered. For the facial expressions and action impulses, I suspect it is less than a second. I make this suggestion based upon observing how quickly people can wipe an expression off their face, reducing the length of its appearance or masking it with another expression. Listening to what people say when they are trying to conceal their feelings, I have noted that such control over the sound of the voice takes longer, but it is still likely to be only a matter of seconds or at most a few minutes, unless the emotion is very strong, or unless something new happens to reinforce it. The changes in our respiration, perspiration, and cardiac activity also have a longer time line, some stretching out to ten or fifteen seconds. The reader should note that this idea that the instructions can't be interrupted does not rest on hard scientific evidence. It does, however, fit my observations about how people behave when they are emotional.

Remember my example of Helen, who got angry when her husband, Jim, told her that she, not he, would have to pick up their daughter after school? The expression of irritation that flashed on her face; the edge in her voice when she asked why he didn't give her more notice; the slight thrust forward of her body; the increase in her skin temperature, blood pressure, and heart rate—these are all the preset changes generated by the affect program. Most of them could vanish the next moment when she learned from Jim why he couldn't give her more notice (the changes in skin temperature, heart rate, and blood pressure will take a bit longer to return to where they were before the episode began). The episode also could continue; she could maintain her anger if the refractory period persists. Perhaps there is a backlog of resentment, or she might import the bullying-by-brother script, or maybe Jim really is inconsiderate and this is just another instance of it. If Helen discounts Jim's excuse, interpreting it as another instance of his thinking his needs have priority over hers, her anger would surge forth again. My point is that the initial preset changes generated by the affect program, when an emotion is aroused through automatic appraisal, are brief and need not persist. Sometimes they fit and are needed to deal with the situation—Jim really is inconsiderate and will walk all over her unless she prevents it. Sometimes they are inappropriate—Jim couldn't have given her more notice; this isn't a pattern of his being dominant; she just didn't have enough sleep last night and woke up in a grouchy mood.

To say we can't interrupt our reactions is not to say we can't manage them, only that we don't have the option of choosing instantly to turn them off completely. Even if we reevaluate what is happening, the emotional responses already active may not end instantly. Instead, the new emotional responses may be inserted over or mixed with the emotions already generated. Suppose Helen's anger at Jim is based on importing the being-bullied-by-brother script. Once Helen hears that Jim really had no choice, that he wasn't dominating her, then she knows that continuing to be angry about it is inappropriate; but if the bullying script is operating, her anger persists, or she may recall that she woke up grouchy, and it is her mood that is sustaining her inappropriate anger. Helen may begin to feel guilty about continuing to feel resentment. We know from scientific study that two emotions can occur in rapid sequence, again and again. Two emotions also can merge together into a *blend;* but in my research I have seen that happen less often than repeated rapid sequences.

Reevaluations are not the only way in which we may for a time bounce back and forth between different emotional responses. Tomkins pointed out that we often have affect-about-affect, emotional reactions to the emotion we initially feel. We may become angry that we were made afraid, or we may become afraid about having become so angry. We could feel afraid of what we might do because we are feeling so sad. This linking of a second emotion with a first emotion can happen with any pair of emotions. Silvan Tomkins also suggested that one way of understanding the uniqueness of personality was to identify whether a person typically had a particular affect about another affect. He also suggested that sometimes we are not aware of our initial emotional reaction, we are aware only of our secondary emotion about the first emotion. We may not realize that we were afraid at first and be aware only of the anger that was aroused in response to the fear. Unfortunately, no one has done any research to determine the merit of these very interesting ideas.

But what's important to remember is that emotions rarely occur singly, or in pure form. What we are reacting to in the environment often changes quickly; what we remember and imagine about the situation may change; our appraising changes; and we may have affect-about-affect. Typically, people experience a stream of emotional responses, not all the same ones. Sometimes each emotion may be separated by a few seconds, so that some of the initial emotional responses come to an end before new ones begin, and sometimes emotions occur in overlapping time, blending.

There is another very important matter to consider further. As I said, affect programs are open, not closed. New emotional behaviors are continuously acquired throughout life, added to the preset emotional behaviors. This feature of our affect programs makes it possible for us to adapt to whatever circumstances within which we live. It is why our emotional responses are linked not just to our evolutionary past, but also to our own personal past and our present. Automobiles were not part of our evolutionary past, but these complex actions that were learned not as children but as young adults were incorporated into the fear response. The learned fear responses—twisting the steering wheel and braking—appear, involuntarily and without thought, when the threat is from another car.

Once learned and entered into the affect programs, these newly acquired emotional responses become involuntary, just as involuntary as the unlearned responses. One of the amazing things about the affect programs is that both learned and innate behaviors can become so tightly joined together and can be brought into action so quickly and involuntarily. However, there is also a downside to having an open emotional response system. These acquired, or added-on, behaviors are hard to inhibit once entered into the affect programs. They happen even when they don't necessarily work, or when we might not want them to occur.

Recall the example from the last chapter in which a passenger's foot shoots out to hit the nonexistent brake pedal when another car lunges toward the car in which the passenger is riding. The passenger can't stop her foot because it shoots out before she knows what she is doing, just like she can't stop the expression of fear that passes across her face. Are these acquired emotional responses permanent, as immutable as those that are preset and not learned? I don't think so. I believe we can unlearn, not just manage, our acquired emotional responses. This will be easier to accomplish with some of the acquired emotional responses than with others.

Any responses that involve bodily movement are more easily unlearned than responses that involve the voice and the facial movement. As I explained earlier, we have great control over the muscles that control our body (the skeletal muscles). Driving teachers learn not to press their foot to the floor when they are sitting in the passenger seat. An involuntary action that had become automatic, part of the instructions added into the fear affect program, can, over time, be modified with practice and effort. Some of the factors that I described in the last chapter that determine how easy it will be to weaken a hot emotional trigger apply also to how readily we can unlearn a pattern of emotional behavior. Behavior patterns that were acquired early in life, that were learned during a highly intense and dense emotional episode or series of episodes, will be harder to modify or unlearn.

As children we may become violent at times, and we almost always are taught not to be. In chapter 6, when discussing anger, I consider whether we need to learn to be violent, whether the impulse to hurt another is a built-in part of the anger response. Most adults do not ever want to be violent unless there is no other way to defend others or themselves from injury. (I realize that there are a few deviant people who wish to be violent, either because it is part of their criminal activity or what they find enjoyable. I will consider them in my discussion of violence in chapter 6.) Can any of us be pushed to the point where we totally lose control, act destructively, and in that sense have no choice over what we say or do? Does everyone have a breaking point? Could any of us commit murder, and the fact that we haven't is simply because we haven't been sufficiently provoked? I believe the answer to these questions is no, but there isn't scientific evidence to prove that to be so. (Can you imagine the experiment in which you attempt to drive a person to violence with ever-increasing provocations?)

Most of us have acquired regulatory patterns that moderate our emotional behavior, setting some brake on what we say and do before it reaches the stage where we engage in extremely harmful behavior. We may do and say terrible things, but there is still a limit—we don't take our life or the life of another in an uncontrolled impulsive emotional peak. Even when enraged or terrified or anguished, we stop before becoming irreversibly destructive. We may not be able to keep the emotion off our faces or out of our voices, we may not be able to prevent ourselves from saying something cruel or kicking the chair (although that should be easier than inhibiting the facial or vocal signs of the emotion), but we can and do prevent that cruelty from growing into physical damage. I do recognize that there are people who have poor impulse control, but I view that as an aberration rather than the norm.

Granting then that most of us will not reach the ultimate form of destructive actions, permanently harming others or ourselves, it is still true that most of us will occasionally say or do things that are harmful. The harm may be psychological rather than physical, and it may not be permanent, but our behavior is still hurtful. The harm may not be motivated by anger; it may not involve harm to others but to us. For example, uncontrolled fear can paralyze us from dealing with danger; sadness may cause us to withdraw from the world. The issue now for us to consider is how and when we can prevent destructive emotional episodes, whether the harm be to us or others or both.

. . .

One of the functions of emotion is to focus our conscious awareness on the problem at hand, the one that has triggered our emotions. Typically, our emotions do not operate outside of our awareness, although that can happen. We have all had the experience of not realizing we have been acting emotionally until someone points it out. Although that does happen, more commonly we are consciously aware of how we are feeling. The emotions we are experiencing feel right, justified. We don't question what we are doing and saying. We are in the swing of it.

If we are to put a brake on our emotional behavior, if we are to change how we are feeling, we must be able to develop a different type of emotional consciousness. We must be able to take a step back—right while we are feeling the emotion—so we can question whether we want to go along with what our emotion is driving us to do, or exercise a choice about how we will act on our emotion. This is more than being conscious of how we are feeling, it is another, more advanced, difficult to describe, form of consciousness. It is close to what Buddhist thinkers call *mindfulness*. Philosopher B. Alan Wallace says this is "the sense of being aware of what our mind is doing."[19] If we are mindful of our emotions, he says, we can make the following choice: "Do we want to act upon the anger, or do we simply want to observe it."[20] I am not using the term *mindful* because it is embedded in a larger, quite different philosophy from what I have described for understanding emotion, and it depends on quite specific practices, different from the steps I have and will suggest.

In writing about memory, psychologists Georgia Nigro and Ulric Neisser described how "in some memories one seems to have the position of an onlooker or observer, looking at the situation from an external vantage point and seeing oneself 'from the outside.'"[21] They contrasted this type of memory to one in which you have the perspective of the person in the memory. In much of our emotional experience we are so much in the experience, so gripped by the emotion, that no part of our mind is observing, questioning, or considering the actions in which we are engaging. We are conscious, aware, but in what psychologist Ellen Langer calls a mindless way.[22]

Nigro and Neisser's distinction between two types of memory is very similar to what psychiatrist and Buddhist thinker Henry Wyner described as the difference between the stream of consciousness and what he called the watcher, "the awareness that watches and responds to the meanings that appear in the stream of consciousness."[23] In order for us to be able to moderate our emotional behavior, to choose what we say or do, we have to be able to know when we have become or, better still, are becoming emotional.

Conceivably, we would have even more choice if we were able to become aware of the automatic appraisal as it is happening, and modify or cancel it at will. Because the automatic appraisers are so fast, I doubt that anyone is able to do that. His Holiness, the Dalai Lama, in my meeting with him, did mention that some yogis are able to stretch time. For them those few milliseconds during which automatic appraisal occurs might be stretched long enough for them to make a conscious choice to modify or cancel the appraising process. But the Dalai Lama was doubtful that this type of *appraisal awareness* is possible for the vast majority of people, including him.

A next step that may be possible, but is hard to achieve, is to become aware of what is happening in one's head immediately after the automatic appraisal but before emotional behavior has begun; aware of the impulses to action and words when those impulses first arise. If one could achieve such *impulse awareness,*[24] one could decide whether to allow the impulse to be realized. Buddhists believe they do achieve impulse awareness, but it requires many years of meditative practice. Let's move on to consider what may be more readily, though still not easily, achievable.

Philosopher Peter Goldie describes what he terms *reflective consciousness* as being aware that one feels afraid. If a person were to say, "Looking back on the experience, I was obviously afraid whilst it was going on, but I didn't feel any fear at the time," that, says Goldie, would be an example of not being reflectively aware.[25] This is a prerequisite for what I want to focus upon, but it is not sufficient, for it leaves out the consideration of whether or not we want to go along with or attempt to change or inhibit our emotion.

Jonathan Schooler, in his account of what he calls *meta-consciousness*, describes the familiar experience we have all had of turning the pages of a book without reading a word as we were instead thinking of what restaurant to go to that night.[26] It is not that we are not conscious; we are quite conscious of thinking about the restaurants, but we are not aware that we have stopped reading the book. If we were, we would have developed meta-consciousness. It is such consciousness of what we are experiencing at the moment that I want to consider, wedded to the choice of whether or not we want to go along with or change that experience.

I have not been able to find a single term to describe this type of consciousness; the best I have been able to come up with is *attentively considering our emotional feelings.* (To avoid repeating the entire phrase I will sometimes abbreviate it by just using the term *attentive* or *attentiveness,* in italics.) When we are being *attentive,* as I mean it, we are able to observe ourselves during an emotional episode, ideally before more than a few seconds have passed. We recognize that we are being emotional and can consider whether or not our response is justified. We can reevaluate, reappraise, and if that is not successful, then direct what we say and do. This occurs while we are experiencing the emotion, as soon as we have become conscious of our emotional feelings and actions.

Most people are rarely so attentive to their emotional feelings, but such attentiveness is possible to achieve. I believe that we can develop the ability to be *attentive* so it will become a habit, a standard part of our lives. When that happens, we will feel more in touch, and better able to regulate our emotional life. There are many ways to develop this type of *attentiveness.*

One method people can use to become more *attentive* to their emotions is to use the knowledge about the causes of each emotion described in chapters 5 through 9. By becoming more familiar with what triggers our emotions, we can increase our consciousness of when and why our emotions occur. A crucial part of taking this route to increasing *attentiveness* is having the ability to identify our own hot emotional triggers and being able to take steps to weaken them. The goal is not to be devoid of emotion, but instead to have more choice once we become emotional about how we will enact that emotion.

Learning about the sensations, the bodily feelings that distinguish each emotion, should also help to focus our *attentiveness.* Normally, we are consciously aware of these sensations, but we don't focus on them or use them as signals to alert us to be *attentive* to our emotional states. In chapters 5 through 9 I provide exercises to increase your consciousness of how these emotions *feel,* so that you can be more aware of these physiological changes and use them as deliberate cues that make us *attentive,* giving us the opportunity to consider, reevaluate, or control our emotions.

We may also be able to become more *attentive* to our emotional feelings by becoming more observant of the emotional feelings of others with whom we are engaged. If we know how they are feeling, if that registers in our conscious mind, we can use that as a cue to better discern our own feelings, and to signal us to become *attentive* to our own emotional feelings.

Unfortunately, my research has found that most of us are not very good at recognizing how other people are feeling unless the expressions are pretty strong. No one needs much help in how to interpret a facial expression when an emotion is at its peak. The expressions are usually uncontrolled by then, showing the appearances I found to be universal. But expressions can be very subtle, just a change in the eyelids or the upper lip. And often we are so focused on what the person is saying that we miss these subtle signs completely. This is a pity, since we are better off if we can detect how another person is feeling early in our interaction with them. The appendix provides a test that allows you to assess how well you recognize the subtle signs of when an emotion is beginning. Chapters 5 through 9 provide photographs to help you become more sensitive to subtle facial expressions, and ideas about how to use that information in family life, in friendships, and in the workplace.

Learning to *attentively* consider our own emotional feelings is not easy, but it is possible, and, over time, with repeated efforts, I believe it becomes easier.* Even when *attentiveness* has become an established habit, it won't always operate. If the emotion is very intense, if we are importing a script that we have not identified, if we are in a mood relevant to the emotion we are feeling, if we have had little

---

*My very limited experience with meditation, and my personal knowledge of a number of friends and colleagues who have had a great deal of meditative practice, has convinced me that this is another means to achieving such *attentiveness.* In research I am just beginning, I will learn more about how this occurs and document the nature of the changes that result.

sleep or are experiencing continual physical pain, we may fail to be *attentive*. We will make mistakes, but when we do, we can learn from them to reduce the likelihood that they will reoccur.

There are a number of techniques we can use to moderate our emotional behavior once we are being *attentive:*

• We can try to reappraise what is occurring; if we succeed, the emotional behaviors will shortly stop, another more appropriate emotion may occur, or, if our initial reaction was appropriate, it may be confirmed. The problem with reappraising is that our refractory period causes us to resist and prevents us from having access to information—stored within us or from the outside—that can disconfirm the emotion. It is much less difficult to reappraise once the refractory period is over.

• Even if we cannot reappraise what is occurring, even if we still believe our feelings are justified, we can choose to interrupt our actions, to halt our speech within a few seconds, or at least not to give our feelings full reign. We can try to reduce the signals in our face and voice, resist any impulses to action, and censor what we say. Voluntarily controlling the involuntary behavior driven by our emotions is not easy, especially if the emotion felt is intense. But it is possible to stop speech and action, more so than to wipe out completely any trace of the emotion in our face or voice. It is *attentiveness,* knowing that one is emotional, that can keep people from losing control over what they say or do, from acting in ways they later regret.

Let's consider how this operates by examining another example, one from my own life. My wife, Mary Ann, was away for four days attending a conference in Washington, D.C. We both follow the practice, when away, of calling the other each day. On our Friday night call I told her that on Saturday I would be having dinner with a colleague and then working with him late into the evening. By the time I expected to reach home, at about eleven o'clock at night, it would be two in the morning for her in Washington and she would already be asleep. Since we would not be able to talk Saturday night, she said she would call me in the morning on Sunday.

Mary Ann knows that I get up early, even on a Sunday, and when she is not home I am always sitting at my computer by eight in the morning. By nine she had not called and I began to worry. It was noon her time; why hadn't she called? By ten I started to become angry. It was one in the afternoon her time, and surely she could have called. Why hadn't she? Was she embarrassed about something she had done the night before that she didn't want to reveal? I didn't like having such thoughts, and that added to my anger. If she had called I would not have started to become vulnerable to jealousy. Might she be sick; had she been in a car accident? I began to feel afraid. Should I call the Washington, D.C., police? Probably she had just forgotten, or was so engaged in the museums she was seeing—she had told me that was what she would do on Sunday—that she had forgotten our telephone appointment. Her thoughtlessness made me angry again, supplanting my fear, as I began to think about her enjoying herself while I was worrying about her. Why should I be vulnerable to jealousy? Why didn't she call!

If I had been smarter, if I had already learned from the lessons I've discussed in this book, I could have begun preventive work on Saturday night or Sunday morning. Knowing that abandonment by a woman is a hot emotional trigger (my mother died when I was fourteen), I would have prepared myself not to feel abandoned if Mary Ann forgot to call. I would have reminded myself that Mary Ann hates to use the telephone, especially the pay telephone, and probably wouldn't call me until she got back to her hotel. I would also have retrieved knowledge that in twenty years of marriage Mary Ann has proven herself to be trustworthy, so I need not be jealous. By thinking of all of these things ahead of time, I might have been able to weaken my emotional triggers so I would not interpret her failure to call in the morning in ways that would make me feel abandoned, angry, jealous, or afraid about her welfare, and angry that she might be needlessly making me have all these feelings.

It was, of course, too late to have the benefit of that kind of thinking, for not having done it ahead of time I couldn't do it Sunday morning. Each time I felt angry, or afraid, or jealous, I was in a refractory period when everything I knew that would defuse the situation was no longer available. The emotions had begun; they were getting stronger each time I experienced them as time passed; and I could no longer access the relevant information about Mary Ann and about me. I could only access information that fit the emotions I was feeling.

I was determined not to let my emotions prevent me from working. Although I was not angry from eight in the morning until one o'clock in the afternoon when Mary Ann finally did call five hours later (four o'clock her time), I had many angry episodes each time I looked at my watch and noted that she still had not called. Given the span of time, however, I also had time to begin to become *attentive* to my emotional feelings. Though I felt quite justified in being angry at her thoughtlessness for not having called me in the morning when she said she would, I decided it would be wise not to express my anger over the telephone, and to wait until she returned home. I could hear the trace of anger in my voice as we talked, but I succeeded in my effort not to complain or make any of the accusations I so sorely wanted to discharge. It was not a very satisfactory talk, and after a few minutes we agreed to hang up, noting that she would be returning late in the evening the next night.

I reflected on what had happened. I felt relieved that I had not said anything accusatory, but I knew she knew from the sound of my voice that I was angry about something. She had exercised control in not pressing me about it. The refractory period had come to an end, so I was able to reappraise the situation. I no longer felt angry, but instead I felt a little foolish for having become angry. Not wanting to leave things distant, when we were actually a few thousand miles apart and would not see each other for nearly two more days, I called Mary Ann back. Perhaps two minutes had passed since the first conversation. This time it was a pleasant, satisfying conversation. A few days later I asked her about this episode, about which she had forgotten. She confirmed that she had realized I was angry, but since I hadn't brought it up, she had decided not to bring it up.

This is an example of an emotional episode in which a person regrets having become emotional. There are, of course, other instances in which we are very pleased about our emotional reactions. But let's focus on what we can learn from this episode that might have application to other situations in which one regrets one's emotional behavior. First is the importance of trying to anticipate what may occur, of knowing one's vulnerabilities. I failed in this instance and so could not short-circuit the whole matter; I could not reduce the likelihood that I would import the anger-about-being-abandoned script into this episode, and thereby extended the refractory period. Happily, I have learned enough from this experience that it is not likely that I will respond with anger when Mary Ann again doesn't call me when she says she will. When *attentive,* I can choose not to become angry, but if I am already in an irritable mood or under a lot of other pressure in my life, I might fail.

There are two parts to the analysis that we need to do to weaken an emotional trigger that we suspect may be about to go off. One part focuses on ourselves, what it is within ourselves that is causing us to respond emotionally in a way we later regret. In this example, it was my recognition that not being called on the telephone was tapping my never-resolved resentment toward my mother for having abandoned me when she died, which I was importing into this situation. The second part is to try to broaden our understanding of the other person. In this example, that involved my reviewing what I knew about Mary Ann that would lead her not to call, such as her dislike of pay phones, which had nothing to do with abandonment.

It may be too much to ask ourselves always to be able to anticipate and defuse emotions, especially at the outset. But part of becoming more skilled in how we deal with our emotions is developing the ability to analyze and understand what has happened once a given episode is over. The analysis should be done at a time when we no longer feel the need to justify what we did. Those analyses can help alert us to what we need to guard against, and they can help us cool down an emotional trigger.

In the previous chapter I recommended keeping an emotion diary of episodes that one regrets. Studying that diary can help to identify not only why such episodes are occurring, but when they are likely to reoccur and what you can do to change yourself so it doesn't happen in the future. It would be useful also to keep in that same diary a record of episodes in which one succeeds, in which one reacts well. Apart from providing encouragement, such diary entries allow us to reflect on why we were sometimes able to succeed, as well as when and why we failed.

Frequently the issue will be what to do once an emotion has begun and we are in the refractory period, unable to reinterpret what is occurring. If we are being *attentive*, we can try not to feed the emotion while inhibiting actions that are likely to cause the other person to respond in such a way as to make our own feelings become stronger. If I had made accusations, Mary Ann might well have responded defensively with anger, which would have made me become angry again, perhaps angrier. I have come to view controlling emotional behavior, whether it is fear or anger, as a challenge, a challenge I almost enjoy, although I don't always succeed. When I do succeed I have a sense of mastery that is very satisfying. Again, I believe practice and thinking about what needs to be done, as well as being self-aware during the emotional episode, can help.

Controlling emotional behavior will not always work. When the emotion aroused is very strong, when we are in a mood that predisposes us toward the emotion, when the event resonates very closely with one of the evolved emotional themes or with an early learned emotion trigger, my suggestions will be more difficult to use. And, depending on the emotion, some people's affective style—those who characteristically become emotional very quickly and very intensely—will make it harder to control some emotions.

The fact that we will not always succeed does not mean that we cannot improve. The key is to understand ourselves better. By analyzing our emotional episodes afterward, we can begin to develop the habit of *attentiveness*. By learning to focus more on what it is we are feeling, by learning some of the internal clues that signal to us what emotions we are feeling, we are more likely to be able to monitor our feelings. Increasing our ability to spot the signs of how others are responding to us emotionally can alert us to be attentive to what it is we are doing and feeling—and help us respond to others' emotions in an appropriate way. And, learning about the common triggers for each emotion, those we share with others and those that are especially important or unique for us, can help us prepare for emotional encounters. The next chapters provide information on all these matters.

5

Sadness and Agony

It is a parent's worse nightmare. Your son suddenly disappears, with no apparent explanation. Months later you hear that the police have uncovered a homosexual mass murder ring that abducted, tortured, and killed young boys. Then you learn that your son's body has been uncovered and identified at the mass burial site.

The police were led there by seventeen-year-old Elmer Wayne Henley. The police had arrested Henley for shooting his friend Dean Corll, thirty-three, after an all-night paint-sniffing party. Henley claimed to be part of a mass murder ring procuring young boys for Dean Corll. When Corll said Henley was to be his next victim, Henley shot him. In custody for Corll's death, Henley told the police about the murder of the boys as "a service to them [the parents] of sorts." He felt the parents should know what had happened to their sons. In all, the bodies of twenty-seven young boys were recovered.

Bettye Shirley is the mother of one of the dead boys. Her grief is stunning, her suffering so intense that looking at her expression can be overwhelming. One can almost hear the sobs that are bursting forth from her deeply unhappy face. The messages conveyed by the face and voice repeat each other when no attempt is made to regulate expression.

The death of one's child is a universal cause for sadness and

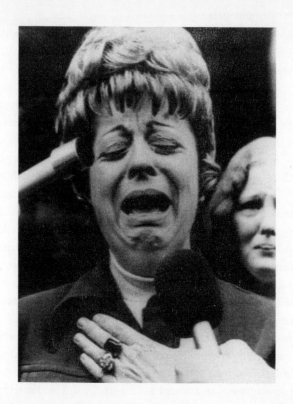

agony.* There may not be any other event that can call forth such intense, recurrent, and enduring unhappiness. In 1967, when I was conducting my research in Papua New Guinea, I asked the Fore to show me what their faces would look like if they learned their child had died. The videotapes of their performances show the same facial expressions as Bettye Shirley, although less intense, as they were imagining rather than experiencing the loss.

Many types of loss can trigger sadness: rejection by a friend or lover; a loss of self-esteem from failure to achieve a goal at work; the loss of admiration or praise from a superior; the loss of health; the loss of some body part or function through accident or illness; and, for some, the loss of a treasured object. There are many words to describe sad feelings: distraught, disappointed, dejected, blue,

*An exception would be if the child has been suffering from an incurable illness, or, in some societies, if the child is a very young infant for whom the family cannot care.

depressed, discouraged, despairing, grieved, helpless, miserable, and sorrowful.

None of these words seems strong enough for the emotion shown by Bettye Shirley. Wally Friesen and I suggested that this emotion has two distinctive sides—sadness and agony.[1] In the moments of agony there is protest; in sadness there is more resignation and hopelessness. Agony attempts to deal actively with the source of the loss. Sadness is more passive. Often agony appears to have no purpose when there is nothing that can be done to recover what has been lost. We cannot tell from the facial expression in this photograph whether Bettye is feeling sadness or agony. It would be more apparent if we could see her expressions for a few seconds, hear what she said, and see her body movements. Indeed, it would be painful to hear Bettye's cries of despair or pain. We can look away from a face, but we cannot escape the sound of an emotion. We teach our children to inhibit the unpleasant sounds associated with some emotions, especially the terrible cries of despair and agony.

Sadness is one of the longer-lasting emotions. After a period of protesting agony, there is usually a period of resigned sadness, in which the person feels totally helpless; and then, again, the protesting agony returns in an attempt to recover the loss, followed by sadness, then agony, again and again. When emotions are mild or even moderate, they may be as brief as a few seconds, or they can last a few minutes before another emotion (or no specific emotion) is felt. Bettye Shirley's intense emotion would come in waves, again and again, rather than being sustained continuously at this high pitch. In such an intense loss there may always be a background sad or dysphoric mood until, over time, that mood begins to fade as the mourning process ends.

Even in such intense grief, there are moments when other emotions may be felt. A grieving person may have moments of anger at life; at God; at the person or thing that caused the loss; at the person who died for dying, especially if the deceased put himself or herself at risk in some way. Anger may be directed inward for not having done something, for not having expressed some important sentiment, for not having prevented the death. Even if rationally there was nothing that could have been done that would have prevented the loved one's death, people who are mourning may feel guilty and angry with themselves for not having had the power to prevent it.

Bettye Shirley almost certainly would have felt anger toward the two men who killed her son, but the photograph catches her at a different moment, at the moment when she feels sadness and agony. We feel angry toward the person responsible for a loss, while we feel sadness and agony about the loss itself. Anger is all that may be felt if the loss is not permanent, as in death, but is due to rejection. Even then there may be sadness when the loss itself is felt. There are no hard-and-fast rules, for it is not unusual for the mourner who feels abandoned to have moments of anger toward the person who died.

There may be moments when the grieving person is afraid of how she will be able to live without the deceased, afraid also that she will never be able to recover. Such fear may alternate with feeling unable to resume life after such a loss. If the loss has not yet occurred, fear may be the predominant emotion rather than sadness or agony.

Even positive emotions may be felt briefly during an otherwise intensely sad experience. There may be moments of amusement when recalling some shared funny moment with the deceased. Often friends and relatives at a memorial service or when visiting the home of the mourning person will bring up such positive memories and there may even be some laughter. There may also be pleasure for a moment in greeting a close family member who has come to share the grief and provide comfort.

When I was working in the New Guinea highlands, I learned about another feature of grief. One day I left the village in which I was living and hiked into the regional center in Okapa, where there was an Australian hospital, so I could take a shower and recharge the batteries for my movie camera. A woman from a village some miles away had come to the hospital with a very sick baby, who unfortunately had died. The Australian doctor was about to take the woman, with her dead child, back to her village, and he invited me to come along. The woman sat in the Land Rover quietly, unexpressive, holding her baby in her arms during the long trip. When we arrived and she saw her relatives and friends, she began to weep, showing intense agony. The doctor thought she was insincere, turning on a ritual display of emotion to impress her fellow villagers. He thought that if she had truly felt despair she would have shown it while traveling with us.

The doctor failed to recognize that we may not truly experience agony unless we are in the presence of others who can and do share our loss. We know what has happened, but its meaning to us becomes enriched when we tell others about it or see their reactions to our loss.* This was a very extreme example of that phenomenon, for this woman was living in a Stone Age culture, with no matches, no running water, no mirrors, and no clothes other than grass skirts. Her baby had died in a context that had no meaning for her. The Western hospital with all its facilities made the experience unreal, as though she had been on Mars and then returned to Earth. Another possibility was that she was holding in her grief in the presence of these two strange men—the doctor and me. She may also have been in shock, and it took time for her to get past that state for the grief to be displayed. If more time had passed, no matter where she was, her grief might have emerged.

There was a period when mental health professionals believed that mourners who did not show intense grief were engaging in denial and would, consequently, be vulnerable to serious psychiatric problems later. More recent research suggests that is not always the case, especially when the person who dies has had a slow decline, and there has been ample time to adjust to the oncoming death. In such cases the mourner experiences little agony, and just occasional sadness, when the death finally happens. If the attachment has been a difficult one, with many stormy periods or considerable dissatisfaction, then death may bring a release, with feelings of relief rather than despair.

When the death of a loved one is sudden or unexpected, with little time to prepare, it is not infrequent for mourners to believe the dead person is still alive. Dr. Ted Rynearson, who has studied how people react to the sudden death of a loved one, found that many such mourners converse with the deceased, believing in a sense that the dead person can hear and is responding to them.[2] When the death occurs by accident, homicide, or suicide, it may take years for

---

*Psychologist Nico Frijda made a very similar point when he said, "Grief often does not emerge when one is notified of death or departure; such notification consists only of words. Grief strikes when one comes home to the empty house."

these conversations to end and for the mourner to accept completely that the loved one is dead.

An intense expression of grief like Bettye Shirley's may even appear when someone who was anticipating a devastating loss gets the good news that the loved one is all right. In that first moment of relief, all the agony that was being held in bursts forth. The grief anticipated, but contained, is now expressed. At that moment the person feels both grief and relief. Postponed emotions, suppressed for one reason or another, emerge when it is safe to feel them, even if the emotion is no longer relevant to the immediate situation.

There is another possible, but unresearched, explanation for why we sometimes see the signs of agony, complete with tears, when a person hears wonderful news. It is conceivable that the most intense joy overwhelms the emotion system, and that extraordinarily strong emotion of any kind produces moments of agony.

Anger can be a defense against agony, a substitute, and sometimes even the cure. When the rejected lover can become angry at being jilted, the despair subsides. In a moment of intense loneliness, the sadness will return and may again be driven away by anger. In some people anger is maintained in reserve, ready to appear at the least sign of loss, to prevent the experience of agony.

Some psychotherapists have held that prolonged sadness and agony in response to loss is the result of anger turned inward. If the suffering person could direct the anger outward, at the deceased, for leaving, at the rejecting lover, spouse, teacher, or boss, then the sadness and agony would be "cured." While this can occur, I doubt it is the usual reaction. It is not uncommon to have feelings of anger toward the person who is lost, but anger is by no means the only feeling, nor is its expression a necessary or certain cure for the sadness and agony that is felt.

These days it is common for people to take medications to alleviate intense sadness or agony, to attenuate the depth of mourning. I have no reservations about the use of medications for dealing with depression, an emotional disorder described later in this chapter. I am much less certain that it benefits a person not to feel sadness or agony about the normal losses we all experience in life if the person is not clinically depressed. Sadness and agony may help heal the loss, and without those feelings the suffering from the loss could endure longer.

If sufficiently medicated, a person won't seem to be suffering, and that can be a drawback. The sadness and agony in facial and vocal expressions call for help from others. That social support, the caring of friends and family members, is healing. A person who is medicated so as not to display sadness and agony might receive less of that healing attention. I don't mean to suggest that the expressions of sadness and agony are in any sense deliberately made to cause others to help. These expressions are involuntary, not deliberate, but one of their evolutionary functions is to cause others who see the expressions to feel concern and want to offer comfort.

Another function of the sadness and agony expressions is to enrich one's experience of what the loss has meant. We are keenly aware of what it feels like to cry, of the suffering we feel in our face after many expressions of agony and sadness. It is not that we would not know what the loss meant if there was no expression; we would know, but we wouldn't feel it fully if medications soothed our despair. Still another function of sadness is to allow the person to rebuild his resources and conserve his energy. Of course, that won't happen when the sadness is alternating with agony, which dissipates resources.

I want to caution the reader. There is no firm evidence, one way or the other, on medicating people to deal with the normal reactions of sadness and loss in mourning, or when suffering another type of loss. We don't know yet what to advise, and I can only raise these issues for the reader to consider. Again, I emphasize that I have been discussing nonpathological reactions to loss, not clinical depression. Later in this chapter I will explain how clinical depression differs from sadness and agony.

It was the summer of 1995 in a Bosnian refuge camp in Tuzla. The Europeans and Americans had declared certain areas safe from Serbian attack, to be protected by NATO troops. But the Serbs disregarded the declaration, and the safe area of Srebrenica fell. The Serbs brutally murdered many of the men. The refugees traveling to Tuzla saw civilian corpses along the road; they passed blackened houses still smoldering after the Serbs had set them on fire, in some

instances while people hid inside them. They also saw hanging from trees the bodies of men who had tried to escape. The people shown here are Bosnian Muslims, in Tuzla, another supposedly safe area. They have just read a list of those who survived, learning that many—most of their fathers, brothers, or husbands—had not.

It is hard not to want to comfort a child who shows such agony. That impulse to reach out and help is fundamental to any sense of community. It is motivated, in part at least, by the suffering we feel when we see another person suffer, especially when we see a child who is helpless and miserable. This is one of the functions or purposes of this expression: to call out for help, to impose one's suffering on others so they will help. And it does feel good to comfort another person; comforting another, reducing his misery, gives the caregiver a positive feeling.

Those same feelings of wanting to help and comfort may have been aroused when you saw Bettye Shirley's expression, but probably not as strongly. Most of us are less inhibited about comforting a strange child than an adult, even when suffering is intensely manifest. The sociologist Erving Goffman observed that there are few barriers to touching children we do not know: comforting them if they are in distress, touching them in a playful fashion when passing them. (He wrote in the 1960s before there was heightened concern about pederasty.)

I myself am perhaps too vulnerable to feeling the suffering of others. A television news account of suffering, even if it is about an event that was satisfactorily remedied, instantly brings tears to my eyes and feelings of suffering. Even rather crass television commercials that show someone in a state of loss start my tears flowing! I was not always that way. I believe it is the result of an extraordinarily painful experience following back surgery thirty years ago. Because of a medical mistake, I was not given any pain medication, and the suffering I experienced was so severe and unrelenting for five days that I would have taken my life if I had had the means. This terrible, traumatic suffering unhinged my own sadness/suffering emotion system. I am like a shell-shocked soldier who overresponds to the least sound of something resembling gunfire. Very intense, dense (repeated again and again) emotional experiences can reset the thresholds for experiencing any emotion.

It is worth noting that not everyone wants to be helped when he is experiencing sadness or agony. Some people wish to withdraw, to be alone, not to be seen in such a state. Such people may be ashamed of being weak and helpless, ashamed of having been so dependent upon a person, so attached, that sadness and agony are experienced when that person is lost. Some people take pride in never showing an unpleasant emotion, instead showing a "stiff upper lip." But the fact that someone does not want to show his feelings does not mean that he will succeed completely; it also does not mean that he isn't feeling the emotions just because he's suppressing (insofar as he can) his expression. As I explained in chapter 4, emotional expressions are involuntary; they begin to appear even when we don't want them to. We can suppress them but not always completely. If we could completely eliminate emotional expressions—so there was no trace in face, voice, or body—then we would have to regard these expressions as being as unreliable as the words we speak.

(I purposely used the masculine pronoun in the previous paragraph because this is more common among males, although it is by no means unknown in females and certainly not evident in all males. Cultural traditions and upbringing within a culture, and perhaps also temperament, play a role in shaping one's attitude about feeling or displaying sadness and agony.)

Each expression conveys a set of related messages. The messages for sadness and agony revolve around "I am suffering; comfort and help me." Our reaction to seeing these expressions is not typically a detached, intellectual matter, even when they are manifest in such an abstract fashion as a still photograph on the page of a book. We are constructed to respond with emotion to emotion; we usually feel the message. That does not always mean we feel the emotion that is being signaled to us.

Not everyone feels the suffering of others; not everyone is drawn to help and comfort a miserable person. Some people become angry in response to another person's misery. They may feel that an unwelcome, improper demand is being made upon them for help: "Why can't he take care of himself. Why is he being such a crybaby?" Silvan Tomkins believed that a fundamental difference among people was how they respond to the suffering of others. Do we feel that suffering ourselves and want to help them, or do we blame the person who is suffering for being in such a predicament and making a demand on us?

Sometimes a person or group of people—the Bosnian Muslims, the Jews, the American Indians, the African slaves, the Gypsies— may be regarded as not being really human, not like the rest of us. They may be called animals, to show how little they matter. Although the suffering of animals moves many people, it does not move everyone, and not everyone is moved by the suffering of those they regard as less than human. Their suffering may seem deserved, or at least not discomforting to witness. There are also people who enjoy the suffering of others. They torment, physically or psychologically, because it feels good to exert their power and to witness the pain and suffering it produces. An expression such as the one this young boy is showing may only whet their appetite to induce more suffering in their victims. (Such people are discussed at the end of chapter 6.)

Tears are apparent streaking the Tuzla boy's agonized face. Tears are acceptable in children and adult women in Western cultures, but until very recently tears of sadness or agony were considered a sign of weakness in adult men. Presidential candidate Edmund Muskie's tears when he described his reactions to a newspaper's attack on his wife were said to have cost him the 1972 primary elections. Today, matters seem to have changed. Bob Dole and Bill Clinton both showed tears in the 1996 election campaign and were not criticized for doing so. The mass media and many teachers emphasize the acceptability of emotions in general and sadness and anguish, in particular, in men. I doubt that this has permeated all segments of American society, but we have no benchmarks to compare what was usual thirty years ago with now.

Tears are not unique to sadness or grief. They can also occur during intense joy, and in bouts of laughter, although a recent review of the literature found more reports, in adults, of crying when people feel helpless.[3] People report feeling better after crying, and although there are differences in what triggers a cry, which may be due to the management of expression, crying appears to be a universal emotional expression. There is a claim that crying is unique to humans; however, there are scattered reports of crying in anguishing situations in other primates.

As discussed earlier, not only do emotions have a role in moods, but most emotions are also central to a specific personality trait and a specific emotional disorder. Considering the duration of each phenomenon is the easiest way to distinguish among emotions (which can be as short as a few seconds or as long as many minutes; moods (which can last hours, or sometimes a day or two); and personality traits (which can color a major section of a person's life, such as adolescence, young adulthood, and sometimes a person's life).* While

*What causes them and how they affect our lives are other ways in which emotions, moods, emotional traits, and emotional disorders differ, but those matters need not concern us now.

emotional disorders can be either episodic, lasting only weeks or months, or pervasive, enduring for years or decades, it is not how long they last but how they impair our ability to live our lives that distinguishes them from emotional personality traits. In a disorder, emotions are out of control, and they may interfere with our capacity to live with others, to work, to eat, and to sleep.

When we have a blue mood, we feel sadness for many hours; a melancholic personality is prone to feeling sad or having blue moods; and depression is the mental disorder in which sadness and agony are central. Of course, people commonly use these words interchangeably, saying, for example, that one felt depressed that a grade on an exam was not very high. But mental disorders have distinctive markers that place them beyond the range of normal emotional responses.

For one thing, they last a lot longer. That "depression" about the grade will dissipate quickly if some other emotional event comes along. True depression lasts for days, months, even sometimes for years. In an emotional disorder, particular emotions dominate life, monopolizing matters, so that few other emotions can be felt. The emotions are felt very intensely, again and again. Emotions are out of control; the person cannot regulate them or escape them. They interfere with the person's ability to carry out the fundamental life tasks of eating, sleeping, cohabiting, and working. It is severe; one could say, metaphorically, that the emotions are flooded.

If sadness dominates the depression, we speak of a retarded depression; if agony is more prominent, it is an agitated depression. People who are depressed not only feel helpless to change their lives, they feel hopeless. They do not believe it will ever get better. In addition to sadness and agony, guilt and shame are strongly felt, for depressed people believe they are worthless, which is why they think they feel the way they do. Depression may be a reaction to some life event, an excessive reaction, or it may appear seemingly without reason or cause, when no event can be identified to have set it off.

Sadness and agony are not the only emotions felt; anger, directed inward or out, and fear are often manifest. If there are swings between depression and extreme elation and excitement, then it is called a bipolar depression or, in the old terminology, manic-depression. There seems little doubt that there is an important genetic contribution that makes one vulnerable to depression, and that medications are helpful in most cases. Psychotherapy with or without medications can be helpful, although there is still argument in the literature about whether psychotherapy alone can be as helpful as medications alone when the depression is severe.

We found no unique facial expressions in our study of people suffering from depression, nothing that one would not see in normal people experiencing sadness and agony. Any thirty-second observational period could show only that the person was miserable, not that he or she was in a clinical depression. It was the repetitiveness and strength of the emotions, shown again and again over an hour, that made it obvious the face expressed depression, not simply sadness and agony over an important loss.

The amount of sadness was related to the patient's diagnosis. There was less sadness shown by those suffering from what is called minor (less severe) depression and more sadness by those diagnosed with major depression. In addition to some sad expressions, manic patients showed much more smiling, but not the smiles of enjoyment. (The distinction between smiles of enjoyment and other kinds of smiling is explained in chapter 9.)

In a study of patients at my own hospital, we found that differences in the type of emotions shown at the time the patients were admitted to the hospital predicted how well they responded to subsequent treatment; that is, how much improvement would be shown three months later.[4]

Recognizing Sadness in Ourselves

Now I want to shift attention to how we experience sadness internally. You may have begun to feel some sadness or agony when you looked at Bettye Shirley's or the Tuzla boy's face. If that happened, look again, and, if you start to feel the emotion, let the feeling grow so you can consider how your body responds. If you did not feel any sadness when you looked at the pictures, try looking again and permit those feelings to occur. If they do begin, let them grow as strongly as possible.

When you look at the pictures, you may have remembered a time when you yourself felt very sad over a loss, and that memory triggered feelings of sadness. For some people a sad event has been so important in their life that they are primed to reexperience easily and to remember that event, to be flooded by those sad feelings. Their sadness story is waiting for an opportunity to be reenacted again. Such people are highly susceptible to sadness; they need to feel it again because the sadness they felt is not completely over. Some experiences are so devastating—such as the death of a loved child—that the sadness may never completely fade away. A person who has endured such trauma may be very easily moved to tears, vulnerable to any hint of suffering in others.

If you still have not had any feeling of sadness, if the photograph did not provoke any empathic feelings, and if no memory spontaneously emerged, try this path: Was there ever a time in your life when someone died to whom you were very attached and for whom you felt sadness? If so, visualize that scene, and let the feelings begin to re-institute themselves. When this begins to happen, let the feelings grow, paying attention to how your face and body feel.

If you still have not felt any sadness then try the following exercise.

Imitate the facial movements of sadness, such as those Bettye Shirley is showing. (You may need to use a mirror to check on whether you are making the correct movements.)

- Drop your mouth open.
- Pull the corners of your lips down.
- While you hold those lip corners down, try now to raise your cheeks, as if you are squinting. This pulls against the lip corners.
- Maintain this tension between the raised cheeks and the lip corners pulling down.
- Let your eyes look downward and your upper eyelids droop.

If you still have not begun to feel any sadness, then try imitating the eyebrows that Bettye Shirley is showing. This is a much harder movement for most people to make voluntarily.

- Pull the inner corners of your eyebrows up in the middle only, not the entire brow.
- It may help if you also pull your brows together and up in the middle.
- Let your eyes look downward and your upper eyelids droop.

Our research shows that if you make these movements on your face, you will trigger changes in your physiology, both in your body and in your brain. If this happens to you, let the feelings grow as strongly as you can.

If you have been able to feel sadness or agony by looking at Bettye's picture, by the memory exercise, or by following the instructions to make the facial movements, try doing it again. Concentrate on what those feelings feel like. Pay attention to what happens as those feelings first begin, how they register, what changes in your body and in your consciousness. Let the feelings grow and become as strong as you can allow. While that happens notice what you feel in your head, neck, or face, in your throat, in your back and shoulders, in your arms, in your stomach, and in your legs. These are the sensations you feel with sadness; they are very unpleasant feelings. They may verge on being painful if they are very strong and last for long.

Your eyelids may become heavier. Your cheeks may start to rise. The back of your throat may begin to feel sore. Your eyes might have moistened with the beginning of tears. These are normal reactions during sadness, and they are also normal when looking at the face of someone who is feeling intense sadness. Empathic reactions are common, and they are a means by which we establish bonds with others, even with total strangers. These feelings make you care about Bettye's or the boy's suffering, and they make you want to help them. Bettye Shirley is experiencing every parent's worst tragedy; the boy is experiencing every child's worst fear.

When looking at Bettye's picture, or following the memory or facial muscle movement exercises, most people will experience sadness, not agony. If the feeling grows extremely strong or is held for long, it may convert into agony. By becoming more familiar with these feelings, by reflecting on what they feel like, you have a better chance of recognizing those feelings when they first begin, of realizing when you are beginning to experience a loss.

I have described the most common sensations experienced during sadness, the theme, if you like, but each individual has his or her own variations on how sadness, or any other emotion, feels. Most of us presume that everyone else feels an emotion the way we do, or that our way is the only correct way. People differ in how readily sadness can be called forth, how rapidly sadness switches to agony and back to sadness, and how long sad feelings usually endure. Knowing your own way and how it differs from those you care about may help you better understand the miscommunications and misunderstandings that might occur in your life involving this emotion.

Some people can enjoy the experience of sadness, although not sadness that is as intense as Bettye's. Such people read novels known as tearjerkers; they go to movies they hear will bring on sadness; they watch such television programs. And there are some people who have an extreme aversion to sadness and agony, who go out of their way to avoid situations in which they might feel these emotions. They may avoid attachment or commitment, since caring about others leaves them vulnerable to loss and sadness.

Recognizing Sadness in Others

Now let's shift our focus to how the emotion of sadness is registered in the faces we have seen. We begin by analyzing what this emotion looks like when it is extreme, and then turn to the more subtle signs of sadness and agony. Look again at Bettye's expression. Her intense sadness or agony is displayed across her entire face. One very strong and reliable sign is the angling upward of the inner corners of her eyebrows. It is reliable because few people can make this movement voluntarily, so it could rarely be deliberately fabricated. (That is not so for some of the other facial movements described later.) Even when people are attempting not to show how they are feeling, these obliquely positioned eyebrows will often leak their sadness. Look at the space between her eyebrows. In most people a vertical wrinkle between the brows will appear, as it does here, when the eyebrows are drawn up and together. In some people that wrinkle is permanently etched in the face, and if that is so it will deepen and darken when the inner corners of the eyebrows are pulled up and together.

To see how powerful the eyebrows are, cover the rest of her face below the eyebrows with your hand. She still looks anguished, even when you can see only her eyebrows. Her eyebrow movement has triangulated her upper eyelids. Sometimes this may be the only sign of sadness.

Her intense sadness is also clearly registered in her lower face. Her lips are stretched horizontally, her lower lip is pushed up, and, I expect, her lower lip was trembling. Her wide-open mouth adds to the intensity of this display. Another crucial registration of her agony is in the raised cheeks, which are another part of the full display of this intense feeling. The lip corners probably are being pulled down, but this action is too weak to see when the lips are so strongly stretched horizontally and the cheeks are pulled strongly upward. Look at the skin between the tip of her chin and her lower lip, what the anatomists call the chin *boss*. It is wrinkled and pushed upward by the action of the chin muscle, the muscle that, when it acts alone, produces a pout. Here the lower lip is not pushed up in a pout because it is being stretched so intensely.

Now take a look at the expression on the younger woman standing behind Bettye Shirley. We see only part of her face, but enough to notice that the inner corner of one eyebrow has been pulled upward and toward the center, and that the cheek has been raised. These two signs repeat what we see in Bettye Shirley's face. The lips in the younger woman's face are not open but might be pressed slightly together, perhaps in an attempt to keep from weeping aloud.

Now look again at the boy from Tuzla. His eyebrows are not angled upward. This is because when crying, the brows may sometimes be pulled down and together, especially during the peak of a crying bout. His raised cheeks and wrinkled chin were also apparent in Bettye's face. The pulling up of the cheeks sometimes causes the lip corners to be slightly raised, as if there is a grin.

Use your hand to cover the boy's upper face so you can just see from the bottom of his lower eyelids down. It is still obvious that the smile is not one of enjoyment, and that the lower part of the face is showing sadness. Some scientists have been confused by such smilelike appearances, asserting that smiles have nothing to do with enjoyment because they appear—as they do here—when someone clearly is in anguish. The key is realizing that the lip corners are being pulled upward by the strong action of the cheek muscle, not by the muscle that underlies smiling. Note that the boy's chin boss is very much like Bettye's. There is a remote possibility that this boy might be trying to mask his agony with a smile to show that he can cope with the grief (perhaps so he will not be a burden to his family).

In the Tuzla picture there are two other women showing despair or grief: The woman on the right shows the archetypal oblique eyebrows, the stretched mouth, slightly lowered lip corners, and raised cheeks. The woman behind the boy mirrors his expression.

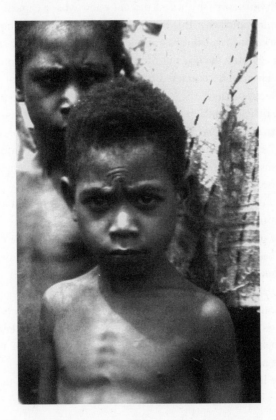

The young boy pictured on page 99 was walking along a trail in the New Guinea highlands when he came across a stranger, me. To the best of my knowledge, he had not seen any other Caucasian; at most another scientist, or, even more unlikely, a missionary might have passed by. He and most of the other people in his culture were visually isolated, which is precisely why I was there studying them. He had never seen a photograph, a magazine, a film, or a video, and so he could not have learned his expressions from such sources.

I was an object of great interest to these people, for nearly everything I did was novel. Even doing such a simple thing as lighting my pipe with a match was a source of wonder, since they had no matches. I was surrounded each night when I would type my experiences into my diary. They thought my portable typewriter was a music machine, emitting but one tone every few seconds. I did not have to worry that he might be camera-shy, for he did not know what a camera was.

I have no idea what this boy was thinking or why he showed this sad expression, for I did not speak his language and the translator who was helping me was not there at this moment. In some people, the muscle that is contracted to raise the inner corners of the eyebrows does not cause the brows to move, but instead produces this characteristic wrinkle pattern. In his book *The Expression of the Emotions in Man and Animals,* Charles Darwin wrote of this pattern: It "may be called, for the sake of brevity, the grief muscle. . . . [It] produces a mark on the forehead which has been compared to a horseshoe."

This same muscular action, albeit weaker, is responsible for the appearance of Bettye Shirley's forehead, but in the New Guinea boy only the skin and not the eyebrows moved upward in the center of the forehead. For some people this is always the way this involuntary expression shows on their faces, presumably because of an anatomical peculiarity. While some people may think the boy is perplexed rather than sad since his eyebrows are drawn together, the horseshoe pattern would not occur unless he was sad. For contrast, look at the fellow behind the boy, whose eyebrows are just drawn together, showing perplexity or concentration.

There is no hint of sadness in either the boy's mouth or cheeks.

This is an example of a *partial* expression. The signal is in just one part of the face, unlike the full expressions shown in the two earlier pictures. This could happen if he were trying to control the display of his emotion, for, as I mentioned earlier, the eyebrows are more difficult to manage than the lower face. Or perhaps the feeling is too weak to be shown yet across his entire face.

Now let us examine some of the components of the sadness expression and its more subtle signs. I am using photographs of my daughter Eve that I took four years ago. I didn't tell her to pose an emotion; instead I showed her on my face the specific muscle movement I wanted her to make. I took thousands of photographs in order to obtain the ones I needed to explain how subtle changes occur in expression. I have used only one person as the model (except for a few pictures of me that appear in other chapters), so you won't be distracted by the specific features of the person you

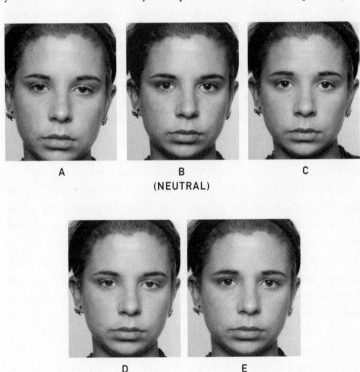

A   B
(NEUTRAL)   C

D   E

see, and so you will be able to focus on how the expressions change.

I'll begin with the eyes—both the eyelids and the eyebrows. Picture B shows a neutral nonemotional pose so you can compare what her face looks like when she shows no emotion with the isolated, and sometimes very slight, changes I describe. Photo A shows the drooping of the upper eyelids, while photo C shows just the hint of the inner corners of the eyebrows raising. When even slight changes like this occur, they seem to change the entire face.

To help you see that it is only the upper eyelid on the left and the brow on the right that is providing the message, I created composite photographs, pasting just those features on the picture in the middle. Picture D shows the upper eyelids from picture A pasted onto the neutral B picture. Photo E shows the brows from C pasted onto the neutral B picture. This should convince you that even a very subtle change seems to affect the appearance of the entire face. Incidentally, E looks a bit less sad than C above it. That is because in C, there is a very slight hint of upper eyelid droop. It would not be apparent without comparing C to E, the picture where just the brows of E have been pasted onto the neutral face.

Photo C is a definite sign of sadness; it may be slight sadness, sadness being controlled, or sadness that is beginning to ebb. Not everyone will recognize it without practice, especially if it is brief. Photo A is more ambiguous. It could be a sign of slight or controlled sadness, but it may also just be a sign that the person is getting sleepy or bored, since the drooping eyelid is the only signal.

Notice, however, what happens when the drooping eyelid is combined with the raising of the eyebrows. Picture F shows a composite in which the eyebrows of C and the eyelids of A have been pasted onto the neutral face. The same combination of drooping eyelids and raised inner corners of the eyebrows is shown in G, but in this natural, not computer-created, picture the movement of the eyebrows is stronger. Now there is no doubt. This is very clear sadness, hard to miss or misinterpret unless it was very brief.

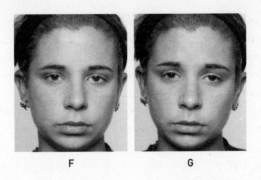

F   G

The next row of pictures shows other changes in the eyes. In picture H on the left, the eyebrows are strong but the gaze is straight ahead, with no upper eyelid droop. In picture I the eyebrows are strong; there is a slight droop of the upper eyelid and a slight tensing of the lower eyelid. Compare the lower eyelids in photo I with the neutral photo B. In picture J we see a typical feature in sadness, in which the gaze is directed down. You saw this as part of the sad display in Bettye Shirley's photograph. Of course, people do look downward when they read, or when they are tired, but when it is added to the sad eyebrows, the message is unambiguous.

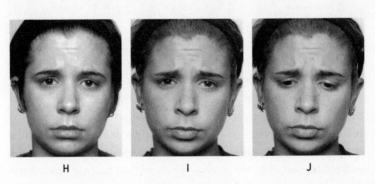

H   I   J

The eyebrows are very important, highly reliable signs of sadness. They rarely are shown in this configuration unless sadness is felt, for few people can voluntarily make this movement. There are exceptions; both Woody Allen and Jim Carrey show this movement often. While most people emphasize speech by raising or lowering their eyebrows, these two actors often use the sad brow to emphasize a word. It makes them seem empathetic, warm, and kind, but that may or may not be a true reflection of what they are feeling. For those who do use the raised inner corners of the eyebrows to accent their speech, it has little significance, but for nearly everyone else it is an important sadness signal.

Now let's focus on what happens to the mouth in sadness. Photo K shows the lip corners pulled downward very slightly. This action is stronger in picture L, and even stronger in the picture M. This is another sign of very slight sadness, or it can happen when people try to limit how much sadness they reveal. Picture M is so strong that when it is shown alone, without sadness shown in the eyebrows or the eyes, it probably isn't sadness. Instead it more likely is a movement some people make as a symbol of disbelief or negation.

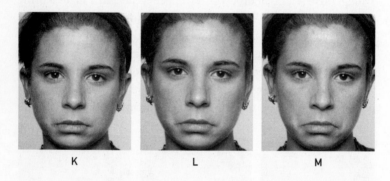

K   L   M

The next photos show the expression that occurs when just the lower lip is pushed up. Photo N is a pout, which can occur alone when the person is just beginning to feel sad, as a precursor to a cry. It also may occur when the person is feeling sulky. In picture O, the movement is too strong to be a sign of sadness when it occurs alone, without the sad eyebrows, eyelids, or downward gaze. Instead, this is more likely to be a symbol of uncertainty, like a shrug with the hands. Photo P combines pushing up the lower lip, as in N and O, with lip pressing. It is often a sign of determination or concentration, and it is a frequent mannerism in some people, such as President Clinton. Some people also throw a bit of a smile into this configuration, and it becomes a grin-and-bear-it symbol.

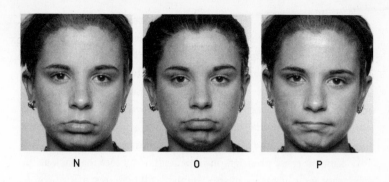

N   O   P

The next pictures show blends of two emotions. Photo Q is the combination of sadness in the eyebrows with quite a full smile. Cover the mouth with your hand and you will see that she looks sad, and by covering the eyes and eyebrows she looks happy. This expression occurs with bittersweet experiences, such as the recollection of a happy moment, which is tinged with sadness because it is in the past, over, no longer in the person's life. It can also occur when a person is using the smile to try to conceal or mask sadness. Picture R shows the combination of fear and sadness expressed by sadness in the eyebrows and fear in the wide-open eyes. Use your hand to cover first the eyebrows, and note the fear in the eyes; then cover the eyes, and you will see that the brows are clearly the sad ones we have seen before. Picture S could be a blend of sadness and surprise because the lips are parted and the eyes are open, though not as much as in the fear-sadness blend in the middle photo.

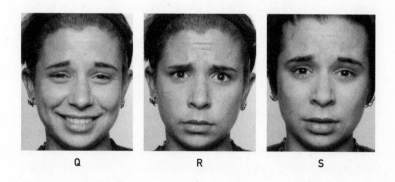

Q   R   S

The last picture, T, shows the combination of all the sadness signs we have seen with one new one. The inner corners of the brows are raised, the upper eyelids are slightly drooped, and the lip corners are pulled down. The new feature is the raising of the cheeks that has produced the wrinkles running down from Eve's nostrils outward beyond the corners of her lips. This is called the *nasolabial furrow*. The muscle that has raised her cheeks produces this furrow and pushes upward the skin below her eyes, narrowing her eyes.

Looking at these photographs repeatedly, and looking back at the news photographs earlier in this chapter, will help to sensitize you to how people are feeling without their telling you. You can increase your skill in recognizing the subtle signs of sadness (and the emotions shown in the other chapters) by checking the Web site emotionsrevealed.com.

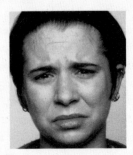

T

Using the Information from Expressions

I want to consider next what you should do now that you will be better able to receive emotional information from people's faces and from your own automatic responses. It is obvious what you should do when sadness is very clearly shown on someone's face, as it was in the boy from Tuzla, in Bettye Shirley, and in some of the pictures shown here of Eve (photos H, I, J, and T). There is no avoiding the sadness expressed; the person showing it is not trying to hide it. When expressions are that extreme, the person showing the expression can feel it on his or her face and would expect that others can see how he or she feels. The expression signals a need for comfort, whether it be an arm placed around the person's shoulder, or simply an offer of comfort in words.

But what if it is only a subtle sign, such as what you saw in pictures A, C, or K? What are you to do with this information? Remember that emotional expressions never tell you their source—there are many reasons why, for example, someone might be sad. Don't presume you know why the person is sad. When you see a subtle expression, it is not certain whether the person wants you to know how he or she is feeling, and you should not assume that you should acknowledge that you know how the person is feeling. It is a very different matter when you see a subtle sign as compared to the complete displays shown by Bettye Shirley or the boy from Tuzla; they know how they feel, they know their feelings are showing, and you have an obligation to respond.

If the expression is a subtle one, the first issue is whether the expression is a sign of sadness that might just be beginning, slight sadness, or anticipation of disappointment, or if it is a sign that strongly felt sadness is being controlled. Sometimes you can tell which it is by when it happens. If it occurs right at the start of a conversation, it is unlikely to be just the beginning of sadness, but anticipatory sadness, sadness imported from a memory or from a prior event. If it emerges during the conversation, it might be the beginning of sadness, or a sign of controlled, more intense sadness. That depends upon what you and the other person have been talking about.

Suppose one of these subtle sad expressions is shown when you deliver the news to someone you supervise about whether he or she will get a promotion. It might be anticipatory sadness; or if the news is not good, slight sadness; or if the news is quite bad, controlled, more severe sadness. Knowing how that person is feeling doesn't mean that you necessarily will want to acknowledge it. It depends on what your relationship is to that person. But it is information you can benefit from in determining how you are going to respond to the person, now or later.

In some situations, with some people, simply acknowledging that you are sorry to have to disappoint them might be helpful. But that might humiliate or even anger some people, and it might be better to say nothing. Would the person think you had a choice, or would the person you are disappointing think you had been unfair? In either case, acknowledging their disappointment or saying you are sorry might seem insincere, and even elicit anger. Alternatively, if there still is another opportunity for that person to be promoted, then acknowledging the disappointment in the context of offering to help them to do better in the next round could strengthen your relationship.

Another matter to consider is just how important is the bad news you are conveying. If it really is a disaster for that person, then the subtle sign of sadness may result from an attempt to diminish signs of much more intense feelings. If that is so, any acknowledgment that you realize how he or she feels might bring on a more intense display of those sad feelings. Do you want that to happen? You are taking from the person's expression information he or she chose to try to conceal from you. Should you bring it up or comment on it?

Suppose you are the person who receives the bad news, not the supervisor, and an expression of slight sadness appears on the supervisor's face when she gives you the bad news about not getting the promotion. That probably means the supervisor is sympathetic to you, is sorry about having to give you bad news. Is she sugarcoating the bad news out of sympathy, or might she not agree completely with the decision; or might she be responding empathetically to the hint of sadness she sees on your face? The hint of sadness doesn't tell you; but it does tell you that she is concerned, and that is worth noting. There is a possibility that it is a fake expression of concern, but most of the muscular movements in sadness are not easy to make deliberately.

If it were a friend, not a supervisor, who showed a subtle expression of sadness when telling you about the bad news he recently got, you might want to go further. You might want to verbally acknowledge your concern, empathize with how he seems to be feeling, and give him a chance to elaborate on his feelings. Again, you must keep in mind that this expression might be the result of an attempt to control and conceal more intense sadness. Do you have the right to invade your friend's privacy? Has your past relationship been one of disclosure, in which your friend expects to receive reassurance and comfort from you? Might it be better just to offer a noncommittal "Is everything OK?" leaving it to your friend to decide whether he wants to reveal anything more about his feelings?

Suppose it is your twelve-year-old daughter who shows that

expression when you ask her how her day went at school. As a parent you have the right, some would say the obligation, to pay attention and acknowledge the feelings of your child. Yet, as kids move into adolescence they increasingly want privacy, the choice as to when they reveal what to whom. Has yours been a close relationship, and can you spend the time, now, if your comment on what she is feeling brings on a flood of tears? I believe it is better to ask, to acknowledge, than to pretend nothing has happened, but that is my style and it may not be yours. There is a fine line between intrusiveness and lack of concern, and you can show concern but not push it. If it is an adolescent, it might be well to give her the chance to regulate what happens by simply saying, "Is everything OK?" or "Need help with anything?"

Sadness is often shown with good-byes, when two people who care about each other anticipate not seeing each other again for an extended period. Most often, in most relationships, acknowledging the regret at the separation is appropriate, but once again, not always. Some people have so little tolerance for sad feelings that it would be difficult for them to have those feelings frankly acknowledged. For others there might be a complete loss of control if the sadness were to be commented on. If you were in a relationship where a separation matters, you would know the person well enough to know how to respond.

These examples are meant to show that having information about how someone feels doesn't itself tell you what to do about it. It doesn't confer the right or obligation to tell that person you know how he or she feels. There are alternatives, depending on who that person is and what your relationship to that person is, the circumstances at the moment, and what you yourself are comfortable with. But spotting sadness when it is subtle does tell you that something important is happening or has happened, that it involves loss, and that this person needs comforting. The expression itself doesn't tell you whether you are the right person to give that comforting, or if this is the right time to offer it.

Brace yourself before turning to the next chapter. It is about the most dangerous emotion—anger. Don't start it until you are feeling relaxed and able to take on this emotion.

6 Anger

The face of attack, of violence, is anger. The separatist demonstrator on the right just hit the Canadian police officer; the demonstrator on the left appears ready to strike. We don't know what happened before this moment, though. Did the policeman attack the demonstrator? Was the demonstrator acting in self-defense, or was his violence unprovoked? Is response to an attack the anger theme, the common, universal trigger for calling forth anger? Emotion theorists have proposed a number of different themes for anger, but there is no evidence to suggest that one is central; in fact, there might be multiple themes for this emotion.

The most effective situation for calling forth anger in infants—something developmental psychologists do to study this emotion—is physical interference, holding the infant's arms so the infant cannot get them free.[1] This is a metaphor for one of the most frequent causes of anger in children and adults: someone interfering with what we are intent on doing. If we think the interference is deliberate, not incidental or required, if it appears the interfering person *chose* to interfere with *us*, our anger may be stronger. Frustration with anything, even an inanimate object, can generate anger.[2] We may even be frustrated by a failure in our own memory or ability.

When someone is trying to hurt us physically, anger and fear are likely responses. If someone tries to hurt us psychologically, insulting us, denigrating our appearance or performance, that, too, is likely to arouse anger and fear. As mentioned in the last chapter, rejection by a loved one can produce not only sadness but anger as well. Some spouses or lovers who become enraged when they are rejected batter their spouses. Anger controls, anger punishes, and anger retaliates.

One of the most dangerous features of anger is that anger calls forth anger, and the cycle can rapidly escalate. It takes a near-saintly character not to respond angrily to another person's anger, especially when that person's anger seems unjustified and self-righteous. So another person's anger can be considered another cause of anger.

Disappointment in how a person has acted may also make us angry, especially when that person is someone we care deeply about. It may seem strange that we can get the angriest at those we love the most, but those are the people who can hurt us and disappoint us the most. In the early stages of a romantic relationship, we may entertain many fantasies about the loved person and become angry when that person fails to meet our fantasized ideal.[3] It may also seem safer to show anger toward an intimate than a stranger.

Another reason why we may be angriest at those about whom we care most is that those are the people who know us intimately, know our fears and our weaknesses, and know what can hurt us the most.

We may become angry with someone who advocates actions or beliefs that offend us, even a total stranger. We need not even meet the stranger; reading about someone who engages in actions or who holds beliefs with which we disagree may arouse our anger.

Evolutionary theorists Michael McGuire and Alfonso Troisi[4] make the very interesting suggestion that people might typically show different "behavioral strategies" in response to the different causes, the themes and variations, of anger. It makes sense to think that the different causes of anger will not arouse the same intensity or type of anger. When someone rejects us or disappoints us, we may attempt to hurt him or her, while an attempt to hurt a would-be mugger might cost us our life.

One could argue that frustration, another person's anger, a threat of harm, and being rejected are all variations on the interference theme. Even anger at someone who advocates what we consider wrong could be considered a variation on interference. But I think it is important for people to consider these as different triggers and determine for themselves which one is the most potent, the hottest trigger for their anger.

The word *anger* covers many different related experiences. There is a range of angry feelings, from slight annoyance to rage. There are not just differences in the strength of angry feelings, but also differences in the kind of anger felt. Indignation is self-righteous anger; sulking is a passive anger; exasperation refers to having one's patience tried excessively. Revenge is a type of angry action usually committed after a period of reflection about the offense, sometimes of greater intensity than the act that provoked it.

When it is brief, resentment is another member of the anger family of emotions, but holding a grudge, a long-standing resentment, is different. If a person has acted in a way you feel was unfair or unjust, you may not forgive him but harbor your resentment—that grudge—for a very long time, sometimes for a lifetime. It is not that you are continuously angry, but whenever you think about or see that person, anger reemerges. Resentment may *fester,* in which case it is never out of mind. The person is preoccupied with the offense, ruminating excessively about it. Presumably, when resentment festers, the likelihood of revenge being taken would be greater.

Hatred is an enduring, intense dislike. We are not angry continuously toward the hated person, but encountering that person or hearing about her or him may easily awaken angry feelings. We are also likely to feel disgust and contempt toward the hated person. Like resentment, hatred is usually long-standing and focused on a specific person, though general in character, while resentment is connected to a specific grievance or set of grievances. Hatred, too, can fester, taking over the hating person's life so he or she becomes preoccupied with the hated person.

It is hard to know how to classify hatred and enduring resentment. They are not emotions, for they last too long. They are not moods for the same reason, and also because we know why we hate or resent someone while we typically don't know why we are having a mood. I have thought of calling resentment an *emotional attitude,* and hatred an *emotional attachment,* along with romantic and parental love. The point is to recognize that these feelings are heavily invested with anger but are not the same as anger.

In the last chapter I said the message of the sadness signal was a cry for help. It is harder to specify a single message for anger. "Get out of my way" seems to capture part of it, the threat to someone who is interfering. However, it doesn't seem to fit the anger aroused by another person's anger, or the anger felt toward a person one reads about in the newspaper who has done something outrageous. And sometimes anger is not merely a feeling of wanting the offending person out of the way; it is a feeling of wanting to hurt that person.

Anger is rarely felt alone for long. Fear often precedes and follows anger, fear of the harm the target of anger may inflict or fear of one's own anger, of losing control, of inflicting harm. Some people often merge disgust with anger, repulsed by the target they also attack. Or disgust may focus on oneself for having become angry, for not having exercised sufficient control. Some people feel guilty or ashamed about having angry feelings.

Anger is the most dangerous emotion, because, as the photograph of the demonstrators shows, we may try to harm the target of our anger. It may be only angry words, shouted or more deliberately delivered, but the motive is the same, to harm the target. Is this impulse to hurt a necessary, built-in part of the anger response system? If it is, we should see attempts to hurt early in life, and observe their diminution only when a child is taught to restrain that impulse. If it is not, the anger impulse could simply be to deal forcefully with the problem, without necessarily trying to hurt the person who is causing it. If that were so, then we would observe hurtful, angry behavior only in those children who learn from caretakers or others that hurting a person is the most successful way to eliminate the problem. It matters which it might be. If hurting is not built in to the anger response system, then it might be possible to raise children in such a way that hitting or hurting wouldn't be part of what they do when they are angry at others.

I asked two leading researchers[5] on anger in infants and children if there was any strong evidence one way or the other, and they said there is not. Joe Campos, a pioneering researcher on emotion in infancy, reported "slashing and thrashing that seems to have the function of removing the obstacle" in newborns, and mentioned what he called "proto-anger" in infants in a variety of situations involving interference with what they were doing, such as removing the nipple when they were sucking. It is unclear whether these movements are yet-to-be-coordinated attempts to hurt the person who is the source of the obstacle or just attempts to stop the interference. There is no information on exactly when and how attempts to hurt emerge, or if they do so in all infants.

There is evidence that hitting, biting, and kicking are evident very early in life in most infants, but begin to come under control at about two years old, continuing to decline each year thereafter.[6] Psychiatrist and anthropologist Melvin Konner recently wrote, "The capacity for violence . . . is never abolished. . . . It is always there."[7] This fits with my own observations, having raised two children of my own; very early in their lives striking out to harm was in place. They had to learn to inhibit that response, to establish other ways of dealing with interference, insults, and a variety of other offenses. I suspect that the impulse to harm, for virtually everyone, is a central part of the anger response. I also believe, however, that there are important differences among us in how strong these violent impulses are.

Although we may condemn people for what they say or do when angry, we understand it. It is the person who harms without anger who is not understandable, and who is often seen as truly frightening. People often regret what they have said in anger. In their apology, they explain that they were seized by anger and claim that what they said was not really what they meant; their true attitudes and beliefs were distorted by the power of this emotion. The common phrase "I lost my head" exemplifies this. Apologies do not come easily as long as a trace of anger remains, and apologies may not undo the damage done.

If we are *attentive* to our emotional state, not only conscious of how we are feeling but pausing to consider whether we want to act on our angry feelings, it will still be a struggle if we decide not to act on our anger. That struggle will be greater for some of us than others, for some of us become angry more quickly and intensely. The struggle is not to damage, not to up the ante, not to return the other's anger with more intense anger, not to say unforgivable things, to decrease the reply from anger to annoyance, or to eliminate any sign of anger. Sometimes we *do* want to act on our anger, and, as I explain later, actions taken in anger can be useful and necessary.

David Lynn Scott III, a twenty-six-year-old man, a self-proclaimed ninja, raped and murdered Maxine Kenny's daughter in 1992. Scott was arrested in 1993, but the trial was delayed for four years. After Scott was convicted, Maxine and her husband, Don, were each given an opportunity to testify during the sentencing phase of the trial. Maxine addressed Scott directly, saying, "So you think you're a ninja? Get real! This is not feudal Japan and even if it were, you could never be a ninja because you're a coward! You sneaked around at night, dressed in dark clothing, carrying weapons, and preyed on innocent, defenseless women. . . . You raped and killed for the false sense of power it gave you. You're more like a dirty, disgusting cockroach that slips between the walls at night and contaminates everything. I have no sympathy for you! You raped,

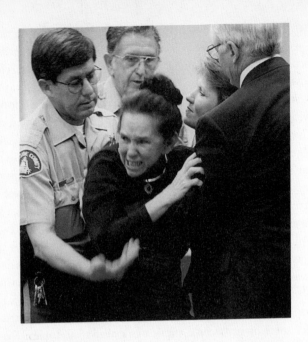

you tortured, and brutally killed my daughter Gail, stabbing her not once, but seven times. You showed no mercy as she desperately fought for her life as shown by the numerous defensive wounds on her hands. You don't deserve to live." Scott, who had not shown remorse, smiled at Mrs. Kenny as she spoke. As she returned to her seat, Maxine Kenny hit Scott on his head before being restrained by her husband and the sheriffs shown in this picture.

Often what motivates us to control our anger and not let it grow into rage is our commitment to continuing our relationship with the person toward whom we feel angry. Whether it is our friend, employer, employee, spouse, or child, no matter what that person has done, we believe we might irrevocably damage our future relationship with them if we fail to manage our anger. In Maxine Kenny's case, there was no prior relationship with this man, and no expected future relationship that would motivate her not to act on her anger.

Surely we can understand and sympathize with Maxine's rage. Any of us in her situation might well have had the same feeling. While we may think she was wrong to attack Scott, it is hard to condemn her. Perhaps she reached her breaking point when she saw that her daughter's murderer showed no remorse or distress, when he smiled at her as she denounced him. Would anyone have acted as she did? Would it be a breaking point for anyone? Does everyone have a breaking point? I don't think so. Her husband, Don, did not act on his violent impulse; instead he restrained her from attacking Scott.

Maxine and Don Kenny suffered every parent's worst nightmare—the cruelly inflicted death of their child, committed by a total stranger, for no understandable reason. Eight years after their thirty-eight-year-old daughter Gail was raped and murdered, they told me they still suffer and miss her. Why did Maxine and Don react so differently at that moment in the courtroom?

Maxine might have a short fuse, an abrupt, very quick onset of anger, but she says that is not typical of her. Her husband, Don, is slow to anger, containing all of his emotions, which rise very gradually. People with a steep anger gradient are burdened by having a much harder time than the rest of us if they want to inhibit their anger responses and prevent their anger from growing into rage. While Maxine does not believe she has a short fuse, she says she could be explosive if "I think my family is being threatened in any way."

Maxine told me that "I always experience emotions very intensely. . . . I think people have different emotional intensities, I think there are different emotional makeups in people and some are more intense." I told Maxine and Don that I was doing research on precisely what she was describing, and finding that she is right (this work is described at the end of chapter 1 and in the conclusion).

Each of us differs in how intensely we can experience each emotion. Some people may simply not have the capacity for extremely intense anger, and extraordinary fury is not something that can ever be a part of their lives. Different expressions of anger depend not just on whether the fuse is short, but how much explosive capacity, how much dynamite—to continue that metaphor—there is, and it isn't the same for everyone. Scientists do not yet know the source of such differences, how much is contributed by genetic inheritance and how much by environment. In all likelihood both play a role.[8] Later in this chapter I will describe some of my research on people known to be unusually angry.

Maxine told me that she did not know ahead of time that she was going to attack David Scott. She thought that she could abuse him verbally and stop at that. But a barrage of verbal abuse can open the door, allowing anger to feed on itself and grow, making it more difficult to put on the brakes and prevent a physical attack. During a break in the sentencing hearing, Maxine explained her attack on David Scott to a reporter: "It was just like temporary insanity. I just couldn't handle it anymore." I asked her if now, when she looks back on it, she still thinks she was insane. Maxine replied, "Yes, I remember feeling so much hate. . . . The anger was so intense I didn't even think of the consequences." (Perhaps unexpectedly, Don condemns himself now for *not* having attacked David Scott.*)

I believe that nearly everyone can prevent acting or speaking when angry, even when enraged. Note I say *nearly,* for there are people who appear unable to control their anger. This may be a lifelong pattern, or the result of an injury to a particular area of the brain. This does not apply to Maxine; she has always been able to regulate her emotions.

Although we may feel impelled to say something nasty or physically attack, most of us can choose not to act. A few words may slip out, an arm may wave in the air, but control is possible for nearly everyone. All of us, or nearly all of us, have the choice not to harm, not to be violent in words or actions. Maxine made the deliberate choice to speak in the sentencing phase of the trial, and to speak in as strong a fashion as she could. She is proud of her hatred, which she still feels.

I expect that most people would act violently if it seemed that such actions could prevent the murder of their child, but is this truly a loss of control? When violence achieves a useful purpose, few people condemn it. It may not be impulsive but carefully planned. Even His Holiness, the Dalai Lama believes that violence in such circumstances is justified.[9]

I realize that not everyone, even in such an extreme circumstance,

---

*Don is still suffering from this shattering experience and, in his severe anguish and unrelenting grief, believes he was a coward for not killing David Scott when he had an opportunity to do so in the courtroom. He told me that he had been a college wrestler and could have broken Scott's neck on one of the many occasions when he passed by him. I explained to Don that attacking Scott would have been an act of revenge. Not seeking revenge is not cowardice. Cowardice would have been not to act to protect his daughter when Scott attacked her. I am sure if he had had the opportunity, he would have acted to protect her. If he feels he is a coward now, it may be because he has not yet really accepted that she is dead; he has not accepted that he could not protect her, because he had no opportunity to do so.

would act violently. It can't be that those who wouldn't act have a higher anger threshold, that a more severe provocation must occur for them to lose control, since it is hard to conceive of a more extreme provocation. In my own research, in which I have asked people to describe the angriest situation they can imagine anyone in the world would ever experience, the threat of death to a family member is mentioned most frequently. Even then, even when acting violently might prevent the death of a family member, I don't believe everyone would so act. Some might not act out of fear, and some out of a strongly held value never to be violent.

Maxine Kenny's attack on the murderer David Scott is different. It could not prevent the murder of her child; it was revenge. We understand her actions, but most of us would not do that. Every day parents confront in the courtroom the person who has murdered their child, and they do not seek violent retribution. Yet it is hard not to sympathize with Maxine Kenny, not to feel that she did what was right; the offense was so great, the loss so severe. And the man who raped and murdered her beloved daughter sat there smiling at her! Can any of us be certain that if we were in her shoes we would not have acted as she did?

Before meeting Maxine and Don Kenny I had written that hatred is always destructive, but now I am not as convinced. Should we really expect ourselves not to feel hatred, not to want to hurt someone who has raped our child, who stabbed her seven times while she tried to defend herself, as the cuts on her hands show, before she died? Might Maxine's continuing hatred of David Scott not serve a useful purpose in her life, binding her own wounds? Maxine's hatred did not seem to be festering, she was leading her life productively, but she maintained her hatred of David Scott.

Most of the time we are not responding to such a severe provocation when we get angry. Yet anger, even intense or violent anger, may occur when the provocation appears to others to be slight. It may be a disagreement, a challenge, an insult, a minor frustration. Sometimes we may choose not to exercise control over our anger, not caring about the consequences or, for the moment, not thinking about any consequences.

Psychologist Carol Tavris,[10] who has written an entire book about anger, argues that getting your anger out—something advocated by other psychologists—usually makes matters worse. Carefully reviewing the research, she concludes that suppressed anger "does not, in any predictable or consistent way, make us depressed, produce ulcers or hypertension, set us off on food binges, or give us heart attacks. . . . Suppressed anger is unlikely to have medical consequences if we feel in control of the situation that is causing the anger, if we interpret the anger as a sign of a grievance to be corrected instead of as an emotion to be sullenly protected, and if we feel committed to the work and people in our lives."[11]

There is a cost to showing our anger.[12] Angry actions and angry words can damage a relationship, momentarily and sometimes permanently, and often brings about angry retaliation. Even without angry actions or angry words, our angry facial expression or tone of voice signals the target that we are angry. If that person then responds angrily, or with contempt, it may be harder for us to maintain our own control and avoid a fight. Angry people are not well liked. Angry children have been found to lose the approval of other children,[13] and angry adults are seen as socially unattractive.[14]

I believe we are usually better off when we don't act on our anger or when we do we take care to act in a constructive fashion, in a way that does not attack the person at whom we are angry. An angry person should consider, and often does not, whether what is making him or her angry can be best dealt with by expressing anger. While that may sometimes be so, there will also be many occasions when the remedy will be easier to achieve if the grievance is dealt with after anger has subsided. There are moments, however, when we don't care that we are making matters worse, when we don't care about any future relationship with the target of our anger.

When anger is intense, we may not initially know, or even want to know, that we have become angry. I am not referring to the failure to be *attentive to our emotional feelings*. It is not that we are unable to take a step back and consider whether we want to go along and act on our anger. Rather, we are not even aware of being angry, even though we are speaking angry words and engaging in angry actions.

It is very unclear why or how this happens. Do we not know we are angry because to know would mean we would condemn ourselves? Are some people more likely than others to be unaware when they are angry? Is such unawareness more common with anger than any of the other emotions? Is there a level of anger that, when reached, always means that the angry person will have to become aware he or she is angry, or does that, too, vary from one person to another? Is it harder to be *attentive* to our emotional feelings when one is angry, fearful, or anguished? Unfortunately, there has been no scientific research on these questions.

The main benefit of being aware of and *attentive* to our angry feelings is the opportunity to regulate or suppress our reactions, reevaluate the situation, and plan the actions most likely to remove the source of our anger. If we are unaware of what we are feeling and simply acting on it, we can't do any of that. Unaware, unable to reflect for a moment on what we are about to do or say, we are more likely to do or say things we will later regret. Even if we are aware of our anger, if we are not able to be *attentive* to our angry feelings, if we do not take a step back, pausing to consider what is happening, we won't be able to exercise any choice about what we do.

Usually we won't be unaware of our anger for long. Others who see and hear our anger may tell us, we may hear it in our voice, or we may figure it out from how we are thinking and what we are planning. Such knowledge does not guarantee control, but it offers that possibility. For some people the old adage of counting to ten before acting may work, while others may need to leave the situation, at least temporarily, to allow their anger to subside.

There is a particular way of responding to anger that causes trouble in intimate relationships. My colleague John Gottman found what he called *stonewalling* in his studies of happy and unhappy marriages.[15] More often shown by men than women, it is a cold withdrawal from interaction, in which the stonewaller won't respond to his partner's emotions. Typically, stonewalling is a response to the anger or complaint of the other person, in which the stonewaller retreats because he feels unable to deal with his feelings and the feelings of his spouse. It would be less damaging to the relationship if, instead, he acknowledged hearing his spouse's complaint, recognized her anger, and asked to discuss it at a later time when he could prepare and feel in better control.

Emotion theorist Richard Lazarus has described a very difficult technique for managing anger, difficult because the aim is not just to control but to defuse anger: "If our spouse or lover has managed to offend us by what they have said and done, instead of retaliating in order to repair our wounded self-esteem, we might be able to recognize that, being under great stress, they couldn't realistically be held responsible; they were, in effect, not in control of themselves, and it would be best to assume that the basic intention was not malevolent. This reappraisal of another's intentions makes it possible to empathize with the loved one's plight and excuse the outburst."[16] Lazarus acknowledges that this is easier said than done.

His Holiness, the Dalai Lama[17] has described the same approach, in which we distinguish between the offensive action and the person who made it. We attempt to understand why the person acted offensively, and we try to sympathize with him, focusing on what it might have been that made him feel angry. That doesn't mean that we do not inform the person that we are unhappy with how he or she has acted. But our anger is directed at the action rather than the person. If we can adopt this framework, we do not want to injure the person; we want to help him or her to not act in this way. There are people who may not want to be helped. A bully, for example, may want to dominate; a cruel person may enjoy inflicting harm. Only anger directed at the person, not just the action, may stop such people.

What Lazarus and the Dalai Lama each suggest might be feasible when the other person is not deliberately, willfully malicious. Even then, when we are not dealing with malicious anger, our own emotional state influences how we can respond. It will be easier to be angry at the action rather than the actor when our anger is not intense, it is building slowly, and we are fully aware of being angry. It takes a moment's pause; and hot, fast, intense anger does not always permit that. It will be especially hard to manage our actions during the refractory period, when information inconsistent with our anger is not available to us. This way of dealing with anger won't always be possible, but if it is practiced, it may become possible at least some of the time.

At a meeting a few months ago I witnessed such constructive anger. Five of us were planning a research project. John objected to our plans, telling us we were being naïve, reinventing the wheel, and were, by implication, poor scholars. Ralph replied, noting what we had indeed taken account of, and the discussion proceeded. John again interrupted, repeating more forcefully what he had said earlier, as if he had not heard Ralph's answer. We tried to proceed without answering him directly, but he would not let us. Ralph then interceded, telling John that we had heard him, that we disagreed with him, and that we could not let him interfere anymore. He could stay if he either would be silent or wanted to help, but if he couldn't, he should leave us alone. I listened carefully to Ralph's voice and watched his face. I saw and heard firmness, strength, and determination, perhaps just the slightest trace of impatience, a trace of anger. There was no attack on John, no mention that he had become obstreperous, which indeed was the case. Not attacked, John did not defend and, in a few minutes, left the room, seemingly, from his behavior later, without any resentment. Ralph told me later, when I asked, that he had felt mildly angry. He said he had not planned what he said; it just came out that way. Ralph's specialty is teaching children how to deal with anger.

Everyone has a harder time controlling their anger when they are in an irritable mood. When we are irritable, we become angry about matters that wouldn't bother us if we weren't irritable. We are looking for an opportunity to become angry. When we are irritable, something that might have just annoyed us makes us angrier, while something that made us just moderately angry makes us furious. Anger felt in an irritable mood lasts longer and is harder to manage. No one knows how to get out of a mood; sometimes indulging in activities we really enjoy can help, but not always. My advice is to avoid people when you are feeling irritable, if you can recognize that you are in an irritable mood. Often that isn't obvious until we have the first angry outburst, then realize it happened because we are feeling irritable.

With so much of this chapter emphasizing the importance of managing anger, it might seem that anger is not useful or adaptive. Or perhaps anger was adaptive to our ancestors who were hunters or gatherers but not to us. Such thinking ignores a number of very useful functions of anger. Anger can motivate us to stop or change whatever caused us to feel angry. Anger at injustice motivates actions to bring about change.

It is not useful simply to absorb another person's anger, or not respond to it at all. The offending person needs to learn that what he or she has done has displeased us if we want the person to stop doing it. Let me explain this with another example. Matthew and his brother Martin have different talents and skills, and both feel stuck in the jobs they now have. They meet Sam, who has many contacts in the business world that could help either of them find a better job. Matthew has been dominating the conversation, interrupting Martin, not giving Martin a fair share of the conversational opportunities. Martin gets frustrated and becomes angry. He says, "Hey, you are hogging the time with Sam; give me a chance." If he says it with anger in his voice or face, he may not make a good impression on Sam. Although he may stop Matthew, it could have a cost, for using the word *hogging* is an insult. Matthew might retaliate with a snide remark, and then they will both lose Sam's help.

If Martin becomes aware of his anger before he speaks, if he can recognize that although Matthew is not being fair, his motivation is not to hurt Martin, he could act differently. He could say to Sam, "You've heard a lot about Matthew's interests, but I want to be certain that I get a chance to describe my situation before you have to go." Later he might tell Matthew he understood how important the meeting was to Matthew, but he thought Matthew was on the verge of getting all the time, not remembering that he, Martin, needed time also. If Martin can say it in a light fashion, with a bit of humor, there is a greater chance Matthew will learn from it. If thoughtlessness and unfairness are not typical for Matthew, Martin might also choose not to bring it up. If thoughtlessness and unfairness *are* typical for Matthew, then Martin certainly might want to point out how unfair Matthew has been. If Martin says this with anger, it might impress Matthew with how serious it is, but it might generate an angry defense, and no progress would be made.

Part of the message we should get from our own anger is "What is it that is making me angry?" It may not always be obvious, it may not be what we think; we have all had the experience of "kicking the dog," of becoming angry with someone who has not offended us, as a result of being frustrated. Such displaced anger may also occur when another person has angered us, but we cannot express our anger toward that person, instead victimizing someone toward whom it is safer to be angry.

Anger tells us that something needs to change. If we are to bring about that change most effectively, we need to know the source of our anger. Was it interference with what we are trying to do, a threat of harm, an insult to our self-esteem, rejection, the other person's anger, or a wrongful act? Was our perception correct, or were we in an irritable mood? Can we actually do anything to reduce or eliminate the grievance, and will expressing and acting on our anger eliminate its cause?

Although anger and fear often occur in the same situations, in response to the same threats, anger can be helpful in reducing fear and providing the energy that mobilizes actions to deal with the threat. Anger has been thought of as an alternative to depression, blaming others rather than the self for the trouble experienced, but it is not certain that this is so, for anger can occur with depression as well.[18]

Anger informs others of trouble. Like all emotions, anger has a signal, a powerful signal in both face and voice. If another person is the source of our anger, our angry expression tells that person that whatever he or she is doing is objectionable. It can be useful to us for others to know that. Not always, of course; but nature did not equip us with a switch to turn any of our emotions off on those occasions when we wish not to have them.

Just as some people enjoy sadness, others can enjoy anger.[19] They seek a good argument; hostile exchanges and verbal attacks are exciting and satisfying. Some people even enjoy a knockdown physical fight. Intimacy can be established or reestablished after a vigorous angry interchange. Some married couples find that after a furious argument or even a violent fight, their sexual relations are more exciting and passionate. Conversely, there are people who find the experience of anger extremely toxic and will do anything to avoid ever becoming angry.

Just as each emotion has a mood saturated with that emotion, and a disorder of that emotion, there is also a personality trait in which each emotion plays a central role. In anger that trait is hostility. My research on hostility has focused on the signs of hostility and its health consequences.

In the first study,[20] my colleagues and I sought to determine whether there was a sign in facial expression regarding whether an individual is a Type A or Type B personality. That distinction, no longer as popular as it was when we did the research fifteen years ago, was supposed to identify those whose aggressive, hostile, and impatient characteristics made them candidates for coronary artery disease (the A's). By contrast the Type B's are more laid-back. More recent research has shown that it is the hostility that may be the most important risk factor. Hostile people should be more likely to show more anger, and that is what we sought to check in this study.

We examined the facial expressions of midlevel executives at a large business, who had already been classified by experts as either A or B. They all underwent a mildly challenging interview, in which the interviewer slightly frustrated the interviewees. Technicians used the technique my colleague Wally Friesen and I had developed for measuring facial movement—the Facial Action Coding System (FACS). As I explained in chapter 1, this technique doesn't measure emotion directly; instead, it objectively scores all facial muscular movements. The technicians who did the FACS scoring did not know who was an A and who was a B. They used slowed and repeated viewing of the videotape to identify the facial muscular movements. Analyzing the results, we found that a particular expression—a partial anger expression that we called a *glare* (shown on page 127), in which just the brows are lowered and the upper eyelids are raised—was shown more often by the A's than the B's.

It was only a glare, not a full anger expression, probably because the A's were trying to diminish any sign of their anger. These business executives were sophisticated; they knew they should try not to appear angry. Another possibility is that they were only annoyed, and because their anger was not intense it did not register across the entire face.

A major limitation of this study—not knowing what was happening to their hearts when these people glared—was remedied in our next study. My former student Erika Rosenberg and I examined patients who had been diagnosed as already having serious coronary artery disease. They were vulnerable to what are called *ischemic*

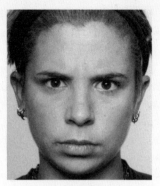

GLARE

episodes, during which the heart does not get enough oxygen for a period of time. When this happens most people experience pain, *angina,* which tells them to stop whatever they are doing because they are at risk of having a heart attack if they don't. The patients we were studying had silent ischemia, no pain, no warning when their heart was not getting enough oxygen.

In this collaborative study[21] with James Blumenthal's research group at Duke University, the patients were again videotaped in a mildly challenging interview. This time a continuous measure of ischemia was obtained from an imaging device pressed against their chest that produced a picture of their heart as they talked. We measured their facial expressions during a two-minute period when they answered questions about how they dealt with anger in their lives.

Those who became ischemic showed a full or partial anger expression on their face much more often than the patients who did not become ischemic. Showing anger in their face when they talked about past frustrations suggests that they were not just talking about anger; they were reliving their anger. And anger, we know from other research, accelerates heart rate and increases blood pressure. It is like running up a flight of stairs; you shouldn't do it if you have coronary artery disease, and not everyone did. Those who didn't become angry were much less likely to become ischemic.

Before explaining why we think we obtained these findings, let me make clear that this study did not show that anger caused heart disease. Other research[22] has found that either the personality trait of hostility, or the emotion of anger (and it is not certain which it might be), is *one* of the risk factors for producing heart disease, but that is not what we did. Instead we found that in people who already *have* heart disease, getting angry increased their risk of becoming ischemic, which puts them at increased risk for having a heart attack. Now let us consider why these people became angry when they talked about being angry in the past, and why that put them at risk.

All of us talk about emotions we are not feeling at the moment. We tell someone about a sad event, a time when we got angry, what made us afraid, and so forth. Sometimes in the course of describing a past emotional experience we begin to experience the emotion all over again. That is what I believe happened to the people who became ischemic. They could not talk about angry experiences without becoming angry again, without reliving their anger. Unfortunately, for people with coronary artery disease, that is dangerous. Why did this happen to some people and not others? Why do some people reexperience past angry experiences while others don't? Presumably, anger is easily provoked, ready to surface with any opportunity, in those who have a hostile personality. It is both a mark and a manifestation of being a hostile personality that remembered angry events would reinstitute the feelings that were felt.

Leaving aside hostile people, any of us may find we are reliving a past emotional experience that we started out thinking we would just describe. I suspect this happens when that event was left unfinished. Take an example in which a wife gets angry with her husband for again coming home late for dinner without giving her any advance notice. If that argument ended without her feeling satisfied that her grievance had been dealt with (he didn't apologize, explain why he couldn't call, or promise not to do this again), she is likely to relive the experience at a later time. Thinking she is raising the topic again because she would now be able to talk about it dispassionately, she might well find her anger reemerging. This can also happen even when a given event was resolved if there has been a history of other unresolved angry events, creating a backlog of resentment waiting to be tapped.

I don't mean to suggest that it is impossible to describe a past angry experience without becoming angry. It is possible if there is no backlog and if the specific event was resolved. It is even possible, when talking about the past emotional event, to use part of an anger expression to illustrate how one felt. I might tell my wife, for example, how frustrated and angry I was earlier in the day when I was trying to deal with the Internal Revenue Service, and was put into one voice mail after another. Let's suppose that I expressed my anger at the clerk who finally did talk to me, and I received a most gratifying apology. I might show an element of anger in my face—what I call a *referential* expression.[23]

A referential expression refers to an emotion one is not feeling now; it is much like saying the word *anger,* but with the face. The expression does have to be transformed somewhat so that the person who sees the expression won't be confused and think the person is feeling angry now. Typically, this is done by using only a portion of the expression, and doing it very briefly. A referential anger expression might involve just the raised upper eyelids, or just pressed lips, or just lowered brows. If more than one of these elements is used, it not only might confuse the person seeing the expression, it might reinstitute the anger. As you should have found out by making the expressions described in the previous chapter, if you put on your face all of the muscular movements for an emotion, that emotion will generally begin to occur.

Violence

Just as each emotion has a related mood that is saturated with that emotion, for each emotion there is a related psychopathological state, in which that emotion plays an important role. The common phrase *emotional disorder* recognizes this to be so. For sadness and agony the disorder is depression. In depression emotions are flooded, depressed people cannot regulate their sadness or agony, and it permeates and interfere with all aspects of their lives. The disorder in which anger is so out of control that it interferes with the person's life is manifest in those who show certain forms of violence.

There is not much agreement about just what constitutes violence. Some scientists consider verbal attacks, insults, and ridicule to be forms of violence, and so their research does not separately examine those who engage in strictly verbal attacks from those who attack physically. Similarly, there are aggressive behaviors that do not involve physical violence, such as being overly assertive or dominating, and many researchers do not separate aggressiveness from either physical violence or verbal abuse. Then there are those who destroy property in an act of violence, breaking chairs, glasses, and so forth. We don't know whether these are all due to the same causes, the same upbringing, for example, or mediated by the same brain activity. If that were so, we might expect to find that people who are verbally abusive are also aggressive and physically violent, but while that can happen, there are also people who show one and never show the other forms of violence. That suggests that it would be wise at this point in our study of violence to examine separately those who engage only in verbal abuse, those who show only highly aggressive but not abusive behaviors (not always easy to distinguish, I realize), and those who show physical violence. Only in that way can we determine if they have the same causes, and if one is a step to another.

Even when restricting our focus to physical violence, there are many types to consider, only some of which might be signs of an emotional disorder. Society considers some violent acts socially useful. All but pacifists believe that sometimes war is justifiable. There also are occasions when individual violence is justified. When a police sharpshooter kills a person who is threatening the lives of the children he holds hostage, few would object to his violence, especially if the person who is shot had already killed one or more of the children. It is not just the police who may be justified in killing; most would agree an individual can be violent if that is required to save the lives of family members, or even of strangers. Violence that does not prevent worse acts of violence, but is motivated by revenge or retribution, is understandable, although we do not approve of it as much.

In a discussion of these ideas with my friend and colleague, the evolutionary philosopher Helena Cronin,[24] she pointed out that in all cultures, and in all times in history that we know of, certain forms of violence have been considered justifiable. Infidelity, suspected infidelity, and the threat of or actual rejection by a sexual partner are the most common causes of murder, and men kill women far more often than women kill men. Cronin, along with other evolutionary thinkers, attributes this to the man's nearly unavoidable uncertainty about whether he truly is the father of any offspring. Consistent with this viewpoint, one of the largest studies of homicides found that one in six solved homicides was a spousal homicide, with women being three-quarters of the victims. To my surprise, spousal killings were equally likely between legally married couples at all stages of a relationship and across all social and economic boundaries.[25]

Murder to avenge unfair treatment by a boss is also committed much more often by men than women, because of the greater importance of status hierarchies in men as compared to women. Before we get too far afield from my focus—which is on violence that is the product of an emotional disorder—let me say that evolutionary thinking can help us understand why certain forms of violence occur, who commits those violent acts, and why it is that the community may approve of them. Such forms of violence may be regrettable, or even legally punishable, but violence that has had adaptive value over the course of our evolution is not likely to be the result of an emotional disorder.

A major difference among acts of violence is whether they are premeditated or impulsive. Either can be normal, even socially approved. Consider the person held captive, knowing that his victimizer has already murdered another one of his captives, who carefully plans an attack on his potential murderer. This is violence that is premeditated but not pathological, and it is socially approved. It may be less obvious that impulsive violence can be socially approved, but it can have its place. When my daughter Eve was a toddler, she often ran out into the street without taking heed of cars coming her way. I cautioned her about this a number of times, but she, I think, had come to see this as almost a game, a way to get Dad really upset. One day it was only by fast action that I succeeded in pulling her to safety. Without thought, acting on impulse, I hit her and yelled at her never to do that again. It was the only time I ever hit her. While a few people might disapprove of my violent act, she never ran out into the street again. More than 90 percent of parents report having physically punished their toddlers.[26]

I have given instances of normal premeditated and impulsive violence, but there also are abnormal versions of each. Killers, rapists, and torturers may plan their actions carefully, selecting whom they will victimize, and when and how they will do it. There are also impulsive spouse batterers, who hit without warning, without planning. Both research on personality[27] and studies of brain activity[28] have found differences between impulsive and premeditated violence. Clearly, both should be considered, although some research has failed to make that distinction. While it is important to consider whether the violence was impulsive or premeditated, that is not sufficient to isolate abnormal violence.

A necessary ingredient is that such violence is also antisocial—disapproved of by society—but that may not always involve a mental disorder. Some have argued that antisocial violence committed in groups during adolescence should not be considered a mental disorder, and the evidence does suggest that many of those who show such behavior do not continue to be violent in adulthood.[29] Simply being antisocial may not be a sign of mental illness of any kind, even when it occurs in adulthood. Instrumental violence, such as violence committed to gain money, although against the law, may not be a sign of what is called an Antisocial Personality Disorder, if the person is from a subculture that supports such behavior. Antisocial violence is necessary, I believe, but not sufficient for identifying violence that is the product of an emotional disorder. I would add the not-always-easy-to-determine requirement that the violence have no social support (thus exempting gang violence), and be either disproportionate to any provocation or without provocation.

Antisocial violence that is the result of an emotional disorder may be chronic, or a single isolated incident in a life. The violent person may feel genuine remorse afterward, or no remorse. The violent person may act coolly, or in the heat of anger or rage. The target of the violence may have been carefully selected or chosen at random. The violence may include torture or not. I suspect that research should consider all of these factors, searching to see if there are different risk factors and different causes for these many different forms of antisocial violence. Regrettably, that has not been the case, as can be seen in the manual of psychiatric diagnostic criteria, *DSM-IV*, which identifies Intermittent Explosive Disorder (IED) as including "several discrete episodes of failure to resist aggressive impulses that result in serious assaultive acts or destruction of property; the degree of expressiveness during the episodes is grossly out of proportion to any precipitating psychosocial stresses. . . . The individual may describe the aggressive episodes as 'spells' or 'attacks' in which the explosive behavior is preceded by a sense of tension or arousal and is followed by a sense of relief."[30] While I commend this definition of a type of violence—chronic, serious, out of proportion to provocation—it is a mistake to combine both violence against people and destruction of property without evidence that both are due to the same causes. There is no way to discover whether that is so when the two are lumped together.

While research on violence has not typically drawn distinctions as finely as I am suggesting, there is evidence that suggests multiple causes for violence. Environmental stress early in life, bad parenting, head injury, and genetic factors all have been found to be associated with many types of violence.[31] Which are most important for which kinds of violence, it is too early to say. It is likely that even when distinctions are finely drawn, more than one cause will be found. For example, even if we were to limit ourselves to studying just chronic, antisocial physical violence, which does not involve torture but is a single brutal act, committed by a single enraged individual, with little provocation, impulsively, against a selected target, with subsequent remorse, we are not likely to find a single cause.

Recognizing Anger in Ourselves

Let us turn now to consider what anger feels like on the inside. You need to feel angry right now so you can compare your feelings with what has been found about angry sensations. I cannot expect that simply looking at the photographs of the Canadian fighting or of Maxine Kenny will awaken feelings of anger in you. This is an important difference between anger and sadness/agony. Even a still photograph of a total stranger's agony calls forth our concern, but this is not so for anger. It takes more to feel angry. If you were there, if that anger was directed at you, you would feel either fear or anger, but seeing photographs won't do it. In a parallel fashion we feel sympathetic concern when we see someone who is in pain or anguish without needing to know the cause, but when we see anger we need to know the source of the anger before we sympathize with the angry person.[32]

Here are two paths that may allow you to experience anger, one using memory and the other making an expression.

Try to remember a time in your life when you were so angry that you nearly hit someone (or did hit someone). If that has never happened, then try to remember a time in your life when you were so angry that your voice got much louder and you said something you later regretted. Since one seldom experiences only anger, you may have felt afraid (of the other person or of losing control) or disgusted (with the other person or yourself for losing control). You might have had a positive feeling such as triumph. For now try to focus on the moments when you just felt angry, and then try to experience those feelings again. It may help if you visualize the scene you remembered. When those feelings begin, let them grow as strongly as you can. After thirty seconds or so have passed, relax and consider what you felt.

It is worth trying to make the movements described in the following exercise to concentrate on what anger feels like in your face. Moreover, if the memory task didn't bring on angry sensations, making the face may achieve that.

Imitate the facial movements of anger. (You might try using a mirror to check on whether you are making all of the muscle movements.)

- Pull your eyebrows down and together; make certain that the inner corners go down toward your nose.
- While holding those brows down, try to open your eyes wide, so that your upper eyelids push against your lowered eyebrows, staring hard.

- Once you are confident that you are making the eyebrow and eyelid movements, relax the upper part of your face and concentrate on the lower part of your face.
- Press your lips together tightly and tense your lips; don't pucker, just press.
- Once you are confident that you are making the right lower-face movements, add in the upper face, lowering your eyebrows, pulling them together, and raising your upper eyelids to produce a stare.

Angry sensations include feelings of pressure, tension, and heat. The heart rate increases, as does respiration; blood pressure rises, and the face may redden. If you are not speaking, there is a tendency to bite down hard, upper against lower teeth, and to thrust the chin forward. There is also an impulse to move forward toward the target of anger. These are the common shared sensations that most people feel. You may feel some of them more strongly than others. Now again try to experience anger (using either the memory or facial movement task, whichever worked better), noting whether or not you feel the heat, pressure, tension, and biting-down sensations.

Recognizing Anger in Others

Turn back and look again at the first picture in this chapter. Both angry men show lowered and drawn-together brows that are part of the anger display. The man on the right also shows the glaring eyes that mark anger. In both of these angry faces the jaw is tightly clenched and the teeth are exposed. The lips take on two different positions in anger. The lips may be open, as they are here, either square or rectangular in shape. Or the lips may be tightly closed, lip pressed against lip.

In Papua New Guinea, when I asked them to show me what their face would look like if they were about to hit someone, people pressed their lips tightly together as they moved their arm to strike with an axe. Charles Darwin, more than a century ago, noted that we press our lips tightly together whenever we engage in any strong physical exertion. When I asked the New Guineans to show me what their faces would be like if they were controlling their anger, they would part their lips, as if talking or ready to talk. With middle-class Americans, I found the reverse pattern: they pressed their lips tightly together for controlled anger and opened their lips for uncontrolled anger. For these middle-class Americans, uncontrolled anger meant hurting with words, not with fists, so the lips were pressed to prevent it in controlled anger.

The two Canadian men in the photograph are showing open-mouth anger, in the moment after one of them has just hit the policeman. I suspect that in the moment before, when he actually hit the policeman, his lips were tightly pressed.

One of the most important clues to anger is hard to see in a photograph, although it is probably present in both angry men. The red margin of the lips becomes narrower in anger, the lips become thinner. This is a very hard action to inhibit, and it may betray anger even when there is no other sign. I have found it to be one of the earliest signs of anger, evident when a person has not yet become aware that he is angry. Nearly everyone has had the experience of someone else noticing that he is angry before he realized it himself. A person responded to a subtle sign in his face, or a tightening of his voice or increase in loudness. Because the lips become thinner in anger, we may mistakenly react to someone who has thin lips as if he is sullen, cold, or hostile.

Look again at the photograph of Maxine Kenny. Her eyebrows are down and together, and her eyes are glaring. Her lips are parted, and her jaw is thrust forward, a fairly common sign of anger, which may be where the warning to boxers, "Don't lead with your jaw," came from. I have no idea why this movement is often part of an anger expression, but I am quite certain that it is.

I photographed this young woman one day in the village that was my base camp in the New Guinea highlands. Although she did not know what a camera was, she obviously saw that I was paying attention to her, and it seemed that such attention was unwelcome. Usually embarrassment would be the response to such attention, but in this instance it clearly was not. I suspect that by paying attention to a single woman in public I was breaking a rule in that society and endangering both of us, but I can't be certain.

I deliberately tried to provoke various emotions in these people, setting up my movie camera to record what would happen for my later analysis. One day I lunged at an adolescent boy with a rubber knife I had brought with me for just that purpose, but he saw immediately what it was, and the film shows his initial surprise and then amusement. For my own safety I decided not to provoke anger again, and I never saw another angry moment among these people. Although they were a peaceful culture, they did get angry, but not in the open, at least not when I was around. This is the only spontaneous photograph I have of someone who is angry in this culture.

The picture shows very well the glaring eyes of anger, with lowered brows drawn together. She is also pressing her lips together. The woman to the left shows just the lowered and drawn-together brow. By itself, without the glaring eyes, this expression can mean many things. It is produced by what Darwin called the muscle of difficulty. He noticed, as have I, that any type of difficulty, mental or physical, causes this muscle to contract, lowering and drawing the eyebrows together. Perplexity, confusion, concentration, determination—all may be shown by this action. It also occurs when someone is in bright light, as the brows are lowered to act as a sunshade.

RESTRAINED ANGER

I have not been able to find news photographs that show a more restrained anger, the kind often seen in ordinary life, before anger has gotten out of control. Yet there can be strong evidence of anger with very slight changes in the face, as this picture I took of myself shows. I took it twenty years ago, trying to produce an anger expression without moving any of my facial features. I concentrated on tightening the muscles without letting them contract in a way that would be sufficient to pull the skin. I first tightened the muscle in my eyebrows, which if contracted would lower and pull them together. Then I tightened the muscles that would raise the upper eyelids. Finally I tightened the muscle in my lips, which did narrow the lips. It is not a friendly face; it is perhaps a highly controlled anger, or just an annoyed expression. Now we'll turn to the pictures showing the subtle signs of anger.

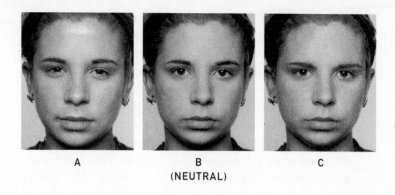

A	B	C
	(NEUTRAL)	

Let's begin with the eyelids and eyebrows. In picture A the lower and upper eyelids have been tightened. It can be a subtle sign of controlled anger, or it may be just slight annoyance. It can also occur when there is no anger at all, but the person is literally or figuratively trying to focus on something or is concentrating intensely. Picture C is a composite photograph made by pasting lowered and slightly drawn-together brows from another picture (not shown here) onto the neutral picture B, which is provided for comparison. Photo C can also be a signal of controlled anger or slight annoyance. It could appear when a person is feeling slightly perplexed, concentrating, or finding something difficult. Which it is will depend on the context.

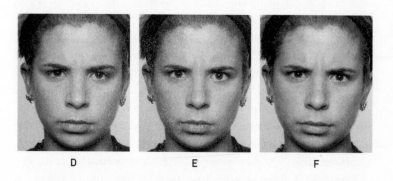

D	E	F

Picture D shows the combination of the two movements you saw above. The eyebrows are slightly lowered and drawn together, and the lower eyelids are slightly tensed. The tensed lower eyelids are not as strong as in picture A. You can see that they are tensed by comparing picture D with the neutral photo B, noting how the lower eyelids have begun to cut off part of the lower rims of the irises. It is still possible that this might be perplexity or concentration, but more likely it is controlled anger or very slight anger.

Picture E shows a very important additional action, the raising of the upper eyelids. This is a glare; and now there is little doubt that this is an anger sign, probably controlled anger. You saw this earlier in this chapter when I described my research on Type A personalities. Picture F shows the combination of the three actions—lowered brow, tensed lower eyelid, and raised upper eyelid—more strongly. This is a clear sign of anger.

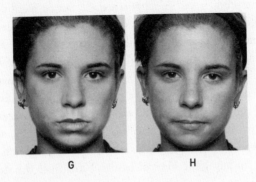

G   H

Now let's look at signals in the jaws and lips. In anger the jaw is often thrust forward, as it is in picture G. This picture was made by pasting that movement (from another photograph not shown here) onto the neutral picture B. You can see this jaw thrust in the picture of Maxine Kenny, although she has also raised her upper lip and lowered her lower lip.

In picture H the lips are pressed together with slight tensing of the lower eyelids. This can happen in very slight anger, or anger that is just beginning. It may also happen when someone is thinking about something. And in some people it is a mannerism that has little meaning. If there were no lower eyelid action, just a lip press, it would be very ambiguous.

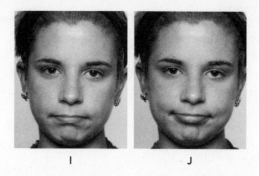

I

J

In picture I both lips are pressed together, as in photo H, plus the lower lip is being pushed up. This may be controlled anger or resignation, and some people use this as a sign of thinking, while in other people it is a frequent mannerism. President Clinton often showed this movement as a mannerism. In picture J the lip corners are tightened, plus the lower lip is being pushed up. When it is alone, as it is here, it is ambiguous; it may have any of the meanings of photo I. Because it is slightly asymmetrical, it might also have a contemptuous element. More about contempt is explained in chapter 8.

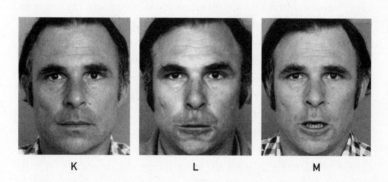

K

L

M

I have used some pictures of myself, taken nearly thirty years ago, to show the very important movement of narrowing the red margins of the lips. Pictures L and M show this action, with picture K there for comparison of what my lips look like when they are relaxed. In photo M the lips are also parted as if in speech. This action of narrowing the lips is a very reliable sign of anger; it is often a very early sign of anger, or it may be highly controlled anger. It also seems to be difficult to inhibit.

The last way in which anger can be registered in the mouth you saw in the Canadian demonstrators and in Maxine Kenny; the upper lip is raised and the lower lip lowered, and the lips are narrowed. The mouth has a square appearance.

Using the Information from Expressions

Let us consider how you can use the information you may pick up from the signs of anger shown in this chapter. Let me repeat again what I said in the last chapter, because it is even more important to consider when dealing with anger than when you spot signs of anguish or sadness. Expressions do not tell you what is generating the emotion, only that the emotion is occurring. When you see that someone is angry, you don't know what made the person angry. It is obvious in the pictures of the Canadian demonstrators and Maxine Kenny. But let's suppose someone shows an angry expression when you are talking with him or her. Is the anger directed at you? Is it something you have done, now or in the past, or something the angry person thinks you are planning to do? Or might the anger be directed inwardly; is the angry person angry with him- or herself? Another possibility is that the anger is at a third party, someone mentioned in the conversation, or perhaps someone not mentioned but who has come to mind.

There is no way for you to tell from the expression itself. Sometimes it will be obvious from what has been happening, what has been said or not said, what has already occurred or is likely to occur. Sometimes you won't know. Knowing the person is angry is itself very important, for anger is the most dangerous emotion to others, but you won't always be certain if you are the target of the anger.

Some of the subtlest signs of anger (photos A, C, and D) might also be signs of perplexity or concentration. There are also anger expressions where it is not certain if the anger is slight, just beginning, or being controlled (photos G, H, I, L, and M, as well as my picture on page 138). I will return to them later. First, let's focus on what you might do when you spot an expression that is clear, where there is no doubt from the expression that the person is angry, such as shown in photos E and F. I have used the same examples I described at the end of the last chapter so the reader will be able to see how different the choices are when you spot anger as compared to anguish or sadness. You will also see that what you consider depends in large part on your relationship to the person who shows anger, whether you are that person's supervisor, supervisee, friend, lover, parent, or offspring.

Most emotional expressions last about two seconds; some are as short as a half second, some may last as long as four seconds, but rarely are they shorter or longer. The duration of an expression is usually related to the strength of the expression. So a long-duration expression typically signals a more intense feeling than a briefer one. There are exceptions, though. A very brief, intense expression (photos E and F) suggests that the person is concealing the emotion; that concealment might be the result of a deliberate effort or unconsciously guided repression. The very brief expression doesn't tell us whether the person is deliberately or unconsciously changing the face, only that the emotion is concealed. A long-duration slight expression (photos G, H, I, L, M, and my picture on page 138) is a sign of deliberately controlled emotion. If one of those expressions were shown for only a half second or a second, it would more likely be a slight feeling of anger or anger just beginning, rather than more controlled anger. What I have been describing about the duration of an expression, and how it relates to the strength of the emotion, whether the emotion is being controlled, or is slight, applies not just to anger, but to all of the emotions.

Let's say you deliver the news to someone you supervise that he is not getting a promotion, and the person shows a clear-cut anger expression. If he shows an expression such as E or F, or an even stronger expression, he probably would know he is angry, especially if it is on his face for more than a fraction of a second. Since you just delivered unwelcome news, you are probably the target of his anger, but not necessarily. Perhaps he is angry with himself for having failed to do what was needed to get the promotion. Before he speaks you don't know if he thinks the decision was an unfair one; even when he does reply you may not know, for he may have decided it is not in his interest to tell you how he is feeling, at least not then.

Unless you know that person well, don't assume he is taking such a step back to consider whether he wishes to go along with his anger, what I called emotional attentiveness; that is not a developed capacity in most people. So, what do you do?

You could ignore his show of anger, acting as if it didn't happen, but taking heed of it and being cautious about what else you say and how you say it. It isn't always or even often the case that you want to confront someone who is angry by saying something like, "Why are you angry with me?" or even the slightly less confrontational, "Are you angry?" Such remarks are an invitation for someone to say something mean-spirited, or act in an angry fashion, and that is not always in your interest or the interest of the angry person. Not that grievances or offenses should be ignored, but they may be more readily dealt with once the moment of anger has passed. A somewhat better version of the "Why are you angry with me?" question would be to say, "My decision may well have made you angry, and I regret that. Tell me if there is anything else I can do that would be of help." In this response you acknowledge his anger rather than challenge it, and you indicate your interest in seeing if you can be helpful despite your unwanted decision.

Returning to the prior example, suppose your teenage daughter showed this same expression when you told her she cannot go to her friend's house that evening, because you need her to baby-sit her younger brother while you and your husband attend a suddenly called neighborhood meeting. Is she angry at you for frustrating her plans? Most likely, but she might be angry at herself for caring so much about it. How you would respond depends on the nature of your relationship with your daughter, her personality and yours, and the past history of your relationship with her. Yet I believe there is more reason to deal with her anger than would generally be so in a work situation. That doesn't mean that you should comment on her anger, or challenge her right to be angry. Quite the contrary, you might sympathize with her frustration and explain further why the meeting is so important, and how, because you had no notice, you had to make this imposition. If that is the consequence, then her anger has done its job. It brought an offense to your attention, let you know it was important, and led you to respond by explaining the circumstances. You could go further and say how you will make it up to her in some other way.

Whenever you see an emotional expression that the person does not also express in words, you are in a sense taking information that the person has not acknowledged, for which the person has not taken responsibility. The supervisee in the work example might be doing all he can to control his anger. You won't make that easier by confronting him about it. In a business setting you might not want to deal directly with a supervisee's anger, especially with someone who is not being advanced. Of course, it could be someone who you still hope will advance, and there might be some benefit from dealing with his feelings, but you might want to deal with them later. The next day you could say, "I know that was bad news, and I expect it was disappointing. I had the impression you were upset [it bothered you], and wondered if it would help to talk about it."

Another choice would be to say, "I would be glad to talk to you now or at a later time about how you feel about it." Again, by not using the label *anger*, you reduce the chance of anger being expressed in a way he might regret, but you also give him the chance to talk about his concerns when he feels comfortable doing so. If you know your daughter to be someone who has a hard time handling her anger, you might use a variant on this response, giving her the choice as to when she wants to talk about it. Couples may also find that they want to note the anger, but reserve discussion about it for a specified later time when there is less likelihood that the anger will generate hurtful words, angry replies, or defensiveness.

We often think we know why someone has become angry with us, but our version of the grievance may not match the other person's version. While avoiding what makes someone angry leads to resentments, building a backlog of trouble, rarely should the matter be dealt with when one or both people are in the heat of their anger. If it is so urgent that the matter must be dealt with at once, and it cannot be postponed until a cooler moment, then it is important that both people try to be certain that they are past the refractory period. Otherwise, the discussion is bound only to fuel the anger, not focus on what the problem is and how it can be solved.

It can also be important to recognize and consider how different the situation can be when the power is reversed from the examples I have discussed. Suppose you were the supervisee who just learned that you didn't get the promotion, and when your supervisor said this, she showed an angry expression. It is likely she is angry with you, but she could be angry with herself about being in the spot of having to deliver such bad news, or at someone else in the organization. In any case, a subordinate in most organizations does not enjoy the right to comment on a superior's anger. The most you might be entitled to say, after expressing your disappointment, is something like, "I would appreciate the opportunity to learn from you, at a time you deem appropriate, about anything I might have done that has displeased you or the organization." The idea here is not to label the anger, but to acknowledge it and show concern for feedback, while making it easy for the supervisor to defer telling you about it until a moment when she is not feeling angry.

All that I have suggested about what to do when you spot an anger expression applies as well to expressions in which it is not certain whether the expression is slight anger, controlled anger, or anger that is just beginning (photos G, H, and I). The only difference is that if you have reason to believe it is anger that is just beginning, let us say just the narrowing of the lips shown in pictures L and M, you have more of an opportunity to consider whether there might be something you could do or say that would interrupt the anger before it gets stronger.

The expression shown in photo C, the lowered, drawn-together eyebrows, merits special comment. You saw another version of this action in the woman sitting to the left of the New Guinea woman who was glaring at me. Although it may be a sign of very slight anger, it may also occur under many difficult situations. If someone is lifting something heavy, or trying to solve a difficult math problem, this action may well be shown. It may be shown with difficulty of nearly any kind. If you are speaking and the other person shows this for a moment, it may be a sign that he or she doesn't quite understand what you are saying, or needs to work hard to follow your line of conversation. It can be a useful signal that you should explain what you are saying in a different way.

I could not explain all that should be considered when you spot an anger expression. My examples are only meant to suggest that there are many possibilities, and some responses you might consider. Which are applicable will depend on who you and the other person are, and the specifics of the situation. Admittedly, much of what I have suggested about how to respond when we note another person's anger is not established firmly by research. I have contradicted ideas prevalent some years ago that we should learn how to fight fairly, but not avoid the fight. My own experience suggests that this is more than can be expected from most people, and isn't necessarily the best or most certain way to deal with whatever is generating the anger. The grievances must be considered, but not, I suggest, in the heat of anger.

7

Surprise and Fear

Surprise is the briefest of all the emotions, lasting only a few seconds at most. In a moment surprise passes as we figure out what is happening, and then surprise merges into fear, amusement, relief, anger, disgust, and so forth, depending upon what it was that surprised us, or it may be followed by no emotion at all if we determine that the surprising event was of no consequence. It is rare to see a photograph of surprise. Because it is unexpected and the experience is brief, a photographer is rarely ready to shoot and even if he is he may not be fast enough to capture it once something surprising happens. Press photographs usually show reenacted or posed surprise.

The *New York Post* photographer Lou Liotta gave this account of how he was able to get this prize-winning photograph of two surprised men:

"I got a call to go over to this building where a woman was doing a promotional stunt. I got there late, as she was being raised up to the top of the building, holding on to a cable with her teeth. I put a long lens on my camera, and I could see there was a strained look on her face. Her body was spinning around. I saw her lose her grip and followed her down—like you do covering a horse race or some other action. I took one picture."

Fortunately, the woman in this photo survived, though in falling

thirty-five feet onto wooden planks she broke both wrists and ankles and injured her spine. Our interest, however, is in the emotion felt by the two fellows facing the camera. Surprise can only be triggered by a sudden, unexpected event, as happened here. When an unexpected event unfolds slowly, we aren't surprised. It must be sudden, and we must be unprepared. The men who saw the stuntwoman fall had no warning, no idea ahead of time of what was going to happen.

Years ago, when I first taught medical students how to understand and recognize the emotions, I would try to arouse a different emotion in each class meeting. To surprise them, I once had a belly dancer emerge from behind a screen, stamping her feet and clanging her finger cymbals. She would not have been surprising if she had come onstage at a nightclub featuring Turkish dancing, but in a medical school class she was out of context, and her sudden and noisy appearance triggered surprise.

We don't have much time to mobilize our efforts deliberately in order to manage our behavior when we are surprised. That rarely is a problem unless we are in a situation in which we shouldn't be surprised. For example, if we have claimed to know all about something, and we react with surprise when a feature we should have known about is suddenly, unexpectedly revealed, then it might be obvious that we were claiming more than we actually knew. In a classroom a student might claim to have read the optional readings that were assigned, when, in fact, she hasn't. Her surprise when the teacher reveals something quite unexpected in those readings could betray her lie.

Some emotion scholars do not consider surprise to be an emotion because they say it is neither pleasant nor unpleasant, and they claim that all emotions must be one or the other. I disagree; I think surprise *feels* like an emotion to most people. In that moment or two before we figure out what is occurring, before we switch to another emotion or no emotion, surprise itself can feel good or bad. Some people never want to be surprised, even if it is by a positive event. They tell people never to surprise them. Others love being surprised; they deliberately leave many things unplanned so that they can often experience the unexpected. They seek experiences in which it is likely they will be surprised.

My own doubt about whether surprise is an emotion arises from the fact that its timing is fixed.* Surprise can't last more than a few seconds at most, which is not so for any of the other emotions. They can be very brief, but they can also endure much longer. Fear, which often follows surprise, can be extremely brief, but it can also endure for quite a long time. When I had to wait for a few days to learn from the results of a biopsy whether or not I had cancer, and if so, how far the disease had progressed, I had long, prolonged periods of fear. I was not afraid for the entire four days I waited, but there were recurrent periods in which I felt afraid for many seconds and sometimes for minutes. Fortunately, the biopsy was negative. I then felt relief, an enjoyable emotion that I discuss in chapter 9.

I think it makes sense to include surprise in our discussion of emotions, just noting that it has its own special characteristic—a fixed,

---

*Another reason to question whether surprise is an emotion is my failure, as described in chapter 1, to find that the New Guineans I studied could distinguish it from fear. When I told them the story about fear, they were just as likely to pick the surprise as the fear photograph. When they were told the surprise story, they did pick the surprise face more often than any of the others. In another study we told them the stories and asked them to show it on their face—to pose the emotions. We then showed these poses to American college students. The Americans recognized the expressions of anger, disgust, sadness, and happiness, but when shown either a New Guinean's fear or surprise pose, they were just as likely to call it fear or surprise. I can't really explain why these problems occurred. The fact that this problem did occur, and that when my colleague Karl Heider tried these tasks with another New Guinea group there were also similar problems with surprise, raises doubts as to how well surprise is really distinguished from fear.

limited duration. Each of the emotions we have considered so far also has its own unique characteristics. Sadness-agony is unique in at least two ways: There are two sides to this emotion that often alternate, the resigned feeling of sadness and the agitated agony; and this emotion can last much longer than others. Anger differs from all other emotions in being the most dangerous to others because of the potential for violence. And we will see that contempt, disgust, and the many types of enjoyment have characteristics not shared with any of the other emotions. In that sense, each emotion has its own story.

While surprise is an emotion, startle is not, although many people use that word interchangeably with surprise. They don't look the same; the startle expression is the exact opposite of the surprise expression. I fired a blank pistol to trigger startle in my unsuspecting research subjects.[1] Nearly immediately their eyes closed tightly (in surprise they open wide), their brows lowered (in surprise the eyebrows are raised), and their lips stretched tensely (in surprise the jaw drops open). In all of the other emotional expressions, the most extreme expression resembles a moderate expression of the emotion, showing more intense muscular contractions. Fury is a more intense expression than anger, terror than fear, etc. The difference in the startled and surprised expressions implies that being startled is not simply a more extreme state of surprise.

Startle differs from surprise in three other ways. First, the timing of the startle is even more constrained than surprise—the expression is always apparent in one-quarter of a second and is over in one-half of a second. It is so fast that if you blink you will miss seeing someone's startle. The timing is not fixed in any emotion. Second, being told you are about to be startled by a very loud noise reduces, in most people, the magnitude of the reaction, but doesn't eliminate it. You can't be surprised if you know what is going to happen. Third, no one can inhibit the startle reaction, even if one is told exactly when a loud noise will occur. Most people can inhibit all but the subtlest signs of an emotion, especially if they are prepared ahead of time. Startle is a physical reflex, rather than an emotion.

The caption with the extraordinary photograph on page 152 says, "In May, a military truck carrying over one hundred youths, keeled

over under its heavy load in Surabaya, East Java. The passengers were supporters of local football club Persebaya, who were enjoying a free ride home and waving flags to celebrate their team's victory. The truck—one of twenty-four made available by a military commander—capsized after only one kilometer. Most of the passengers escaped unharmed, but twelve of them had to be hospitalized with minor injuries." Fear is shown on the faces of these youths, most clearly on the driver. If the photograph had been taken a moment earlier, we might have seen surprise on their faces, unless the truck began to tip over slowly.

There has been more research on fear than any other emotion, probably because it is easy to arouse fear in nearly any animal, including the rat (a favorite species for researchers because they are inexpensive and easy to maintain). The threat of harm, either physical or psychological harm, characterizes all fear triggers, theme and variations. The theme is danger of physical harm, and variations can be anything that we learn is likely to harm us in any way, whether physical or psychological threats. Just as physical restraint is an unlearned trigger for anger, there are unlearned triggers for fear: something hurling through space quickly, which will hit us if we don't duck; the sudden loss of support, so that we fall through space. The threat of physical pain is an unlearned trigger for fear, although during the moment of pain itself no fear may be felt.

The sight of snakes could be another unlearned, universal trigger. Remember the studies by Ohman that I described in chapter 1, which showed that we are biologically prepared to become more afraid of reptilian shapes than guns or knives. Yet a substantial number of people do not appear to be afraid of snakes; just the opposite, they enjoy physical contact even with poisonous snakes. I am tempted to suggest that being in a very high place where a false step might lead to a fall is another unlearned trigger. I have always been terrified of such situations, but this is not a fear trigger for a substantial number of people.

Perhaps there is no inborn fear stimulus present in everyone. There always are a few people who don't show what we see in nearly everyone else, whether it is in the stimulus that calls forth any emotion, or in the most common emotional response. Individuals differ in nearly every aspect of human behavior, and emotions are no exception.

We can learn to become afraid of nearly anything. There is no question that some people fear things that, in fact, do not pose any danger, such as a child's fear of the dark. Adults, as well as children, can have groundless fears. For example, attaching electrodes to someone's chest to measure cardiac activity (an EKG or electrocardiogram) can alarm people who do not know that the apparatus records but does not deliver electrical activity. People who think they will be shocked will experience real, though groundless, fear. It requires a well-developed capacity for compassion to respect, feel sympathetic toward, and patiently reassure someone who is afraid of something of which we are not afraid. Instead, most of us dismiss such fears. We do not need to feel another person's fear to accept it and help the other person cope with his or her fear. Good nurses understand their patients' fear; able to see the patients' perspectives, they are able to reassure them.

We can do nearly anything or nothing when we are afraid, depending upon what we have learned in the past about what can protect us in the situation in which we find ourselves. Studies of other animals, and what we find in research on how humans are bodily prepared to act, suggest that evolution may favor two very different actions—hiding and fleeing. During fear, blood goes to the large muscles in the legs, preparing us to flee.[2] That doesn't mean we will flee, only that evolution has prepared us to do what has been most adaptive in the past history of our species.

Many animals first freeze when confronted by a danger, such as a potential predator, presumably because that decreases the likelihood that they will be noticed. I saw this when I approached a group of monkeys in a large cage. Most of the monkeys froze as I got close, in an effort to avoid detection. When I moved even closer, so that the direction of my gaze made it obvious which monkey I was looking at, that monkey then fled.

If we do not freeze or flee, the next most likely response is to become angry at whatever threatened us.[3] It is not uncommon to experience fear and anger in rapid succession. There is no certain scientific evidence about whether we are capable of experiencing two emotions at the same instant, but in practice it may not matter. We can alternate between fear and anger (or any other emotions) so rapidly that the feelings merge. If the person threatening us seems to be more powerful, we are likely to feel fear rather than anger; but we may still, at moments, or after escaping, be angry with the person who threatened harm. We may also be angry with ourselves for becoming afraid, if we believe that we should have been able to deal with the situation without fear. For the same reason we may be disgusted with ourselves.

Sometimes there is nothing we can do when faced with great harm—the truck driver in the Surabaya photo is in that situation. Unlike the people sitting on top of the truck who could focus their attention on how to jump, he could do nothing; yet the threat of harm was great. However, something very interesting happens when we *are* able to cope with an immediate, severe threat, which is the situation the people on top of the bus experienced. The unpleasant sensations and thoughts that characterize fear may not be experienced, but instead consciousness may focus us on the task at hand, coping with the threat.

For example, when I first went to Papua New Guinea in 1967, I had to charter a single-engine airplane to take me on the last leg of my journey to a missionary landing strip, from which I would walk to the village where I would be living. Although by then I had taken many flights to many different parts of the world, I remained a bit afraid of flying, enough not to be able to relax, let alone sleep, even on a long journey. I worried about having to take a single-engine plane, but there was no choice; there were no roads to where I was going. Once we were up in the air, the eighteen-year-old bush pilot, next to whom I was sitting in the two-seater plane, informed me that the ground people had radioed him that the wheels had fallen off the airplane on takeoff. We had to return, he said, and slide into the dirt on the side of the runway. Because the plane might catch fire on impact, he told me I should be prepared to jump. He instructed me to open the door slightly to prevent it from jamming on impact when we crash-landed, which might prevent me from getting out. He told me to be careful not to let the door swing completely open, for then I might be thrown out. Needless to say, there were no seat belts.

As we circled the airfield preparing to land, I felt no unpleasant sensations and had no frightening thoughts about my possible doom. Instead, I thought about how amazing it was to have come so far, to have traveled for more than two days, and now less than an hour from my destination not make it. It seemed ludicrous, not frightening, in the minutes before we crash-landed. I watched as the fire brigade pulled onto the landing strip to greet our return; as we tore into the dirt, I gripped the door handle tightly, keeping the door ajar but not fully open. Then it was over. No fire; death and injury were avoided. Within fifteen minutes we had unloaded my gear from the badly damaged plane, put it into another plane, and taken off. Suddenly, I felt worried that this scene would be replayed, literally, and this time I wouldn't make it.

Since my crash-landing experience, I have interviewed others who, though in extreme danger, did not experience unpleasant sensations and thoughts. What distinguishes their experiences and mine from dangerous situations in which fear was felt is whether or not anything could be done to cope with the danger. If so, then fear may not have been felt. If not, if there is nothing to do but wait to see if one survives, then people are likely to feel terror. If I had not had to concentrate on holding that airplane door slightly ajar, tensed, ready to jump, I think I would have been terrified during the crash landing. It is when we can't do anything that we are most likely to experience the most overwhelming fear, not when we are focused on dealing with an immediate threat.

Recent research has found three ways in which fear differs depending on whether the threat is immediate or impending.* First, the different threats result in different behavior: immediate threat usually leads to action (freezing or flight) that deals with the threat, while worry about an impending threat leads to increased vigilance and muscular tension. Second, the response to an immediate threat is often analgesic, reducing pain sensations, while worry about an impending threat magnifies pain. And last, there is some evidence to suggest that an immediate threat and an impending threat each involve different areas of brain activity.[4]

Panic stands in marked contrast to a person's response to an immediate threat. Writing this chapter was interrupted when I had to undergo abdominal surgery to remove a portion of my colon. I felt no fear until the date of the surgery was scheduled. Then, during the five days between the date being set and the surgery being done, I experienced a series of panic attacks. I felt extreme fear, shortness of breath, and coldness, and I became totally preoccupied with the dreaded event. As I mentioned in chapter 5, I had had major surgery thirty years earlier, and due to a medical mistake experienced extreme unrelieved, unmedicated pain, so I had reason to dread going into an operating room once again. These panic attacks lasted anywhere from ten minutes to a few hours. On the day I reported into the hospital for the surgery, however, I felt no panic or fear of any kind, for now I was doing something about it.

The family of fearful experiences can be distinguished in terms of three factors:

- intensity—how severe is the harm that is threatened?
- timing—is the harm immediate or impending?
- coping—are there actions that can be taken to reduce or eliminate the threat?

*Some researchers use the term *anxiety* to refer to response to an impending threat, a personality trait, or an emotional disorder, but I reserve the term *anxiety* to describe a mood.

Unfortunately, no research has considered all three factors at once, making it difficult to know exactly which type of fearful experience has been studied. News photographs of fear provide some clues, often revealing the intensity of the threat, whether it is immediate or impending, and the potential for coping. In the bus photograph we can presume the driver is feeling terror—the danger is intense and he cannot cope, trapped in the bus and unable to jump free. The driver's facial expression is one I had identified as universal for fear. Some of the others who are coping with the threat, those in the midst of jumping or preparing to jump, do not show this expression but show more of an attentive, focused look, which I suspect characterizes coping with an immediate threat. Photographs of people anticipating a threat show an expression similar to but less intense than the bus driver's terror.

When we feel any type of fear, when we are conscious of being afraid, it is hard to feel anything else or think about anything else for a time. Our mind and our attention are focused on the threat. When there is an immediate threat, we focus until we have eliminated it, or if we find that we can't, our feelings may turn into terror. Anticipating the threat of harm can also monopolize our consciousness for long periods of time, or such feelings may be episodic, returning from time to time, breaking into our thoughts when we are dealing with other matters, as it did during those days when I waited to learn the results of the biopsy. Panic attacks are always episodic; if they were to continue unabated for days, the experience might be so debilitating that the panicked person would die from exhaustion.

An immediate threat of harm focuses our attention, mobilizing us to cope with the danger. If we perceive an impending threat, our worry about what might happen can protect us, warning us, making us more vigilant. The facial expressions when we are worried about impending harm, or terrified if the threat is severe, notifies others that a threat is lurking, warning them to avoid harm or recruiting them to help us deal with the threat. If we look worried or terrified when someone attacks us or is about to attack us, that may cause the attacker to back off, satisfied that we will not further pursue whatever provoked the attacker. (Of course, that may not always be the result. An attacker looking for an easy victim may interpret a fearful expression as a sign that we won't fight back and will be easily overcome.) Signs of our panic should motivate others to help or reassure us.

The core of fear is the possibility of pain, physical or psychological, but pain itself is not considered by any emotion theorist or researcher to be an emotion. Why, some might ask, is pain not an emotion? It certainly can be a very strong feeling that focuses our attention. Silvan Tomkins's answer to this question, written forty years ago, is still a good one. Pain, he said, was too specific to be an emotion. With many kinds of pain we know exactly where it hurts. But where are anger, fear, worry, terror, or sadness/agony located in our body? Like erotic feelings, when we feel pain, we make no mistake (unless it is referred pain) about where we feel it. If we cut our finger, we don't rub our elbow to soothe the pain, any more than we are indiscriminate about which parts of our body we want to stimulate when we are sexually aroused. Pain and sex are both extraordinarily important, and we feel many emotions about them, but they themselves are not emotions.

Earlier in this chapter, when discussing surprise, I said that some people enjoy being surprised. Each of the so-called negative emotions can be positive in the sense that some people enjoy experiencing them. (That is why I think it is misleading just to divide emotions into positive and negative, as many emotion theorists do.)

Some people actually appear to enjoy feeling fearful. Novels and movies that scare people are very popular. I have sat in movie theaters turned away from the screen to watch the faces of audiences and seen worry, sometimes even terror, along with enjoyment. In our research, we have shown people scary movie scenes while they sat alone in a room, their expressions recorded with a hidden video camera. We found that those who are showing the fearful face display not just the expression but also the physiology—increased heart rate and blood going to the large muscles in the legs—of being fearful.[5]

One could argue that these people are not really in danger, and they know that they will not be harmed. But there are people who go beyond the vicarious, who seek fearful experiences, who even enjoy risking death in the sports they pursue. I don't know if it is fear that they enjoy, or the excitement often associated with taking such risks, or the relief and pride in their accomplishment they feel afterward.

There are also people who are just the opposite, for whom fearful feelings are so toxic that they take extraordinary efforts to avoid feeling them. For every emotion there are people who enjoy experiencing the emotions and their opposites, people who can't tolerate feeling them, as well as many people who do not seek to experience the emotion but who do not find its experience in most instances particularly toxic.

Each of the emotions we have considered so far plays a role in a more enduring mood that may last for many hours. When we feel sad for a long time, we are in a blue mood. When we are easily angered, looking for something about which to become angry, we are in an irritable mood. I use the term *anxiety* for the mood in which we feel worried and don't know why we are feeling that way; we can't point to the trigger. Although we feel as if we are in danger, we don't know what to do about it since we can't identify the threat.

Like the blue mood, melancholic personality, and depression related to sadness-agony and the irritable mood, hostile personality, and pathological violence related to anger, fear has anxious moods, shy or timid personalities, and a number of disorders that I describe below. Extreme shyness, for example, is said to characterize about 15 percent of the population.[6] Such people are preoccupied with how they may fail to deal with social situations; they avoid social contact and have low self-esteem, elevated stress hormones, and high heart rate. They are also at increased risk for heart disease.[7] One prominent researcher, Jerome Kagan, suggests that parents typically distinguish three different fear-related traits: parents call children who avoid people shy, those who avoid unfamiliar situations timid, and those who avoid unfamiliar food finicky.[8] Many researchers distinguish two types of shyness, rather than three: the self-conscious shy, who are conflicted about whether to approach or avoid strangers and novel situations, and the fearful shy, who avoid strangers and novel situations.[9]

There are a number of emotional disorders in which fear plays a major role.[10] Phobias are the most obvious and perhaps the best known; they are characterized by fear of interpersonal events or situations, of death, injury, illness, blood, of animals, and of places such as crowds, closed spaces, etc. Posttraumatic stress disorder (PTSD) is considered to be the result of having been in extreme danger, which is followed by persistent reexperiencing of the traumatic event and avoiding events associated with the trauma. PTSD is usually accompanied by difficulty in sleep and in concentration, as well as angry outbursts. Panic attacks that occur repeatedly are another emotional disorder involving worry or terror. They often appear with no apparent reason and can be quite incapacitating. Pathological anxiety is still another emotional disorder that differs from normal anxious moods in terms of being more recurrent, persistent, and intense, interfering with such basic life tasks as working and sleeping.

Recognizing Fear in Ourselves

In the sadness chapter I suggested that looking at the picture of Bettye Shirley might generate sad feelings in the viewer. I don't think that happens when we look at people who show anger; I also don't think it happens when we look at people who show fear. However, give it a try. Look at the truck driver's expression, and if that begins to generate any sensations, let them grow. If that doesn't work, try imagining yourself in his situation, and if that begins to generate sensations, let them grow.

If looking at the picture didn't work, try to remember a time in your life when there was an intense, immediate danger, and there was nothing you could do to reduce the threat. Perhaps you were on an airplane flight, and the weather got choppy, and there were sudden drops during air pockets. As you begin to remember the experience, let your sensations grow.

If trying to remember a scene from your past didn't work, then try the following exercise:

> Imitate the facial movements of fear. (You may need to use a mirror to check on whether you are making the correct movements.)
>
> • Raise your upper eyelids as high as you can, and if you are able, also slightly tense your lower eyelids; if tensing your lower eyelids interferes with raising your upper eyelids, then just focus on raising your upper eyelids.

- Let your jaw drop open, and stretch your lips horizontally back toward your ears; your mouth should look like the bus driver's mouth.
- If you can't do this after trying a few times, then just let your jaw hang open and don't try to stretch your lips horizontally.
- With your upper eyelids raised as high as they can go, staring straight ahead, raise your eyebrows as high as you can; try to see if you can also pull your eyebrows together while you keep your brows raised; if you can't do both, then just keep the eyebrows raised with your upper eyelids raised.

Pay attention to the feelings in your face, in your stomach, in your hands and your legs. Check on your breathing, and whether your face and hands feel cool or warm.

You may find that your hands get colder, that you begin to breathe more deeply and rapidly, that you begin to sweat, and perhaps that you feel trembling or tightening of the muscles in your arms and legs. And you might feel your face or body beginning to move back in the chair.

Usually when you are terrified you know it, but you may not be as familiar with the sensations that accompany slight worry, when the threat is in the future and is not severe. (I believe that the sensations are similar to terror, but much less intense. However, no research has yet been done to see if worry and terror are associated with different subjective experiences.)

Let's try now to evoke the sensations you feel when you are worried. Recall a situation in which you were anticipating something harmful happening, something that wouldn't be a disaster, but certainly something you would like to avoid. You might have worried about having a wisdom tooth pulled or a colonoscopy performed. The worry might be about whether the report you wrote will be evaluated as highly as you hope. You might be worried about how you did on the math final exam. When you have such an experience in mind—remember it is in the future, you are anticipating it, and at this point you can't do anything to prevent the possible harm—again focus on what the sensations are that you feel within your face and body. They should be a much weaker version of the terror feelings.

Recognizing Fear in Others

The caption for this picture when it appeared in *Life* magazine in 1973 said: "In New York, a fall from grace. Eyes apop, eight wheels and ten fingers raking the air, San Francisco Bay Bomber Charlie O'Connell assumes the position every Roller Derby daredevil dreads most. He has just taken a fancy bump-and-grind from Bill Groll of the New York Chiefs during the world championship at Shea Stadium last May. O'Connell and his team ended up sore losers."

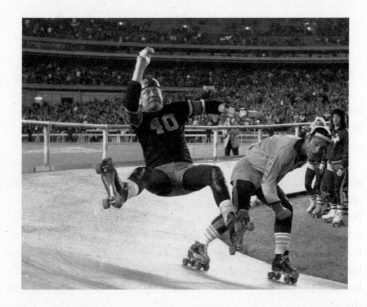

O'Connell shows the same terror expression you saw on the truck driver, although here you can get a better look at it. His upper eyelids are raised as high as they can go, his eyebrows are raised and drawn together, and his lips are stretched horizontally toward his ears, while his chin is pulled back.

The caption for this photograph when it appeared in *Life* magazine said: "Dallas, November 24, 1963. The precise instant of a historic act of revenge is captured as Jack Ruby shoots Kennedy assassin Lee Harvey Oswald."

Detective J. R. Leavelle, the man on the left, has just heard the gunshot. He shows both fear and anger on his face. His eyebrows are pulled down and together, pressing against his raised upper eyelids, producing what I called a "glare" in chapter 6, a clear anger expression. The lower half of his face and the position of his head show fear. The lips are stretched back horizontally, and his chin is pulled backward as his head tilts away from the gunshot. Try covering the lower half of his face with your hand so you can see just the anger in the upper part of his face. Then reverse it, covering the upper part of his face so you can see the fear in the lower part.

It makes sense that he would feel momentary fear, perhaps terror, when he saw the gun, not knowing if it would be turned next on him. (From the pain expression on Oswald's face, we know that the gun has already been fired, and Leavelle's startle reaction to that loud noise has already occurred). Detective Leavelle would also be angry with the assassin Ruby, for Leavelle's job was to prevent such an attack on Oswald. Earlier, I mentioned that it is not uncommon to be both angry and afraid when we are threatened, and that is what has happened here.

Now let's look at the pictures showing the subtle signs of fear and surprise in the face.

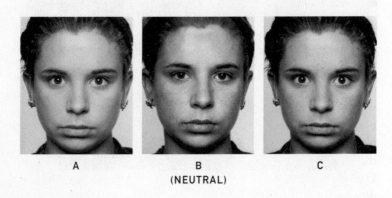

A   B   C
(NEUTRAL)

The eyes are crucial for both surprise and fear and for distinguishing between them. In photo A, the upper eyelids have been raised just a slight amount, compared to her neutral face shown in picture B. This could be a sign of surprise, but probably it is more simply a sign of attention or interest. In picture C, the upper eyelids are raised more, and now it is very likely to be either surprise, worry, or fright; which one would depend on what was happening in the rest of the face. (None of the Eve pictures show terror, which I believe to be the very extreme expressions shown by the truck driver and the roller-derby fellow).

If the expression were limited just to the eyes, as it is in photo C, then what it is signaling would depend on how long it appears. If the eye widening shown in C appeared for just a second or two, it would more likely be surprise than worry or fright.

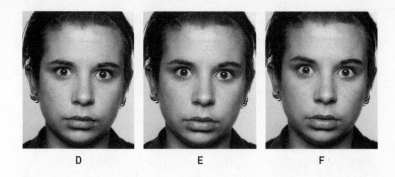

D   E   F

It should be apparent at first glance that now Eve is showing fear in her eyes. Although it is common to speak of expression in the eyes, usually it is not the eyeball itself we are referring to but what we see of it due to changes in the eyelids. Here the clue that this is not surprise or attention but fear are in the lower eyelids. When tensed lower eyelids accompany raised upper eyelids and the rest of the face is blank, it is almost always a sign of fear. Going from photo D sequentially to photo F, the intensity of the fear increases. This is due to the increase in the raising of the upper eyelids. In picture F the upper eyelid raise is extreme, the most that Eve can do deliberately. This could occur in terror, not fright or worry, but it would be highly controlled terror, in which the person showing the expression is trying very hard not to reveal how she feels.

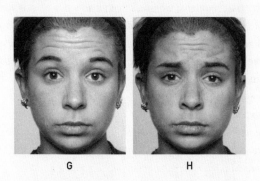

G   H

Now let's look at how the eyebrows express surprise and fear. When the brows are simply raised, as they are in photo G, it is an ambiguous signal. Most often this movement is an emphasis sign, accenting a word when someone is speaking. If this is the case, there will be an increase in the loudness of the emphasized word at the same time. Photo G may also be a question-mark signal, inserted near the end of a questioning statement. Recall in the last chapter I mentioned that lowering and drawing together eyebrows, as shown in picture D on page 165, can also be used as a question-mark signal. Some of our research has suggested that if the person knows the answer to the question he or she is asking and uses a brow movement, it will more likely be the one depicted in photo G; if the person does not know the answer to the question he or she is asking, the movement will more likely be the brow lowering and drawing together shown in chapter 6. Picture G may also be an exclamation sign or a sign of disbelief, especially when the person who is listening to something that the speaker is saying shows it. Rarely will these raised eyebrows without raised eyelids be a sign of surprise.

Photo H, however, is a very reliable sign of worry or fright, in the sense that if it is shown there is little doubt that fear is felt. But no single facial expression can be relied upon always to be present when any emotion is felt; fear may be felt and the raised and drawn-together brows shown in H may not be shown. Sometimes, of course, the absence of this expression may be due to efforts to inhibit the expression; but even when no effort is made to control expression, not everyone shows every sign of an emotion when it is felt. As yet we can't explain why that happens; we don't even know if a person who is unexpressive of fear would be unexpressive of other emotions, but that is a problem I am currently working on. It would be rare, however, for the expression shown in photo H to be shown and for fear *not* to be felt.

 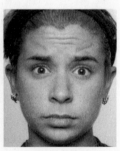

I   J

Usually, the upper eyelids would be raised and the lower eyelids would be tensed and accompanied by the fear eyebrow, as in picture J. Compare photo I with photo J, in which the eyebrows are slightly raised, not as much as in photo G, and the eyes are widened due to the raised upper eyelids. The comparison shows the importance of the eyelids and the eyebrows in differentiating between fear and surprise. We know photo I shows surprise rather than fear because the lower eyelids are not tensed and the eyebrows are not drawn together, though they are being raised; both of these signs are evident in picture J.

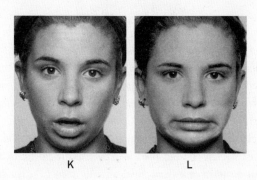

K   L

Now let's focus on the signs of surprise and fear in the lower part of the face. In surprise the jaw drops down, as shown in photo K, while in fear the lips are stretched back toward the eyes, as shown in photo L. (Note that I had to use a composite photograph in L, because Eve found it hard to make this fear lip movement without tensing her lower eyelids.)

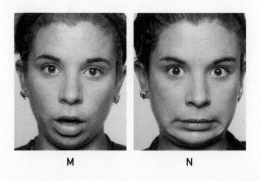

M   N

Earlier you saw that the eyebrows and eyelids by themselves could signal fear, as in photo J, or surprise, as in photo I. When the eyelids are joined by the movements of the mouth, these emotions can also be shown, even without the eyebrow movements. Photo M shows surprise, and photo N shows worry or fright; in both the brow movements for those emotions are absent.

O

Picture O shows how important the raised upper eyelids are in signaling fear. Even though the lower eyelids are not tensed, and the eyebrows and mouth are the actions usually seen in surprise, there is so much upper eyelid raise in this picture that it creates the impression of fear. (This also is a composite in which the brows from photo G were pasted onto another photograph.)

Because fear and surprise are so often confused with each other, the pair of pictures below provides yet another contrast of these two expressions, registered intensely across the entire face in each picture; P shows surprise and Q shows fear.

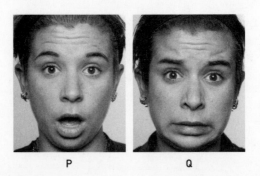

P   Q

Using the Information from Expressions

Now let us consider how you might use the information you pick up from another person's expressions of fear. (I won't deal with surprise, since most of the time I wouldn't think there would be much of an issue about how to respond to another person's surprise, unless you're dealing with the scenario I presented earlier of a person surprised by something he or she should have been—or claimed to be—aware of.[11]) I will use most of the same situations I described in earlier chapters to emphasize how differently we might want to use knowledge that the other person is afraid, as compared to the person being sad or angry.

In the last two chapters I emphasized the need to be careful not to assume that we know what is generating an emotional expression. Emotional expressions don't tell us their cause; usually, but not always, we can figure that out from the situational context in which they are shown. In chapter 3 I described what I called Othello's error,* assuming you know the cause of an emotion without considering the possibility that there might be an entirely different cause. Our emotional state, our attitudes, our expectations, what we want to believe, even what we don't want to believe can all bias how we interpret an expression or more specifically what we think caused the emotion shown by the expression. Taking account of the situation in which the expression is shown may help to reduce the possibilities, but even then it may not be certain. It didn't help Othello. If you keep in mind that emotional expressions do not reveal their cause, and that there may be causes other than the one you expect, you may be able to avoid Othello's error.

Consider the expressions shown in photos D, E, F, H, I, L, and N. Each of them could be a sign of worry, but you would not know from the expression whether the threat is immediate or impending. You would also not know how intensely the fear is felt, for these expressions can occur when the emotion is slight to moderate, or when the emotion is more intense but an attempt is being made to control the expression.

---

*Othello, you will remember, killed his wife because he didn't understand that the fear of being disbelieved looks the same as the fear of being punished for being caught committing adultery. Othello made this mistake because of his jealousy.

Suppose you are the supervisor delivering the bad news to an employee that he will not get a promotion, and that someone else was promoted instead. If he shows any of these expressions before you tell him the news, that would suggest he is anticipating failure. If the expressions are shown during or after you give him the information, that suggests he is concerned about how this affects his future. Although I would not suggest you mention your perception of his fear, it might be a reason for you to reassure him about his future in the organization if his future is not in jeopardy, or to raise the issue of how he may want to consider his future plans. It is possible, however, that his fear has nothing to do with the failure to get the promotion, but that he was anticipating your discovery of something else that would adversely affect him. Maybe he had taken sick leave when he was taking a holiday and is afraid you have found out about that; perhaps he has been embezzling. Or maybe he is worried about his upcoming physician's appointment, and his mind drifts to that for a moment. The most conservative way for you to respond is to say, "Is there more that you would like to discuss with me about the situation?" Or you could go further and say, "I sense that there may be more about this that we need to talk about."

Let's reverse the situation: You are the employee and your supervisor shows one of these worry or fright expressions for a moment before she gives you the news that you did not get the promotion. Is she worried about your reaction? Is she showing empathy for how you might be feeling, showing her sense that you might be worried about your future? Or might there be something else entirely on her mind that she momentarily recalls? You can't know from the expression itself, but in knowing these possibilities, you at least know that she is not dismissive of you, which would be signaled by a contempt expression (which will be discussed in the next chapter), or angry with you.

If your twelve-year-old daughter shows the expression when you ask her how school was that day, or a friend shows one of these expressions when you ask him or her how things are going, your relationship to them gives you reason to be much more direct. You won't know whether their fear is in response to you, or whether something has happened in their lives or is about to happen about which they are worried. My suggestion would be to say, "I sense something is worrying you; can I help in any way?"

If your spouse shows a worried expression when you ask her where she was in the afternoon when you couldn't reach her by telephone at the office, don't jump to the conclusion that she was up to some mischief. If that thought came to mind, you might be an overly suspicious person (unless there has been a pattern of infidelity, in which case, why are you still there?), and the fear might be that you are about to become jealous or accusatory for no reason. Or it could be that your spouse was getting a medical checkup, doesn't know the outcome yet, and has some reason to be worried about it. As I have said earlier, emotions don't tell you what triggered them. If the expression doesn't fit the situation or the words spoken, it is reasonable to be concerned about what is happening, and whether it is something you should know about. It might be wisest for you to follow the suggestion I made for how to respond to your child and ask your spouse if something is worrying her.

8 Disgust and Contempt

He was watching me eat from a can of American food I had brought with me to this remote village in the highlands of Papua New Guinea where the Fore people lived. When I saw him watching me, and the expression that swept over his face, I dropped my fork and raised the camera I always wore around my neck. (Fortunately, the Fore did not yet know what a camera did, and they were accustomed to my holding this odd object to my eye for no apparent reason, so he did not become self-conscious and turn away before I got my shot.) Apart from showing one of the classic disgust expressions, the story behind this picture emphasizes the importance of eating offensive material in generating disgust. He wasn't even eating the food; just seeing me do it was enough to generate his feelings.*

Writing thirty years ago I described disgust as:

> . . . a feeling of aversion. The taste of something you want to spit
> out, even the thought of eating something distasteful can make
> you disgusted. A smell that you want to block out of your nasal

---

*Although over the years I have collected dozens of news photographs showing each of the other emotions, I have none of disgust. A commercial photo research firm I hired could find only posed pictures of disgust, though I've had no problem finding spontaneous news photographs of the other emotions. No wonder; disgusting scenes are not attractive. Newspaper and magazine editors and their advertisers must have decided that such pictures would not sell their products.

passage, or move away from calls forth disgust. And again, even the thought of how something repulsive might smell brings out strong disgust. The sight of something you think might be offensive to taste or smell can make you disgusted. Sounds might also make you disgusted, if they are related to an abhorrent event. And touch, the feel of something offensive, such as a slimy object, can make you disgusted.

It is not only tastes, smells, and touches, or the thought, sight, or sound of them that can bring forth disgust but also the actions and appearance of people, or even ideas. People can be offensive in their appearance; to look at them may be distasteful. Some people experience disgust when seeing a deformed, crippled person, or an ugly person. An injured person with an exposed wound may be disgusting. The sight of blood or the witnessing of surgery makes some people disgusted. Certain human actions are also disgusting; you may be revolted by what a person does. A person who mistreats or tortures a dog or cat may be the object of disgust. A person who indulges in what others consider sexual perversion may be disgusting. A philosophy or way of treating people that is considered debasing can make those who regard it that way feel disgusted.[1]

My observations have since been supported and extended in a series of studies by virtually the only scientist who has focused most of his research on disgust. Psychologist Paul Rozin, a man who is especially fond of very good food, believes that the core of disgust involves a sense of oral incorporation of something that is deemed offensive and contaminating; in my terms, this would be the disgust theme. However, there are large differences across cultures in what food products are considered offensive. The photograph of the New Guinea man illustrates this point: he is disgusted by the sight and smell of food I found appetizing. And there are differences within cultures as well. My wife loves raw oysters, but I find them disgusting. In areas of China, dogs are a succulent delicacy, while most Westerners find that prospect revolting. But there also are universals in what triggers disgust.

Rozin found that the most potent, universal triggers are bodily products: feces, vomit, urine, mucus, and blood. In 1955, the great American psychologist Gordon Allport suggested a disgust "thought experiment," an experiment you perform in your own mind to verify whether what he suggests does happen. "Think first of swallowing the saliva in your mouth, or do so. Then imagine expectorating it into a tumbler and drinking it! What seemed natural and 'mine' suddenly becomes disgusting and alien."[2] Rozin actually did this experiment, asking people to drink a glass of water after they had spit into it, and he found that Allport was right. Even though the spit was inside their own mouth a moment before, they would not drink the glass of water containing their own spit. Rozin says that once a product leaves our body, it becomes disgusting to us.

Disgust does not appear as a separate emotion until somewhere between the ages of four and eight. There is distaste, the rejection of things that taste bad, but not disgust. Rozin asked children and adults to touch or eat chocolate that had been shaped to look like dog feces. Kids aren't bothered until between ages four and seven, but most adults won't do it. Similarly, if you drop a sterilized grasshopper into milk or juice, that won't stop kids under four from being willing to drink it.*

---

*Rozin explains this difference by proposing that the younger child doesn't have the cognitive capabilities necessary for disgust—the ability, for example, to recognize that appearance is different from reality, as in the chocolate dog feces. This is also consistent with his view that other animals do not feel disgust. In my mind it would be extraordinary to have such a fundamental way of responding to the

Children and adolescents have a fascination with disgust. Rozin reminds us that novelty stores sell realistic imitations of vomit, mucus, slime, and feces, and it is mostly young boys who buy these objects. There is a whole genre of jokes centering on disgust. The television program *Beavis and Butt-head*, which was so popular with adolescents, and the *Captain Underpants* and *Garbage Pail Kids* franchises for younger children dwell on disgusting situations.

Law professor William Miller, in his fascinating book *The Anatomy of Disgust*, notes that it is not just children who are so fascinated by the disgusting. "[Disgust] . . . has an allure, a fascination which is manifest in the difficulty of averting our eyes from gory accidents, . . . or in the attraction of horror films.[3] . . . Our own snot, feces and urine are contaminating and disgusting to us, [but we are] . . . fascinated in and curious about them . . . we look at our creations more often than we admit . . . how common it is for people to check their Kleenex or handkerchief after blowing their nose."[4] The box-office success of raunchy movies like *There's Something About Mary* wasn't entirely fueled by teenagers.

Rozin distinguishes what he calls interpersonal disgust from core disgust.[5] He lists four groups of learned interpersonal triggers: the strange, the diseased, the misfortunate, and the morally tainted. My research with Maureen O'Sullivan gives some support to Rozin's proposal. We asked college students to write down the most intense experience of disgust they could imagine anyone in the world would ever have had. Rozin's oral contamination theme was described (e.g., you are forced to eat someone else's vomit), but only by 11 percent. The most frequently mentioned trigger for extreme disgust (mentioned by 62 percent) was in response to morally objectionable behavior, such as how the GIs felt when they discovered the atrocities in the Nazi concentration camps. Almost half of the morally objectionable behaviors mentioned were sexually repugnant actions, such as seeing someone have sex with a young child. The last set of

---

world be unique to humans, so I asked the expert on animal behavior, Frans de Waal. He wrote back: "The emotion must occur in other primates. Disgust originally must have had something to do with rejection of food, and of course primates are capable of this. As for specific expressions, that's harder to answer." For now the issue remains unsettled, it would seem, because no one has looked specifically at whether an expression unique to rejecting food occurs in other primates, and if it does, whether it is also shown in response to social offenses.

examples, mentioned by 18 percent of the respondents, was physical repulsion that did not involve food, such as finding a corpse with maggots coming out of it.[6] Our results suggest that for adults, it is the interpersonal, in particular the morally repugnant, which they *think* is most disgusting, rather than the core disgust of oral incorporation.

Earlier, I said that Rozin's core disgust was the emotional theme, and if he is correct that the four interpersonal forms of disgust— strange, disease, misfortunate, and morally tainted—are learned, then these would be the variations on the theme. It seems possible to me, however, that these four interpersonal forms of disgust are also themes, to be found in every culture, with only the specifics filled in by learning that would vary with individual, social group, and culture. For example, everyone may have disgust reactions to the morally tainted person, but what is considered morally tainted would vary. What is strange and familiar, and what is misfortunate should also vary with circumstances, but disease might not. Those showing severe disfigurement, oozing sores, and the like might be disgusting in every culture.

Miller points out that cultures have more leeway in admitting things or actions to the realm of disgusting than in excluding certain ones from it. This fits exactly with the ideas discussed in chapters 2, 3, and 4, in which I argued that people's emotion alert databases are open, not closed. These databases, together with the programs that guide our responses to our varying emotions, are not empty when we are born; evolution has written instructions for how we respond and sensitivities for what we respond to. As Miller points out, these are hard to change, but because they are open we can learn new triggers and new emotional responses.

Although both Japanese and Americans react with disgust to waste products and oral incorporation, Rozin found differences in social disgust. A person who doesn't fit into the social order, or who unfairly criticizes others, disgusted the Japanese. Americans were disgusted by people who act brutally or by racists. However, not all social disgust varies with culture. Rozin found that in many cultures politicians disgust people!

In addition to the four kinds of interpersonal disgust described by

Rozin, another type of disgust—what I call *fed-up disgust*—is suggested by the findings of psychologists John Gottman, Erica Woodin, and Robert Levenson. Their research merits special attention because they are the only scientists who have precisely measured the expression of emotion during one of the most emotionally laden, important social interactions in life—that between husband and wife.*

Amazingly, a wife's expressions of disgust, directed toward her husband during a conversation in which they were trying to resolve a conflict, predicted the amount of time over the next four years they would spend separated.[7] Gottman found that the wife's disgust expressions usually occurred in response to the husband's withdrawal (stonewalling, which I described in chapter 6), when he wouldn't deal with her feelings. In colloquial language, she had had it; she was fed up. Note how an eating metaphor seems so appropriate. If your spouse repels you, it is no wonder that the future is bleak. (We will return to more of Gottman's findings later in this chapter when I describe contempt.)

Miller makes the very interesting point that in intimacy we lower the threshold for what we consider disgusting. The prime example is ". . . changing diapers, cleaning up regurgitated food, otherwise caring for sick and infirm kin. . . . Parents are those who will care no matter what; will cart away the excrement, risk getting it on their hands and clothing; suffer being shat upon. . . . Overcoming the disgust inherent in contaminating substances is emblematic of the unconditional quality of nurturing parental love."[8]

The same suspension of disgust occurs between sexual intimates. Again I quote from Miller: "Someone else's tongue in your mouth can be a sign of intimacy because it can also be a disgusting assault. . . . Consensual sex means the mutual transgression of disgust-defended boundaries. . . . Sex is only one kind of boundary crossing, involving one kind of nakedness. There are other strippings, exposures, and knowledges upon which intense intimacies are founded, the intimacies of prolonged, close, and loving contact. One thinks of sharing and revealing doubts, worries, concerns; of

---

*By comparison, most emotion scientists examine emotion in people who are alone or engaged in a trivial encounter, and rather than observing what people actually do, they ask their subjects to answer questionnaires about what they imagine or remember feeling.

admitting aspirations, confessing shortcomings and failures; of simply being seen as having warts, weaknesses, and needs. . . . We could define friends or intimates as those persons whom we let whine to us so that in return we may whine to them, with both parties understanding that such whining is the privilege of intimacy which our dignity and disgust would prevent in the absence of the privilege . . . [L]ove . . . privileges another to see us in ways that would shame us and disgust* others without the intervention of love."[9]

Miller's quite extraordinary insight suggests a social function of disgust not otherwise apparent. The suspension of disgust establishes intimacy and is a mark of personal commitment. This acceptance of what the other might find shameful, the involvement in physical activities that would with anyone else be disgusting—not just sex; think of cleaning up the vomit of a stranger rather than a loved one—may not be just a mark of love but a means of strengthening love.

Another very important function of disgust is to remove us from what is revolting. Obviously it's useful not to eat something putrid, and social disgust in a parallel way moves us away from what we consider objectionable. It is, Miller proposes, a moral judgment, in which we can make no compromise with the disgusting person or the disgusting actions. Legal scholar Martha Nussbaum writes that "most societies teach the avoidance of certain groups of people as being physically disgusting."[10] Unfortunately, it can be a dangerous emotion because it dehumanizes the people we find disgusting, and by doing so allows those found disgusting not to be treated as human.

Certain actions have often been deemed illegal because they offend (disgust) public morality, such as child pornography or obscenity. Nussbaum believes that laws should not be based on what anyone finds disgusting, and suggests that we should use outrage, rather than disgust, as the basis for legal judgment. "[Outrage] . . . is a moral sentiment far more pertinent to legal judgment, and far more reliable, than disgust. It contains reasoning that can be pub-

*My editor points out that there is a difference between the suspension of disgust by the parent and by the lover. As far as I can see, baby's diapers are always disgusting, even if it's one's own baby; loving parents overcome their disgust to take care of the child, but they still feel disgust. In sex, however, there's a change; having the right person's tongue in one's mouth is not disgusting at all—quite the opposite. Thus, in the first case disgust is overcome, or suspended, while in the second it is transformed into something else altogether.

licly shared, and it does not make the questionable move of treating the criminal like an insect or slug, outside of our moral community. Instead, it firmly includes him within the moral community and judges his actions on a moral basis."[11]

Noting that a person's emotional state at the time of a crime may be considered a mitigating factor, Nussbaum also argues that disgust is not an emotion that should be so considered. "[O]ne homicide is not worse than another because it is more disgusting. . . . [12] The reasonable response to disgust," she says, "is to get out of the area not to kill the person who makes you disgusted—e.g., homosexual pass. [Just] . . . feeling contaminated or 'grossed out' by someone is never a sufficient reason to conduct oneself violently against that person."[13]

Those who justify the worst degradation of others often refer to their victims as animals (and not the cute variety); sometimes the victims are spoken of as inanimate offensive matter, such as filth or scum. I fear that indignation or outrage might also justify slaughter and even torture, but it would not put the barrier between self and other imposed by disgust. (Nussbaum, of course, focused on the use of emotions to justify laws, not to justify actions legal or not.) One of the barriers or inhibitors that could retard violence, one would think, is the sight and sound of the victims' suffering, their screams, and their blood. But that doesn't always happen, perhaps because the evidence of their suffering makes them disgusting. Even if we do not start out thinking of someone as disgusting, the sight of the person's blood, the deformation of the person's body as a result of injury or torture, can bring forth disgust rather than concern.

In the very early days of my research on expression across cultures, I found that films of people who were suffering—a film of an aboriginal circumcision rite and another of eye surgery—produced disgust expressions in the majority of the college students I studied in Japan and America. I edited other medical training films, one showing the cutting of flesh with a lot of blood as part of an operation, and another showing a man with third-degree burns standing while burned skin was stripped off his body. Again, most people showed and reported being disgusted. The films could be used interchangeably, since they produced the same emotion, and are among the most commonly used film stimuli in emotion research.

There was a minority group (about 20 percent), however, who displayed very different reactions to the sight of another person's suffering during the films. Instead of showing disgust, they reacted with sadness and pain, as if they were identifying with the victim.

It appears that nature designed us to be revolted by the sight of the insides of another person's body, especially if there is blood. That disgust reaction is suspended when it is not a stranger but an intimate, our kin, who bleeds. Then we are motivated to reduce the suffering rather than get away from it. One can imagine how revulsion at the physical signs of suffering, of disease, might have had a benefit in reducing contagion, but it comes at the cost of reducing our capacity for empathy and compassion, which can be very useful in building community.

Neither empathy nor compassion is an emotion; they refer to our reactions to another person's emotions. In *cognitive* empathy we recognize what another person is feeling. In *emotional* empathy we actually feel what that person is feeling, and in *compassionate* empathy we want to help the other person deal with his situation and his emotions. We must have cognitive empathy, in order to achieve either of the other forms of empathy, but we need not have emotional empathy in order to have compassionate empathy.*[14]

Contempt is related to but different from disgust. I was not able to find any news photograph to illustrate this emotion; like disgust, it is not often shown in newspapers or magazines. Picture H near the end of the chapter shows an example.

Many years ago I distinguished contempt from disgust in the following ways:

> Contempt is only experienced about people or the actions of
> people, but not about tastes, smells or touches. Stepping onto dog

---

*The Tibetan Buddhist use of these terms is different but related. The term they use to refer to our capacity for empathy translates, according to the Dalai Lama, as "the inability to bear the sight of another's suffering." It is not that one retreats from that sight, just the opposite: "It is what causes us . . . to recoil at the sight of harm done to another, to suffer when confronted with other's suffering." The Buddhist use of the term *compassion* involves considerably more than we mean by that word in English. Explaining that would take us far away from disgust, but it is worth noting that the Buddhists view both empathy and compassion as human capacities that do not need to be learned, but do need to be cultivated, if they are to come to the fore. I take that to mean that if we are to regard all human beings as our kin, to suspend disgust at the bloody signs of suffering and the impairments of disease, we need to work at it, for nature did not make it easy for us to do so.

droppings might call forth disgust, but never contempt; the idea of eating calves' brains might be disgusting, but it would not evoke contempt. You might, however, feel contemptuous toward people who eat such disgusting things, for in contempt there is an element of condescension toward the object of contempt. Disdainful in disliking the persons or their actions, you feel superior (usually morally) to them. Their offense is degrading, but you need not necessarily get away from them, as you would in disgust.[15]

Unfortunately, there is no Paul Rozin for contempt, no one who has focused his or her research on this emotion. Miller has made the interesting observation that although we feel superior to another person when we feel contempt, those who occupy a subordinate position may feel contempt to their superiors. Think of "the contempt teenagers have for adults, women for men, servants for masters, workers for bosses, . . . blacks for whites, the uneducated for the educated. . . . [16] Upward contempt . . . allows the lower to claim superiority regarding a particular attribute. . . . The persons below know they are below in the eyes of the others, know they are in some sense held in contempt by those others. . . ."[17]

To get some sense of the importance of contempt, consider this extraordinary set of findings from the study of marital interaction by Gottman and his colleagues. The wives whose husbands showed contempt:

- felt flooded
- believed that their problems could not be worked out
- believed their marital problems were severe
- became ill often over the following four years

The fact that the husband's disgust or anger expressions did not yield these findings underlines the importance of distinguishing contempt as a separate emotion (not a distinction recognized by all who study emotion).

Contempt, like all the other emotions we have considered, can vary in strength or intensity, as can disgust. I suspect that the high end is a lot more extended in disgust than in contempt, that is, the maximum contempt does not come near the maximum disgust in its strength.

Disgust is clearly a negative emotion; it doesn't feel good, even though, as mentioned earlier, we are more fascinated by what is disgusting than would be expected for an emotion that doesn't feel good. Certainly when disgust is intense, there is no question that the sensations are unpleasant, leading to nausea. I am less certain that contempt is negative; indeed, I believe it feels good to most people to feel contemptuous. We may be embarrassed afterward that we felt that way, but the feelings we experience during the emotion are more pleasant than unpleasant. This is not to say that it is an emotion that has beneficial effects on others; Gottman's results show that it does not. But the sensations felt during the experience of contempt are not inherently unpleasant. It is hard to specify a function for contempt other than signaling the feeling of being superior, of not needing to accommodate or engage. It asserts power or status. Those who are uncertain about their status may be more likely to manifest contempt to assert their superiority over others.

Contempt will often be accompanied by anger, a mild form of anger such as annoyance, although it may be felt without any anger at all. Anger may also alternate with disgust, if the disgusted person is angry about being made to feel disgusted.

We do not have words to describe moods related to either disgust or contempt, but that doesn't mean we don't experience such moods, only that we don't have an easy way to refer to them. My hunch is that such moods do exist, but there has been no research or theorizing on them that I know of.

Let us consider now whether there are emotional disorders that implicate either disgust or contempt. In an article entitled "Disgust—The Forgotten Emotion of Psychiatry," psychiatrists Mary L. Phillips, Carl Senior, Tom Fahy, and A. S. David suggest that although disgust has not been recognized as important in psychiatric disorders, it does play an important role in a number of such problems.[18] A disturbance in disgust is likely to be of import in obsessive compulsive disorder, as manifested in obsessional thoughts concerning dirt and contamination and the need for excessive washing. Animal phobias may be based on disgust, social phobias in which a person fears being humiliated may involve self-focused disgust, and blood phobias would also involve a disturbance in disgust. People with eating disorders, such as anorexia nervosa and bulimia, have strong feelings of disgust toward their own body parts, sexuality, and certain foods. To date, no one has suggested that there are any psychiatric disorders involving contempt.

Recognizing Disgust and Contempt in Ourselves

Let us now consider the internal sensations we experience with disgust and then contempt. It should be easy to experience feelings of disgust by thinking of one of the oral incorporation themes or of some morally repugnant act. Pay attention to the feelings in your throat, the beginning of a slight gagging. The sensations in your upper lip and nostrils are increased, as if your sensitivity to these parts of your face has been turned up so you feel them more. After relaxing try again to experience disgust, but as slightly as possible, again focusing on the sensations in your throat and in your nostrils and upper lip.

It is much harder to identify the sensations associated with contempt. Think of someone's actions that don't revolt you but that cause you to feel contemptuous toward him or her. Perhaps it is a person who jumps place in line, who plagiarizes, who name-drops. Make certain you don't feel any anger or disgust, simply contempt. Notice that the tendency to want to raise your chin, as if you are looking down your nose at someone. Feel the tightening in one corner of your lips.

Recognizing Disgust and Contempt in Others

Let's now consider how these two emotions appear on the face. Turn back and look again at the New Guinea man's expression at the beginning of this chapter. The upper lip is raised as high as it will go. The lower lip is raised, also, and is protruding slightly. The wrinkle extending from above his nostrils downward to beyond his lip corners is deep, and its shape forms an inverted U. His nostril wings are raised, while wrinkles appear on the sides and bridge of his nose. The raising of his cheeks and lowering of his brows creates crow's-feet wrinkles. These are all the marks of extreme disgust.

Eve's pictures show more subtle versions of disgust, and also examples of contempt. There are two very different facial expressions that signal disgust, nose wrinkling and raised upper lip, and often they occur together. I've included picture A, showing the neutral expression, for comparison.

A
(NEUTRAL)

First, let's look at the nose-wrinkling signal. Photo B shows just the slightest sign of nose wrinkling; photo C shows the same action a bit stronger; photo D shows intense nose wrinkling. Notice that when it gets as strong as that expressed in D, the eyebrows are also pulled down, leading some people to think anger is being shown. But if you look closely, you'll see that the upper eyelids are not raised and the brows are not drawn together. (For comparison, look at photo E in chapter 6.) This is disgust, not anger. In these disgust pictures, the cheeks are raised, pushing up the lower eyelids, but it is the changes in the nose, mouth, and cheeks that are important, not the changes in the eyes. The eyelid muscles are relaxed rather than tensed.

 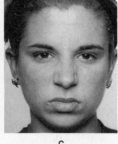 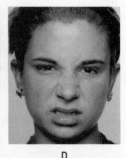

B   **C**   **D**

Now, we'll look at disgust signaled in a raised upper lip. Photo E shows a slight upper lip raise, which is shown stronger in photo F. Picture G shows this same action, but just on one side of the face. When the expression is unbalanced as it is here, it can signal disgust or it may also be a sign of contempt.

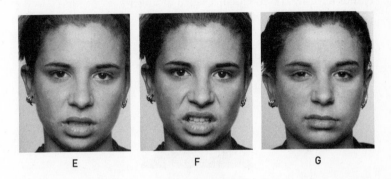

E F G

Compare photo G with the picture of contempt, photo H, shown below. In picture H, the action is also on only one side of the face, but the action is completely different. The lip corner is tightened and slightly raised. This is a clear contempt expression. Photo I shows the same action as photo G, but the action is stronger, causing the lips to part slightly on one side. I, like G, can signal disgust or contempt.

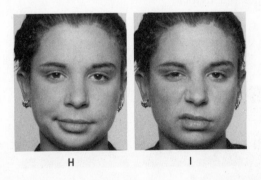

H I

Picture J shows a blend or merging of two emotions into one expression. The nose is wrinkled, a sign of disgust, and the eyebrows are not only lowered but also pulled together, and the upper eyelids are raised—signs of anger. The raised upper eyelids are not very apparent because the brows have been pulled so far down; comparing photo J with the neutral photo A—or even with photo C, which involves changes only in the eyebrows, cheeks, and nose—should make it clear that the upper eyelids have been raised and the lower eyelids have also been tensed, a signal of anger.

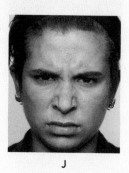

J

Lips being pressed together, another sign of anger, might often accompany the expression shown in photo J and is shown in a composite photograph, K, in which lip pressing has been added to the expression shown in J. Another possible blend of emotions, contempt and enjoyment, is shown in picture L. The expression combines the tightened lip corner with a bit of a smile, producing a smug contemptuous look.

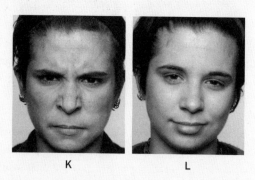

K   L

Using the Information from Expressions

Before considering how you can use information that someone is feeling disgust or contempt, remember that it is possible that the person showing the disgust might be not be feeling disgust with you; it might be targeted toward him- or herself or he or she might be remembering a past disgusting experience. Although it also is conceivable that a person who shows contempt might be feeling that emotion about his or her own actions or thoughts, I have not encountered it.

Because anger is the emotion most often confused with disgust, and anger reactions can over time turn into disgust, I will highlight the difference in how you might react if you picked up signs of disgust or contempt as compared to anger. Suppose you have told your supervisee that he is not getting a promotion; he reacts by showing a definite disgust reaction such as the one shown in photo D, a clear-cut contempt response as shown in photo H, or one of the clear-cut anger expressions shown in chapter 6. Since you just delivered unwelcome news you are probably the target of his disgust, contempt, or anger, but you have to consider the possibility that he is reacting to something else.

If the supervisee shows disgust, it is probably toward you or the situation—the business setting—and it indicates, more than anger would, no interest in trying again to get that promotion. It is not just that your decision was wrong; you did more than make a mistake, you acted immorally in not giving him the promotion, and to him the whole situation stinks. If he shows contempt, it suggests that in some way he thinks he is better than you. Perhaps he feels that he's superior to you: he knows more about the job, about the company, about the type of work he does; he dresses better, and so forth. Or his superiority could be related to something that has nothing to do with the workplace.

In the anger chapter I suggested that in this situation you might not want to confront anger directly; instead you may say something such as, "My decision may well have made you angry, and I regret that. Tell me if there is anything else I can do that would be of help." If it was disgust that you saw, you might try a different tack: "I expect my decision might have been upsetting. Is there anything more I can explain, or other matters we can consider in terms of your future?" I suggest that you do not directly confront the likelihood that he feels repulsed by you, since that is hard for most people to acknowledge even if they know that is how they feel. But it still may be helpful to give him a chance to talk about his feelings, especially if you want to retain him at the firm. The contempt reaction might be what I described earlier as "upward contempt," how a subordinate person attempts to assert that he or she is really not powerless or inferior. It might be worth leaving alone, telling him you would like to set another time to talk about future options.

Staying with this situation, if the facial signs were more subtle, showing the expression in photo B rather than D, or photo G rather than I, and they are the first responses shown when you deliver the bad news, then you have a bit more leeway. When the expressions are this slight, the emotion is either being suppressed or it is just beginning. If it emerges immediately in response to your bad news, I think it is likely that the emotional reaction is just beginning, and you might benefit from approaching the matter more directly. For example, you might say, "I sense that it is hard for you to accept this because you think it was in some way unjustified. Can we talk about that?" Or you might not want to comment at all, waiting to see if the feelings became stronger or if there was something else you could say to decrease his feelings of disgust. Although the research has not been done, I expect the Gottman group's findings on marriage would carry over—when a person in a somewhat subordinate position begins to show disgust or contempt toward a superior, the work relationship is not likely to endure.

Let's consider one more situation that I discussed in chapter 6. Your teenage daughter showed these same expressions when you told her she couldn't go to her friend's house tonight because you needed her to baby-sit her younger brother while you and your husband attend a last-minute neighborhood meeting. In the chapter on anger I suggested that there was more reason for you to deal with her anger than with the anger of one of your employees who learned he didn't get the promotion. That doesn't mean that you should comment on her anger, or challenge her right to be angry. Quite the contrary, you might sympathize with her frustration and explain why the meeting is so important and why you have to impose on her.

If she shows disgust, I also believe that you should not ignore it. Is she feeling fed up, or does she feel you are in some way morally tainted? First, you must consider if this is the time to talk, or if you should let your feelings simmer down. Watch out, if you decide to wait, for the temptation is never to deal with it. A very direct way to address her disgust would be to say, "You feel I am acting pretty unfairly toward you," or "Are you sick of having to deal with me?" If you can, try not to defend yourself, and allow her to say fully what she is feeling. Then try to explain your feelings and actions calmly, without lashing out verbally.

If she shows contempt when she hears she can't go to her party and has to stay home while you go to the meeting, I would be more likely to leave it alone. It may just be an instance of upward contempt, an adolescent's assertion of being as good as or better than the parent. There might be a time when you want to deal with it, but it might not be necessary.

So far, I have assumed in all the examples with your daughter that her expression was quite definite (e.g., photo D not B). If it is a more subtle reaction of disgust, contempt, or anger, it is possible that she might not yet know how she is feeling, or the emotion is just beginning. If you can be open and accepting, it will make it easier for you to follow the suggestions in the above paragraphs. Just be careful not to put her on the defensive. Let her know by what you say that you accept the reason for her having these feelings and that you want to talk about them to explore what you can jointly do so she won't feel that way often.

Notice that in my scenario I made the parent the good guy: the meeting was suddenly called so you didn't have time to make other arrangements; it is not just to indulge your pleasures that you ask for her sacrifice. Of course, that won't always be the case, and your child's reactions, whether they be anger, disgust, or contempt, can get you to examine whether you are being fair, thoughtless, or selfish. If you discover that you acted selfishly and are able to acknowledge it, then explain what happened to her and thank her. You have a great opportunity to teach her how to use a negative emotion, such as disgust or anger, in a positive way.

9
Enjoyable
Emotions

Loretta Stirm and her children had waited patiently on the tarmac at Travis Air Force Base as a group of returning airmen left the plane that had brought them back to America. Because he was the senior officer, Lt. Col. Robert Stirm, who just had been released from a prisoner-of-war camp in North Vietnam, had to give a short speech before the families could be reunited. Again, his family waited. Sal Veder, the photographer who won a Pulitzer Prize for this photograph, wrote: "When he finished his speech, he looked about and saw his family dashing toward him, arms outstretched, smiles glowing in a true burst of joy."[1] *Joy* is a better word than *enjoyment* for the emotion shown in this picture, as it denotes more intensity than enjoyment or happiness. However, like those words, the word *joy* does not tell us exactly which of the enjoyable emotions were felt.

I believe that there are more than a dozen enjoyable emotions, each universal, each as different from the other as sadness, anger, fear, disgust, and contempt are from one another. Just as there is a set of distinctive emotions that we usually don't enjoy feeling, there is a set of distinctive emotions that we do enjoy feeling. The problem with the words *enjoyment* and *happiness* is that they're not specific enough; they imply a single state of mind and feeling, in the same way that the terms *upset* and *negative* don't reveal whether someone is sad, angry, afraid, or disgusted. The English language does not

have single words for all of the enjoyable emotions I describe in this chapter, so I have borrowed from other languages to denote some of the most important of the enjoyable emotions we feel.

We don't know much about most of the enjoyable emotions yet, for nearly all emotion research, including mine, has focused instead on the upsetting emotions. Attention has been focused on emotions when they cause problems to others and ourselves. As a result, we know more about mental disorder than about mental health. That is changing now, as there is a new emphasis on what are called the positive emotions.[2] I believe that we can benefit greatly by knowing and understanding more about our enjoyable emotions, as they are so essential in motivating much of our lives.

Let's begin with the *sensory pleasures*. There are things that feel good to touch, and being touched can feel very good, especially when the touch is from someone we care about and is done in a caring or sensual fashion. There are sights that are enjoyable to behold, such as a beautiful sunset. There are sounds that are pleasurable, such as ocean waves, water running over rocks in a brook, wind in the trees, and a wide variety of music. Tastes and smells we considered in part when we covered disgust, but sweet things taste good to most people, while the ability to enjoy sour, bitter, or spicy tastes seems to be acquired over time. Decay smells bad to most people, but some much-appreciated cheeses do have what most people consider a terrible smell. I expect there are some universal themes and many learned variations for each of the five sensory pleasures.

It is an open question whether the sensory pleasures are just different routes to the same emotional experience, and therefore should be considered one single emotion, or if we should consider them as five different emotions—visual, tactile, olfactory, auditory, and gustatory pleasures. Research will someday settle the matter by determining whether or not each of these sensory pleasures differs in their subjective sensations, the signals shown to others, and in the physiological changes that characterize them. For now I will treat them as five different emotions, because my hunch is that such research will show they differ, and not just in the sense organ that is involved.

My mentor, Silvan Tomkins, did not consider the sensory pleasures emotions. He maintained that an emotion can be triggered by nearly anything, and each of these pleasures is restricted to a single sensory source. That isn't convincing to me, for within any one of the sensory sources, such as sound, there are many, many different triggers. Although some are universal, many are not, as remarkably different tastes, sights, smell, touches, and sounds generate pleasure within and across cultures.

Psychologists Barbara Fredrickson and Christine Brannigan have also argued that the sensory pleasures should not be considered emotions, but they raised a different objection.[3] They argue that sensory pleasures just happen to us without requiring appraisal, and if there is no appraisal, there is no emotion. I disagree, however, as many commonly accepted negative emotions can be triggered by immediate sensory events. Does the automatic pleasure most people feel upon seeing a sunset involve less appraisal than the automatic fear most feel if the chair they are sitting on collapses, or a car suddenly veers toward them at high speed when they are crossing a street? I don't think so. Moreover, most of what provides us with sensory pleasure, whether it be through sight, hearing, taste, or smell, and to a lesser extent touch, are learned triggers, often involving extended appraisals. The pleasure felt, for example, when viewing an abstract painting by Picasso is not devoid of appraisal processes. Sensory pleasures are enjoyable, and I don't see any reason not to consider them as emotions.

One of the simplest enjoyable emotions is *amusement.* Most of us like to be amused by something that we find funny; some of us are very amusing, with jokes effortlessly flowing forth. Large parts of the entertainment industry are dedicated to bringing forth this emotion, so we can easily choose when we want to be amused. Amusement can vary from slight to extremely intense, with peals of laughter and even tears.[4]

When everything seems right in the world, when there is nothing we feel we need to do,* we are contented or, in the vernacular, we are laid-back, for those moments. I am not certain there is a facial sign of *contentment;* perhaps a relaxation of the facial muscles may occur. More likely is that contentment is heard in the voice. I will explain later how the differences among these enjoyable emotions are signaled more by the voice than the face.

Excitement, on the other hand, arises in response to novelty or challenge. Tomkins thought excitement was the most intense form of the emotion of interest, but interest is largely cerebral, a thinking state, rather than an emotion. However, it is true that matters that start out as simply interesting can become exciting, especially when changes happen quickly or are challenging, unexpected, or novel. It is not easy to specify a universal excitement trigger or theme. All those that I think of—downhill skiing, shooting stars—are probably, for some people, terrifying. I think there is often a close relationship between excitement and fear, even if the fear is only vicarious and not brought about by actual danger. Excitement has its own unique flavor, different from any of the other enjoyable emotions. Although it may be felt alone, it often merges with one or more of the other enjoyable emotions. Excitement can also merge into angry outbursts as rage, or with fear into terror.

Relief, often accompanied by a sigh, a deep inhalation and exhalation of breath, is the emotion felt when something that had strongly aroused our emotions subsides. We are relieved to find out the test for cancer was negative, to find our child who was lost for a few minutes in the mall, to know that we passed a difficult test on which we thought we might have done poorly. Relief may also follow

*I don't mean a mood, in which one feels relaxed, calm, and contented for a number of hours, as described in pages 50–51.

positively valued experiences, such as the relief from sexual tension and excitement felt after orgasm, sometimes mixed in with the relief felt if there was worry about sexual performance. Fear is a frequent precursor of relief, but not always, since there may be no good resolution of whatever is frightening us. Moments of anguish can precede relief felt when someone is able to reassure or comfort us about our loss. And moments of intense pleasure may precede relief. Relief is unusual in that it is not a stand-alone emotion; unlike any of the other emotions, it must always be immediately preceded by some other emotion.

Yet another enjoyable emotion is *wonder*.* We know very little about it, but an experience of intense wonder about fifteen years ago led me to propose that it is a distinctive emotion.[5] Within five minutes of meeting Richard Schechner, a professor of theater from New York University, I discovered a number of life coincidences, too many, in fact, to grasp: We had both grown up in Newark, New Jersey. Both attended the same grammar school, but never met since Richard was one year behind me. We had both moved to the same suburb, and to the very same street address! Even writing about it now, I begin to feel the wonderment I felt then. Richard's parents bought our home from my father after my mother died, and Richard's room was what had been my bedroom!

The defining characteristics of wonder are its rarity and the feeling of being overwhelmed by something incomprehensible. Unlike most others who have written about wonderment, I think it is important to separate it from fear, although the two emotions can merge when we are threatened by something overwhelming, hard to understand fully or grasp. It is an intense, intrinsically enjoyable state. Nearly anything that is incredible, incomprehensible, and fascinating can be a source of wonderment. We don't understand what it is, or how it could happen, but we are not frightened by it, unless it poses a threat to our safety, and we then have fear as well. As Dacher Keltner and Jonathan Haidt said in their recent theory about

---

*In earlier discussions I have used the term *awe* for what I now name as *wonder*. I have made the change because writer Claudia Sorsby pointed out that the *Oxford English Dictionary* tells us that awe has a strong component of fear and dread, while wonder does not.

awe (which they and others use to refer to the combination of wonderment and fear), it is about "objects the mind has difficulty grasping . . ."[6] It may be that wonder was not rare in earlier times in our history, when humans understood much less about the world about them. There have been virtually no scientific studies of wonder; think how difficult it would be to arrange for wonderment to occur in a laboratory, where it could be carefully measured.

Darwin wrote about the goose bumps that occur in wonder, and that is one of the strongest physical sensations associated with this emotion. Based on personal experience, I think a tingling on the shoulders and back of the neck also occurs when wonder is triggered. There may also be a change in respiration, not the sigh of relief but deep inhalations and exhalations. Shaking the head in incredulity may occur. No one knows as yet if there is a distinctive signal in face, voice, or body movement for wonderment.

Admiring people or finding them inspiring or charismatic generates feelings that are related to wonderment, but again, I maintain they are different. Admiration does not generate the same internal sensations as feeling wonder—the goose bumps, respiration changes, sighs, or head shakes. We want to follow inspiring people, we feel attracted to them, but when we feel wonder, we stand still, we are not impelled to action. Think of the reaction of the people in the film *Close Encounters of the Third Kind* when they saw the lights of the space ships.

Ecstasy or bliss, that state of self-transcendent rapture, achieved by some through meditation, by others through experiences in nature, and by still others through a sexual experience with a truly loved one, can be considered another enjoyable emotion. Similar to excitement and wonderment, ecstasy is an intense experience, not something one can experience in small amounts, just slightly.[7]

Jennifer Capriati, pictured on page 196, has just won the French Open tennis championship. She has accomplished something terrific, something challenging, especially as it came after she had left professional tennis for a few years because of personal problems. What's the word for that? We could say she feels great, or pleased, or happy, but those terms cover too many enjoyable emotions. She has

met a challenge and done very well. It is a lot more than a feeling of satisfaction, it is a kind of pride, but that word covers too much. In this emotion the person has stretched to accomplish something difficult and the feeling about having done so and succeeded is very enjoyable and quite unique. Others need not know about your accomplishment, you bask in it yourself. Italian psychologist Isabella Poggi identifies this emotion, which has no name in English, as *fiero*.[8]

The posture shown by Capriati is often shown by athletes who win a difficult match, although athletics is not the only challenge that can trigger fiero. I feel fiero when I figure out the solution to a difficult intellectual problem. There is no audience whose adulation I am seeking. Fiero requires a difficult challenge, and a very good feeling one has about oneself at the moment of accomplishment. Triumph would not be the right word to describe this emotion, because that implies winning a contest, and that is only one of the contexts in which fiero will be felt.

I believe this emotion is distinctive; it's not like the sensory pleasures, nor relief, nor amusement. Excitement may precede fiero as we begin to meet a challenge, but it isn't excitement either. It is its own emotion. Indeed, while pride is traditionally listed as the first of the seven deadly sins, the desire to experience fiero has been essential throughout human history, as it has helped to motivate great efforts and great achievements.*[9]

How do you feel when you hear that your son or daughter was accepted by the best college, performed beautifully in a recital, got an award from the scout troop, or accomplished anything else that matters? We could say proud, but it isn't specific enough to the pattern of physical sensations parents feel when their child accomplishes something important, perhaps even exceeding the parents themselves. In Yiddish, however, there is a specific word for just this experience: *naches*. Author Leo Rosten defines naches as "the glow of pleasure-plus-pride that only a child can give to its parents: 'I have such naches.'"[10] A related Yiddish word is *kvell*, which Rosten defines this way: "To beam-with-immense-pride-and-pleasure, most commonly over an achievement of a child or grandchild; to be so proudly happy your buttons can bust."[11] Naches is the emotion, kvelling is its expression. My daughter suggested that children could feel naches about their parents' accomplishments. Her insight gives me naches, and I am now kvelling.

Naches ensures parental investment in facilitating the growth and achievements of their children. Unfortunately, some parents don't feel naches when their children excel, reaching beyond what the parents have done. Such envious parents are often competitive with their children, which can be very destructive to both parent and child. I have also seen this kind of competition more than once between mentor and students in the academic world. "Why did they invite her to the conference? I am the expert; she was my student." A teacher, like a parent, must feel naches if the student is to learn to feel fiero, and be motivated by fiero to greater heights, fully expecting their mentor to kvell. These examples raise the interesting possibility that there might be enjoyable emotions that some people never experience. Certainly that would be so with physical handicaps that block one or another of the sensory pleasures, but perhaps there are psychological handicaps that also block the ability to experience some of the enjoyable emotions.

*Psychologist Michael Lewis retains the term *pride* for what I am calling fiero, distinguishing pride from hubris, but he does note that many fail to distinguish the fiero type of pride from hubris pride, feelings of satisfaction, or efficacy.

Anthropologist Jonathan Haidt has suggested that what he calls *elevation* be considered another one of the enjoyable emotions. He describes it as "a warm, uplifting feeling that people experience when they see unexpected acts of human goodness, kindness and compassion."[12] When we feel elevated, we become motivated ourselves to become a better person, to engage in altruistic acts. I have little doubt that what Haidt has identified and named exists, but I am not certain it meets all the criteria for establishing that it is an emotion. Not everything we experience is an emotion; we also have thoughts, attitudes, and values, for example.

Richard and Bernice Lazarus describe *gratitude* as "appreciation for an altruistic gift that provides benefit."[13] They point out that when someone does something nice for us, and it is an altruistic act, not one that seems to benefit them, we are likely to feel gratitude. However, we could also feel embarrassed about being singled out for attention, resentful for feeling in their debt, or even angry, if we felt that the person who was so nice to us did so because she thought we were so needy.

Indeed, gratitude is a complicated emotion, since it is difficult to know when it will arise. I expect there are major cultural differences about the social situations in which gratitude is experienced (the question of when to tip, for example, has very different answers in the United States and, say, Japan). In the United States, when people are just doing their job, they often say they don't expect to be thanked; if a nurse is just being a nurse when she takes excellent care of a very sick patient, one could say she doesn't expect or need gratitude. My experience, however, has been the opposite; the expression of gratitude is often appreciated in just such situations.

I doubt that there is a universal gratitude signal. The only one I can think of is a slight bow of the head, but this movement can signal many other matters, such as acknowledgment. I also doubt that there is a unique physiological pattern of sensations that characterizes gratitude. This is not to doubt that gratitude exists, just to question whether we should put it in the same bin with amusement, relief, sensory pleasures, etc.

The feeling you experience when you learn that your worst enemy has suffered may also be enjoyable, a different kind of enjoyment than the ones we have considered so far. In German it is named *schadenfreude*. Unlike the other enjoyable emotions, schadenfreude is disapproved by some, at least, in Western societies (I don't know the attitude of non-Western societies about this emotion).[14] We are not supposed to gloat over our successes, not enjoy the misfortunes of our rivals. Should gloating be considered a distinctive enjoyable emotion? Probably not; it is too much like fiero, displayed in front of others.

Are there really *sixteen* enjoyable emotions? Do the five sensory pleasures, amusement, contentment, excitement, relief, wonderment, ecstasy, fiero, naches, elevation, gratitude, and schadenfreude all qualify as distinct emotions? Only research that examines when they occur, how they are signaled, and what occurs internally can answer those questions. For now I believe that we should investigate every one of them. Some might argue that if we don't have a word for an emotion then it doesn't qualify. Surely we should not be so narrow as to insist that it has to be an English word! I don't think it is essential that there be a word in any language, although I expect emotions would be named in some language. Words are not emotions; they are representations of emotions. We do need to be careful that our words do not mislead us about what are the emotions. The way we use words sometimes can be confusing. I have used the word *amusement* for the enjoyable emotion we feel in response to something funny, typically a joke, but other matters as well that have a humorous quality. Now, however, consider the emotions we feel at an *amusement* park. There aren't usually too many jokes, although if comedians perform there we might be amused. Fun houses and roller coasters are more likely to generate excitement, fear, and relief than amusement. We might feel some fiero, as well, in having endured challenging experiences. If we knock over the bottles or score well at a shooting gallery, fiero might also be felt. If our children win in such games, we could feel naches. And there may be sensory pleasures of one kind or another, in the experiences offered. It would fit my use of words better to call it an enjoyment park.

These enjoyable emotions motivate our lives; they cause us to do things that by and large are good for us. They encourage us to engage in activity that is necessary for the survival of our species—

sexual relations and facilitating the growth of children. This is a far cry from hedonism, since altruistic acts, doing good, and creating wonderful things may be learned sources of fiero, excitement, amusement, sensory pleasures . . . in fact, nearly all the enjoyable emotions. Pursuing enjoyment need not be solitary or selfish. Indeed, I believe just the opposite, that without friendship, without achievements, without the contact with others that generates sensory pleasures, life would be quite arid.

Along with Tomkins, I believe the pursuit of enjoyment is a primary motivation in our lives. But which enjoyable emotions do we most pursue? Each of us can experience all of these emotions, unless we are sensorily deprived, but most of us are specialists, craving some more than others. People organize their lives to maximize the experience of some of these enjoyments. I tend to concentrate my efforts so I can feel fiero, naches, and some of the sensory pleasures; when I was younger I was more focused on excitement than naches (since I didn't have children yet). I expect that over the course of a lifetime we shift our focus several times, but this, too, remains to be studied.

The pursuit of contentment has always been low for me, but I have friends for whom it is a major goal, who seek moments of calmness and equanimity. Others I know deliberately enter threatening situations, magnifying their alarm, to experience excitement, fiero, and relief. And then there are still others for whom amusement, being amused and amusing others, is the centerpiece of their personality. Altruistic people, who often choose to work in organizations such as Habitat for Humanity or the Peace Corps, might be seeking elevation and gratitude, and perhaps also fiero.

Turn back and look again at the picture of the Stirm family reunion. Let's try to identify which of the enjoyable emotions were being felt by the daughter racing with her arms outstretched to embrace her father. There is excitement, as well as anticipation of the sensory pleasures she will soon feel when she holds him and reexperiences the familiar feel and smell of him. She probably felt relief a few moments earlier, when she saw her father really had come back home without war injuries. There might also have been a moment of wonder at the sheer incomprehensibility of his returning after a five-year absence, a long segment of this young woman's life.

Reunions with a person to whom you are very attached may be a universal theme for enjoyable emotions. In New Guinea, I found reunions with neighbors from friendly villages to be the best situation for me to film spontaneous enjoyment. I would sit by the edge of a path, nearly concealed by the undergrowth, my movie camera ready to shoot, waiting for friends to meet. Reunions strengthen the bonds among people. Absence can indeed make the heart grow fonder; it feels good to see again people you care about.

Sexual relations is another universal theme, in which many enjoyable emotions may be felt. Obviously a number of the sensory pleasures occur, plus excitement early on and relief after climax. Lust and sexual desire are loaded with erotic anticipation, anticipation of some of the sensory pleasures, and excitement at the prospect of what is desired.

The birth of a wanted child was mentioned more than I had expected by college students, both male and female, whom I asked in an unpublished research study to describe the happiest event they could imagine anyone in the world would ever have experienced. Excitement, wonder, relief, fiero, and perhaps gratitude are likely among the most relevant enjoyable emotions.

Being in the presence of a loved one is another universal theme. Both parental love and romantic love involve long-term commitments, intense attachments to a specific other person. Neither is itself an emotion. Emotions can be very brief, but love endures. However, while romantic love can endure throughout a lifetime, it often does not. Parental love more typically is a lifelong commitment, although there are exceptions in which parents disown their children. There is another meaning of love, which refers to a brief, momentary surge of extreme pleasure and engagement with the loved one.[15] This is what I earlier described as ecstasy or bliss, and it can be considered an emotion.

In loving family relationships we often feel many of the enjoyable emotions, but not without sometimes feeling nonenjoyable emotions as well. We can be angry, disgusted, or disappointed with loved ones, and we often feel despair and anguish if a loved one is seriously injured or dies. I believe parents may never stop worrying about the safety and welfare of their children, although they worry more when the children are young. Contact with one's children, real, remembered, or imagined, can generate many enjoyable emotions: sensory pleasures, naches, moments of contentment or excitement, relief when he or she gets out of jeopardy, and certainly, at times, amusement.

In romantic love one can also feel all of the nonenjoyable emotions, but hopefully not as often as the enjoyable emotions. Disgust and contempt are rarely felt, and when they occur it is a sign that the relationship is in trouble. Romantic relationships differ in terms of which of the enjoyable emotions occur most often.[16] Some couples jointly pursue fiero by working together, or by finding special satisfaction in what each other achieves. Others may focus more on excitement, or contentment, to give just a few examples.

While I believe the themes I have mentioned are universal, they are elaborated by our experiences. Also, many, many other variations on these themes are learned and become major sources of the different emotions of enjoyment.

There are moods related to some of the enjoyable emotions, specifically excitement, contentment, and amusement. These feelings can be extended for long periods, for hours, in a state in which one can very easily feel the emotions related to the mood.

At the beginning of this chapter I said the word *happiness* didn't tell us which kind of happiness was occurring. A further ambiguity is that happiness can also refer to an entirely different matter, which is the person's overall sense of subjective well-being. Psychologist Ed Diener, the leader in the study of subjective well-being, defines it as people's evaluations of their lives. It has been primarily measured by their answers to such questions as, "In most ways my life is close to my ideal," or, "So far I have gotten the important things I want in life." A number of different factors seem to enter into well-being: satisfactions in specific domains such as work and how often the person experiences enjoyable as compared to nonenjoyable emotions.

Subjective well-being has been extensively studied with questionnaires all over the world. It would take us too far afield to give more than a taste of the findings, but one universal finding is a positive correlation with purchasing-power income. A cultural difference is that self-respect is more related to subjective well-being in Western cultures than in non-Western cultures. Across cultures, having a close relationship is also associated with well-being.[17]

There is also a set of personality traits that are related to the enjoyable emotions. People whose personality test scores are high on extraversion and emotional stability report greater happiness.[18] Research on how such personality traits would lead to greater happiness have not considered the different types of enjoyment I have delineated, but they have suggested how being extroverted might predispose one to be happier. Extroverts may be less sensitive to rejection or punishment or more prone to make favorable comparisons between themselves and others. It may also be that extroverts fit better than introverts in American culture.[19]

People also differ in their usual levels of optimism and cheerfulness, and this appears to be an enduring characteristic rather than a reaction to a specific situation or event. Christopher Peterson, one of the experts in the field, suggests that optimism is an attitude about the likelihood of experiencing enjoyable emotions.[20] While not everyone is very optimistic, having such an outlook is good for you—it is found in people who have more enjoyment in their lives, greater perseverance, and higher achievements. Remarkably, a number of studies suggest that optimistic people have better health and actually live longer![21] Peterson suggests that one's overall optimism about life "may be a biologically given tendency, filled in by culture with a socially acceptable content, it leads to desirable outcomes because it produces a general state of vigor and resilience."[22] Peterson also asks, "How does optimism feel? Is it happiness, joy, hypomania [a mental disorder in which there are very high spirits], or simply contentment?"[23]

In earlier chapters I described how an overabundance of certain upsetting emotions—fear, anger, and sadness were the easiest to exemplify in this regard—was a sign of an emotional disorder. The total absence of an enjoyable emotion—not being capable of feeling fiero, naches, sensory pleasures, etc.—is labeled as the psychiatric disorder of *anhedonia*. Excessive, unremitting excitement, mixed sometimes with bliss and fiero, are components of the emotional disorder of mania.

Recognizing Enjoyment in Others

It is obvious from even a cursory glance at the pictures shown in this chapter so far that a smile is *the* facial signal of the enjoyable emotions. Amusement, fiero, naches, contentment, excitement, sensory pleasures, relief, wonderment, schadenfreude, ecstasy, and perhaps elevation and gratitude, all involve smiling. Those smiles may differ in intensity, how quickly they appear, how long they stay on the face, and how long it takes for them to fade.

If these different enjoyable emotions all share the smiling expression, then how do we know which one is being felt by another person? Recent work, which I mentioned in chapter 4, has supported my hunch[24] that it is the voice, not the face, that provides the signals that distinguish one enjoyable emotion from another. English psychologists Sophie Scott and Andrew Calder have identified different vocal signals for contentment, relief, sensory pleasure involving touch, and fiero. They established that these emotions are signaled by the voice, posing each voice sound and finding that people who listened had no trouble identifying one emotion from another. They have not yet described precisely what it is in the sound of the voice that signals each of these enjoyable emotions. I expect they will find vocal signals for the other enjoyable emotions as well.

Smiles can be confusing, not only because they occur with each of the enjoyable emotions, but also because they are shown when people do not feel enjoyment of any kind, for example in politeness. One difference separates enjoyment smiles from nonenjoyment smiles. It is a subtle difference, and our research with psychologist Mark Frank suggests that most people miss it.[25] If you don't know what to look for you may be misled, confused, or reach the conclusion that smiles aren't really very reliable. That is untrue; smiles unambiguously, if subtly, tell us whether they spring from enjoyment or not.

More than one hundred years ago, the great French neurologist Duchenne de Boulogne discovered how the true enjoyment smile differs from all of the nonenjoyment smiles.[26] He had been studying how each facial muscle changes people's appearances by electrically stimulating different parts of the face and photographing the resulting muscular contractions. (He conducted the experiment with a man who felt no pain in his face, so he wasn't bothered by the procedure.) When Duchenne looked at the smiling photograph produced by activating what is called the *zygomatic major muscle*—it goes from the cheekbones down at an angle to the corner of the lips, pulling the lip corners up at an angle into a smile—he noted that the man didn't really look happy. A good experimentalist, Duchenne told the man a joke and photographed his reaction. The comparison revealed that in true enjoyment, as shown in response to the joke, the man didn't just smile, but also activated the muscle that circles around the eye. Compare for yourself the picture in which the man has electrodes on his face (on the left) with the picture without electrodes, in which he is smiling in response to the joke (on the right).

THE DUCHENNE SMILE

Duchenne wrote: "The emotion of frank joy is expressed on the face by the combined contraction of the *zygomaticus major* muscle and the *orbicularis oculi*. The first obeys the will but the second is only put in play by the sweet emotions of the soul [remember, he was writing in 1862]; the ... fake joy, the deceitful laugh, cannot provoke the contraction of this latter muscle. ... The muscle around the eye does not obey the will; it is only brought into play by a true feeling, by an agreeable emotion. Its inertia, in smiling, unmasks a false friend."[27]

Our research[28] confirmed Duchenne's assertion that no one can voluntarily contract the *orbicularis oculi* muscle (it "does not obey the will"), although it is only part of that muscle that is hard to contract voluntarily. There are two parts of this muscle, an inner part that tightens the lids and the skin directly below them and an outer part that runs all around the eye socket—pulling down the eyebrows and the skin below the eyebrows, pulling up the skin below the eye, and raising the cheeks. Duchenne was correct about the outer part of the muscle; very few people can voluntarily contract it (only about 10 percent of those we studied).

The inner part, the eyelid tightener, everyone can do, and therefore its absence cannot "unmask a false friend." Actors who convincingly look as if they are enjoying themselves are either among that small group who can contract the outer part of this muscle voluntarily, or, more likely, they are retrieving a memory that generates the emotion, which then produces the true involuntary expression.

Although Charles Darwin quoted Duchenne and used some of his photographs to illustrate the difference between smiles, the scientists who studied facial expressions over the next hundred years ignored Duchenne's discovery.[29] My colleagues and I reintroduced Duchenne's discovery twenty years ago,[30] and we and others have since shown its importance. For example, when a ten-month-old infant is approached by a stranger, the baby's smile will not involve the muscle around the eye; the eye-orbiting muscle *is,* however, involved in the smile when the mother approaches the infant.*[31] When happily married couples meet at the end of the day, their smile involves the muscle around the eye, but it is absent in the smile shown when unhappily married couples meet.[32] People discussing the recent death of a spouse who manage to show smiles that involve the muscle orbiting the eye have reduced grief two years later.[33] (It is not that they are enjoying their spouse's death, but they are able to remember enjoyable experiences, and for a moment reexperience

---

*While I don't expect that ten-month-old babies are lying when they make a non-Duchenne smile at strangers, they are capable at that age of showing a social smile, the kind of smile that throughout life we show when first meeting a stranger.

that enjoyment.) Women who showed smiles involving the muscle around the eye in their college yearbook photographs reported less distress thirty years later, as well as greater overall emotional and physical well-being.[34] In general, people who frequently show smiles involving the muscle around the eye report feeling more happiness, have lower blood pressure, and are reported by their spouses and friends to be happy.[35] And in our own research we found that smiling with both the eye muscle and the lips activated areas of the brain (left temporal and anterior regions) found in spontaneous enjoyment, but smiling with the lips alone did not do so.[36]

In his honor I have suggested that we call the true smile of enjoyment, in which the outer portion of the muscle that orbits the eye is involved, a *Duchenne smile.*

A   B

At first glance it might seem that the only difference between these photos is that the eyes are narrower in photo B, but if you compare A with B carefully you will see a number of differences. In B, which shows real enjoyment with a Duchenne smile, the cheeks are higher, the contour of the cheeks has changed, and the eyebrows have moved down slightly. These are all due to the action of the outer part of the muscle that orbits the eye.

When the smile is much broader, there is only one clue that distinguishes between enjoyment and nonenjoyment smiles. A broad

C   D

smile, such as in photo C, pushes up the cheeks, gathers the skin under the eye, narrows the eye aperture, and even produces crow's-feet wrinkles—all of this without any involvement of the muscle that orbits the eye.

In comparison, photo D shows the eyebrow and eye cover fold (the skin between the eyelid and the eyebrow) have been pulled down by the muscle orbiting the eye. Photo D is a broad enjoyment smile while C is a very broad nonenjoyment smile. Photo C, incidentally, is a composite photograph made by pasting D from the lower eyelids down onto the neutral photograph E. Photo F, below, is another composite photograph, in which the smiling lips from picture D have been pasted onto the neutral photograph E. Human beings cannot produce the expression shown in photo F. It should look strange to you, and the reason it looks so strange is because when the smile is this broad it produces all the changes in the cheeks and eyes that you see in D. I made this composite illustration to underline the fact that very broad smiles change not only the lips but also the cheeks and the appearance of the skin below the eyes.

There are many different nonenjoyment smiles. Some, such as the polite smile, involve just the smiling lips. That is also shown in smiles used to indicate that the listener agrees with or understands what the speaker is saying during a conversation. Some nonenjoyment smiles require other facial actions in addition to the smiling lips.

E
(NEUTRAL)

F

This New Guinea man was a respected elder in his village. His hesitant or cautious smile signals that he means no harm, but that he is not yet certain about what is going to happen next. I was a very unpredictable person for the people in this village, doing amazing, strange things—lighting a match, shining a flashlight, making

HESITANT SMILE

music come out of a box. He had been confronted with such wonders and was attracted to me as a source of such astonishment, excitement, and amusement, but he could not know when I might startle or awe him. The parting of the smiling lips, as well as his crossed arms, help to convey the hesitance.

Barbs had been flying all day. President Ronald Reagan finally finished his speech to the NAACP, but during his introduction, Chairman Margaret Bush Wilson jabbed him several times, recalling that he had failed to appear at the group's convention during the presidential campaign. She also brought the delegates to their feet cheering when she issued this disclaimer: "The NAACP does not necessarily subscribe to the views that are about to be expressed." After his speech the president hugged Wilson, a perfect occasion for what can be called a miserable smile or grin-and-bear-it smile.[37] This smile acknowledges unenjoyable emotions; it shows you are a good sport, that you can take the criticism and still smile about it. It is not an attempt to conceal emotion but a visible comment on being miserable. It means that the person who shows it is not, at least for the moment, going to protest much about his misery.

Notice that in addition to smiling broadly, former President Rea-

GRIN-AND-BEAR-IT SMILE

gan has pressed his lips together; from the wrinkling on his chin we can also tell that he has pushed his lower lip upward. From the photograph we can't tell if the muscle that orbits the eye had acted; Reagan could have been enjoying his predicament. Miserable smiles typically occur when no real enjoyment is present, but it is possible, as in this instance.

MANAGING EMOTION WITH A SMILE

After he resigned, former president Richard Nixon showed this expression in a tearful farewell to those who had served his presidency, moments before he left the White House for the last time. No one would question Nixon's unhappiness at this moment, but the trace of a smile shows that he is not breaking down, he will manage his regret and likely despair. The lips are turned down very slightly, a sign of sadness, an expression that would have been more intense if he had not also been trying to smile. There is no sparkle in his eyes, a sign often produced in enjoyment smiles by the actions of the *orbicularis oculi* muscle. There is also slight lip pressing, as the former president attempted to control his emotions.

Now we'll turn to some final pictures showing blends of enjoyment with other emotions.

Each of the pictures in the row on page 212 show mixed smiles. The combination of brow lowering and smiling visible in photo G is rarely shown. It is not an angry smile, because the lips aren't narrowed and tensed and the upper eyelid hasn't been raised. I can't be certain what it might signal, because I have not seen it in any of my research. Photo H is easier, for it clearly shows disgust, due to the

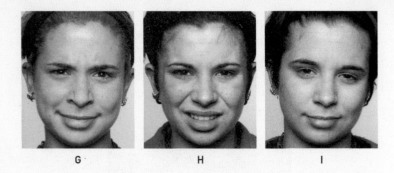

G   H   I

raising of the upper lip; the smile adds a bit of hesitation to the expression, but it is not an instance of someone who is actually enjoying her disgust. In picture I there is a blend of enjoyment and contempt, forming a smug expression. You saw this picture before in the previous chapter on disgust and contempt.

Using the Information from Expressions

In earlier chapters I have discussed how to use the information you derive from subtle facial expressions in various relationships. I won't do that here, since it is rare that sensing that someone is having one or another kind of enjoyable experience creates a problem. Often it does not even matter whether a person is showing a Duchenne smile, actual enjoyment, or a polite or even a fake smile. If your boss tells you a joke that you don't find very funny, you will still smile, and in all likelihood your boss wouldn't scrutinize your expression carefully to be certain you really liked her joke. What matters is that you made the attempt to look as if you enjoyed yourself. There may be times, however, when you really care whether the other person is truly enjoying himself or herself, and the place to look, you now know, is the eye cover fold directly below the eyebrows.

Conclusion: Living with Emotion

We each experience the same emotions, but we all experience them differently. The way in which I experience anger is not, for example, the same in all ways as the way in which my wife experiences anger. We know that, having lived together for more than twenty years, but we would have a hard time describing the differences. Like most people, we don't have a framework for examining how our experiences differ and how they may be the same. We do know that we don't have all of the same specific triggers for our anger, and that I get angry more quickly than she does, but beyond that we couldn't say much. When we are confronted by our differences because one or both of us is angry, we are too much caught up in the moment to recognize the other ways in which we differ in how we experience anger. And yet, when angry we also have some aspects of the experience in common—it is usually an obstacle to what we are doing that makes us angry, we show fairly similar expressions on our face, our voices get the same edge, our hearts beat faster, our hands get warmer. Our individual differences circle around these universals in emotion.

It is fitting that I describe individual differences in emotional experience in the last chapter of this book, because it is based on the research I am doing right now, and have been working on for much of the last decade with my friend and colleague Robert Levenson. While my best-known work is on the universal elements in emotion,

I am now examining the exact opposite, how each individual's emotional experience is unique. Individual differences were present in my study of universals, as they are in virtually any study of emotion, but because the evidence for universals was so strong, the individual differences could be set aside.

I had been attracted to the universals question because it had such a distinguished history, with famous people in disagreement. Having resolved that dispute to my own satisfaction, the study of individual differences attracted me as a way to deepen my understanding of my own life and the lives of my family and friends. I am not trying to find out why we have differences in how we experience emotions. Instead, the first step is to identify those differences, to find out what they are, to establish the basis for individual emotional profiles of the unique ways in which we experience each emotion. It is amazing to me that some of the most fundamental questions about how individuals differ in emotional experience haven't yet been asked, let alone answered.

We do know that people differ in the typical strength of their experience of a particular emotion. Some people typically have a very intense anger response, while others have moderate or mild anger (and not just because they are deliberately controlling their anger). Some people get angry much more quickly than others, and some people's anger usually lasts a long time, while others have very brief bursts of anger. Once anger begins to subside it can disappear quickly, or it can ebb very slowly. So considering just these four ways in which an emotional experience can differ—speed of emotional onset, strength of emotional response, duration of the emotional response, and how long it takes to recover and go back to a baseline state—there are a lot of interesting questions to ask. Does everyone who gets angry quickly get over it quickly, or can you have a fast onset with a long recovery time? If you have a fast onset, does that mean you will have a very strong angry response, or can you have a fast onset and weak or low-intensity anger? And if the anger is very intense, does that mean it typically lasts a short time, in very brief bursts of intense but short duration, or can it last a long time?

I have some answers to these questions, from data I have just finished analyzing and am preparing for scientific publication. Amazingly, everything that could happen did happen. Take the relationship between strength of response and speed of response. I had expected to find that fast responders were usually strong responders, but about just as many were weak responders. And slow responders were split between strong and weak responders. The same was so for the relationship between the duration of response (how long an emotion lasts) and the strength of response. I thought that if you have a strong response, it would take longer for it to end. Not so. The strong response people were split between short and long duration, and the weak response people were also just about split between short and long duration responses. We are still working on this research, asking other questions about how individuals differ.

The frequency of our emotional episodes is another crucial feature in understanding an individual's *emotional profile*. You might be a person who gets angry slowly, never getting furious, whose anger lasts a fair amount of time, and then immediately disappears, but you might have such angry episodes only a few times a year. Alternatively, you might have them a few times a week. How well we can control what we do and say and feel during an emotional episode is also an important element in each individual's emotional profile, while another aspect is how clearly we signal others how we are feeling. Some people have very subtle signs of how they feel, even when they are not trying to control how they are feeling. Others have very strong, clear emotional facial and vocal expressions, even when they are trying to control them. Last are the events that most readily trigger each of our emotions.

Will whatever we find about one emotion, let's say anger, also apply to fear or sadness? Will a person have the same profile—fast onset, moderate strength, long duration, quick recovery, frequent occurrence, easy to control with a clear signal—for anger, fear, and sadness? On still another level we can ask: If a person has strong emotional facial or vocal signals, would that person also have strong changes in his or her autonomic nervous system, or are these two systems of emotional responding disconnected? We don't know the answers to all of these questions, but we do know enough to believe that there are important differences in how people experience emotions, and that they are often not recognized.[1]

If you are interested in charting your own emotional profile, and perhaps the profile of another person with whom you are intimately involved, you can find a tool that will allow you to do so on the Web page: emotionsrevealed.com

Now let me describe the common characteristics found in emotions. Bringing together the ideas that appeared in the early chapters, an emotion has the following defining characteristics:

- There is a feeling, a set of sensations that we experience and often are aware of.
- An emotional episode can be brief, sometimes lasting only a few seconds, sometimes much longer. If it lasts for hours, then it is a mood and not an emotion.
- It is about something that matters to the person.
- We experience emotions as happening to us, not chosen by us.
- The appraisal process, in which we are constantly scanning our environment for those things that matter to us, is usually automatic. We are not conscious of our appraising, except when it is extended over time.
- There is a refractory period that initially filters information and knowledge stored in memory, giving us access only to what supports the emotion we are feeling. The refractory period may last only a few seconds, or it may endure for much longer.
- We become aware of being emotional once the emotion has begun, when the initial appraisal is complete. Once we become conscious that we are in the grip of an emotion, we can reappraise the situation.
- There are universal emotional themes that reflect our evolutionary history, in addition to many culturally learned variations that reflect our individual experience. In other words, we become emotional about matters that were relevant to our ancestors as well as ones we have found to matter in our own lives.
- The desire to experience or not experience an emotion motivates much of our behavior.

• An efficient signal—clear, rapid, and universal—informs others of how the emotional person is feeling.

Before closing, I'd like to mention a few emotions I have not covered in this book: guilt, shame, and embarrassment.*[2] These emotions do not seem to meet this last criterion, since they do not have efficient signals that make them readily distinguishable from one another or from sadness. In guilt and shame, however, this makes sense, since when feeling these emotions the person does not want others to know how he or she feels, and so perhaps a signal did not evolve. Embarrassment is more problematic. The blush doesn't qualify as an embarrassment signal because it is not observable in dark-skinned people. Dacher Keltner has shown that there is not a single momentary expression for embarrassment, as there is for anger, fear, disgust, contempt, sadness, and enjoyment. Instead, embarrassment is shown through a sequence of expressions over time.[3] Perhaps embarrassment came late in our evolutionary history, and there has not yet been enough time for an efficient signal to have been developed.

Envy is another emotion that meets most of the characteristics listed above, with the exception that there does not seem to be a signal.[4] Jealousy I don't consider an emotion, but an emotional scene or plot, in which there are three actors, the one who fears losing the attention of another, the other, and the rival. Within this plot we can say something about what emotions each person may feel, but that isn't fixed. The rival could feel guilty, ashamed, afraid, angry, or contemptuous, depending upon the circumstances. The person concerned about losing the interest of the other person might feel angry, afraid, sad, or disgusted. And the person whose attention is being sought could have a number of different emotions.

Even though they do not have clear and efficient signals, I have no doubt that embarrassment, guilt, shame, and envy are also emotions. I have chosen not to devote chapters to them because I have not done research on them myself.

*In 1872, Charles Darwin claimed, rightly, I believe, that it is attention to the self, particularly to appearance, that brings forth embarrassment, felt just as much in response to praise as disparagement.

. . .

I have described many of the emotions that fill our lives, explaining the usual triggers for each of them, when and why they are useful to us, how to recognize the most subtle expressions of those emotions in others, and how to use the information we can glean from such subtle expressions in the workplace, family life, and friendships. The early chapters addressed two of the toughest problems most of us experience in our emotional life. I explained why it is so hard to change what we become emotional about. It is not impossible, just difficult. We need to identify our own hot triggers and to understand what factors determine how likely we are to be able to weaken them. Equally difficult, but not impossible, is to change how we act when we are emotional so our emotional behavior is not harmful to others or ourselves. The key here is to develop a kind of awareness, which I called *attentiveness,* so we know when we are becoming emotional before a lot of time has elapsed. Exercises I provided to heighten our awareness of the physical sensations we experience during each emotion can help in becoming attentive, as well as other approaches that I mention.

When I began research on emotion decades ago, there were fewer than a handful of us—worldwide—doing such research. Now there must be thousands. A handbook just published has more than forty separate chapters, each describing a different set of findings and questions about emotions, moods, and emotional traits.[5] Here, I have not tried to cover all that is known but have sifted out what I think is most relevant to understanding and improving emotional life, and what I know most about. There will be many new findings in the next decade to add to what I have written.

Afterword

I want to share some further thoughts I have had about two of the emotional skills I outlined at the start of this book. First, being attentive—consciously aware—of when you are becoming emotional; and second, developing more awareness of how others are feeling.

Nature doesn't make it easy for us to achieve conscious awareness of the first moments when an emotion arises, let alone how we automatically make the appraisals of the world around us that generate our emotions. It is nearly impossible for most people ever to become aware of the automatic appraisal processes that initiate an emotional episode. Dan Goleman called this *appraisal awareness*.[1] But through hard work, by developing skills nature doesn't provide and doesn't make it easy for us to acquire, some people can learn *impulse awareness*, that is, becoming aware of an emotion-driven impulse before actions are taken. I don't believe emotions evolved in a way to facilitate impulse awareness. It is as if the emotion system doesn't want our conscious mind to interfere in the matter.

More than forty-five years ago Frank Gorman, my psychotherapy supervisor, said that my goal should be to help my patients increase the gap between impulse and action. The Buddhists talk about recognizing the spark (that arises to initiate an emotion) before the flame (by which they mean the emotional behavior that enacts the emotion). They do not ask us to recognize the appraisal that generates the spark. The Western and Buddhist views on this are the same.

Impulse awareness is a high standard. I don't believe everyone can reach it, and it is unlikely that even those who meet this standard will always do so.[2] But the work we go through to develop impulse awareness will benefit what is achievable for nearly all of us—*emotional behavior awareness*, or recognizing our emotional state once it has begun to be expressed in words and actions. If you can become aware that an emotion has begun to drive your behavior, you can consciously consider whether your emotional reaction is appropriate to the situation you are in, and, if it is, whether your reaction is at the right intensity and manifesting itself in the most constructive way.

Because this is so important, I would like to summarize here the ways in which we can increase *emotional behavior awareness*, and for some of us, some of the time, *impulse awareness*:

- Practice the exercises to heighten awareness of the physical changes within your body when an emotion arises, so they will signal to you that you are becoming emotional. (These exercises appear in the middle of chapters 5, 6, 7, and 8.)
- Identify when you are likely to become emotional, especially in a way you will regret later, by keeping a log of regrettable emotional episodes. This will allow you to anticipate hot triggers before you encounter them, and, by considering whether you are importing any scripts from past emotional experiences, begin to cool down those triggers. (For more on this, refer back to pages 41–51.)
- Learn to spot the emotional reactions of the person with whom you are conversing so you can use their reaction to tip you off to your heightened emotions.

I'd like to also mention an approach that is complementary to these, mindfulness meditation. I did not say much about it in *Emotions Revealed*, for two reasons. There isn't hard scientific evidence that mindfulness meditation actually improves emotional life, although there are many studies in which people claim that it has had such benefit. Also, I previously couldn't understand why focusing our awareness on breathing would benefit emotional life.

Like the proverbial bolt out of the blue, just a few weeks before writing this afterword, the explanation struck me. The very practice of learning to focus attention on an automatic process that requires no conscious monitoring creates the capacity to be attentive to other automatic processes. We breathe without thinking, without conscious direction of each inhalation and exhalation. Nature does not require that we divert our attention to breathing. When we try paying attention to each breath, people find it very hard to do so for more than a minute, if that, without being distracted by thoughts. Learning to focus our attention on breathing takes daily practice, in which we develop new neural pathways that allow us to do it. And here is the punch line: these skills transfer to other automatic processes—*benefiting emotional behavior awareness* and eventually, in some people, *impulse awareness*. I checked my explanation with renowned experts in meditation, and with those in emotion and the brain, and they think it makes sense.[3]

I recommend trying mindfulness meditation to see if it works for you. As I said, it won't be easy, and it probably won't be of much benefit to your emotional life unless pursued regularly. In every large city the telephone book lists meditation teaching, often available without cost. There are many different kinds of meditation; what you are looking for is mindfulness meditation. There are also many books that will allow you to learn about this on your own.[4]

Let's turn now to increasing awareness of how others are feeling.

When emotions first begin, they may become evident in a very *subtle* change in facial expression, as described in the book. If you know what to look for you may sometimes know how people are feeling before the people who are showing the subtle expressions are aware that they are becoming emotional. Sometimes subtle expressions occur when the people showing them know exactly how they are feeling but don't want to show it. The subtle expression is all that escapes their attempts to censor their expressions. In my book on lying I have called this *leakage*.[5]

The test in the appendix and the pictures of Eve in chapters 5 through 8 show all of the subtle expressions I have uncovered. The new CD I produced—the Subtle Expression Training Tool (SETT)

—makes these photographs come alive, flashing before your eyes. You will get better the more you practice with it.

Micro expressions are also very difficult for most people to see. Typically they are very intense and very brief, as short as 1/25 of a second. Micro expressions are always the result of concealment. It may be deliberate, in which the people showing them know exactly how they are feeling but don't want others to know. Or the concealment may be the consequence of repression, in which case the person is totally unaware of the concealed emotion the micro expression is displaying. It is important to note that not everyone who is concealing emotion shows a micro expression, so its absence does not mean you are getting the full story. But its presence is highly informative if you are able to see it.

Another CD I developed, the Micro Expression Training Tool (METT), shows fifty-six different people, males and females, whites and Asians (we are in the process of adding blacks), showing seven different emotions very quickly, from 1/15 to 1/30 of a second each. Our evidence from a new study shows that in less than an hour of practice nearly everyone improves.[6] Since they became available in June 2004, hundreds of people have contacted www.emotions revealed.com to get the METT and SETT CDs, and a number of government agencies are using them.

METT, SETT, and study of the pictures in *Emotions Revealed* can empower you to recognize how another person is feeling. But, as I have mentioned before, you will be using information that has not been given to you. That is why you have to consider carefully how to use that information if that knowledge is not going to be destructive to you and the other person. Don't presume you know what is causing the emotion you have spotted. Emotional expressions don't reveal their source. A micro expression of anger doesn't tell you the person is angry with you. The person might be angry with him- or herself. Or the person might be remembering an earlier event about which he or she felt angry. The first issue to consider is toward whom the emotion is directed.

Chapters 5 through 8 give examples of what to consider in family life, the workplace, and friendships about how to use the information you obtain from micro and subtle expressions concerning each of the emotions. Here I want to give some general guidelines that apply to any emotional information you pick up in a subtle or micro expression.

Often the best course is to say nothing about what you have seen. Instead, be alert to the possibilities. Or you might say: "Is there anything more you want to say about how you are feeling?" A further step could be: "I had the impression you were just feeling something more than what you said." You might even be more specific, asking about the emotion you spotted. How you respond depends on the nature of the relationship, its past history and intended future, and your knowledge of that person.

You may not always be entitled to comment, even vaguely, on the emotion you have detected. Although I believe that generally relationships work better when people understand and acknowledge how each other feel, that isn't always so. Be cautious; don't make the other person feel that he or she has no privacy.

Skills are hard to acquire; some of them require continued practice to maintain, such as the awareness skills I have just described. Some of them are like learning to ride a bicycle; once learned it sticks, and you don't need to continue practice. I suspect that what you learn from METT and SETT is more like that. Practice will help for a while, but it quickly tapers off and then you have it—your eye is educated.

But skills without knowledge aren't enough. To improve your emotional life you have to understand each emotion: its story line, the universal themes that trigger that emotion, some of the more common variations on those themes, the function of the emotion— what it does for us—how it relates to moods, and when and how it can become involved in emotional disorders, as explained in chapters 5 through 9. In a few more years, with the continuing rapid growth of research on emotion, I'm sure there will be more to come. Stay tuned.

Appendix:
Reading Faces—
The Test

I suggest that you take this test *before* you read the book, before you see the pictures in chapters 5 through 9, as well as after you've had time to study them. If this is your first time taking the test, and especially if you haven't delved into the book yet, then don't look at the photographs on the next pages until after you've read this introduction on how to get the most from the test.

Why would you want to take this test? Doesn't everyone already know how to read facial expressions? Doesn't my research show that it's an inborn ability? While I am convinced that we don't need to learn how to make the facial expressions of emotion (they are preset by our evolution and occur spontaneously when an emotion is aroused), it is less certain whether the ability to recognize those signals also operates from preset instructions or is instead learned early in life. There may be an intermediate ground, as well, in which preset instructions may be damaged or destroyed by severely disturbed early experience. Although we cannot be certain exactly what is responsible for the deficits, we do know that neglected and abused children are not as accurate as well-treated children in recognizing different facial expressions of emotion.[1]

Fortunately, most people had a childhood in which they were not neglected or abused and can recognize emotional expressions in the face and voice if the expressions are intense and the person showing the expression is not attempting to diminish or conceal signs of emotion. Often that is not the case. My research[2] has shown that most people don't appear to utilize the information contained in the more subtle expressions shown in this book. And in many conversations, subtle expressions occur much more often than full and intense expressions; and the subtle ones are often the most important ones, for they can tell us what is not yet being said in words or may not ever be said.

When an emotion is just beginning to be experienced, and that emotion is not intense, it may show in a very *slight* expression in which the muscles are not contracted very much, or it may register as a *partial* expression, evident in just one area of the face but not across the entire face in a *full* expression. (Note that not all emotions when they first begin to be experienced are low intensity; it is possible for an emotion right from the start to be very strong.) When people are trying to regulate their emotional expressions so as to diminish any sign of what occurs, then that may also result in a slight or partial expression. When we see a slight or partial expression, we can assume it is either just beginning or is being regulated to appear weaker.

If we are trying to eliminate any sign at all of the emotion, that may also result in a *micro* expression, in which the expression is shown very briefly, typically for only one-fifth of a second or less. Micro expressions occur when a person is consciously trying to conceal all signs of how he or she is feeling (the person knows how he or she is feeling but doesn't want you to know). Micro expressions may also occur when the inhibition of expression occurs outside of consciousness, when the person doesn't consciously know how he or she is feeling.

Micro expressions may be very brief full expressions or they may be very brief partial and/or slight expressions. The combination of all three—micro (very brief), partial (only registered in one area), and slight (not much muscular contraction)—are the hardest to recognize. But you can learn to do so.

Instructions for Taking the Test

You will need a sheet of lined paper, with lines numbered from 1 to 14. At the top of the paper write the following words: anger, fear, sadness, disgust, contempt, surprise, enjoyment. These are the possible choices for the expressions in each of the fourteen photographs on the following pages. You can write any word down on the line for the photograph if you don't think one of these words fits what you have seen. You will also need a slip of paper to use as a bookmark.

You need to look at each picture for just a fraction of a second, so it will be similar to a micro expression. Later, you will have a chance to look at them longer and see if you do better.

The face that you see should be the same size it would be in real life, that is, the size of a normal person's face. Because the picture is smaller, you will have to hold it at arm's length, so it will have the same image size on your retina as it would if a person was sitting at usual conversational distance from you.

It is important that you look at only one picture at a time. Look at each picture as briefly as you can and immediately close the book. (Leave in the bookmark, so you will be able to get back to that spot easily.) Often you won't know what emotion a picture showed, but don't look a second time. Play your hunch, use your intuition, and guess if you have to, because you may have recognized the expression—these are universal and ingrained, remember—without your realizing it. Write down one of the emotion words that you listed at the top of your page or another word that you think fits better. Do this until you have completed viewing all fourteen pictures.

Now it is time for you to have a second chance in which you will look longer. It is better to take a break for a few minutes and use a fresh piece of paper so you are less likely to remember your first impressions of each photo. When you are ready, hold the book at arm's length and look at each photo one at a time, glancing, for one second only (say "one-one-thousand" to yourself slowly), and writing down your interpretation of the face. You might wonder why you are told to look for only one second, for surely expressions often last longer. We have found that during conversation most expressions are between one-half of a second and two and a half seconds. While many are longer than the one second, those expressions often compete for your attention with the other person's words, voice, and body movements, as well as your thoughts about what the person is saying and doing, let alone other distractions.

Having done this twice, if you have the patience, you might go through the test one more time, taking as long as you want to interpret the expressions.

When you are ready to look up the answers, turn to page 243. Keep a tally of how many you got right by intuition and by practice.

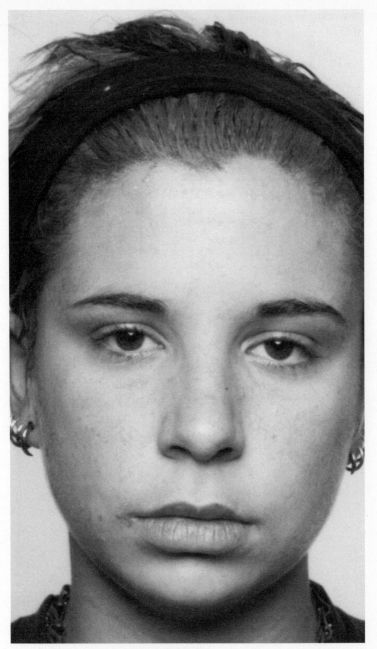

PHOTO 1

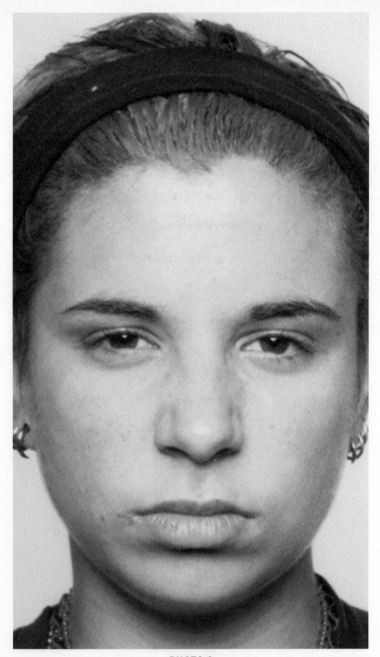

PHOTO 2

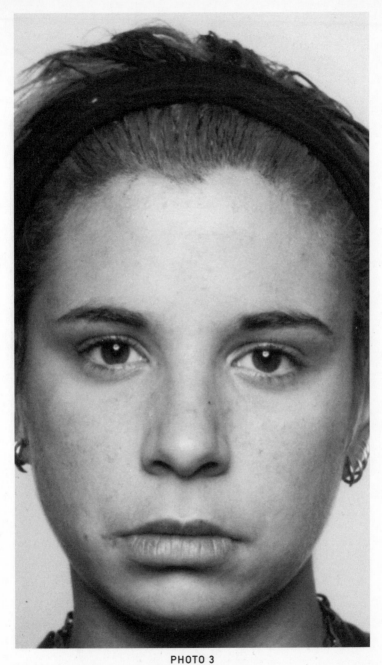

PHOTO 3

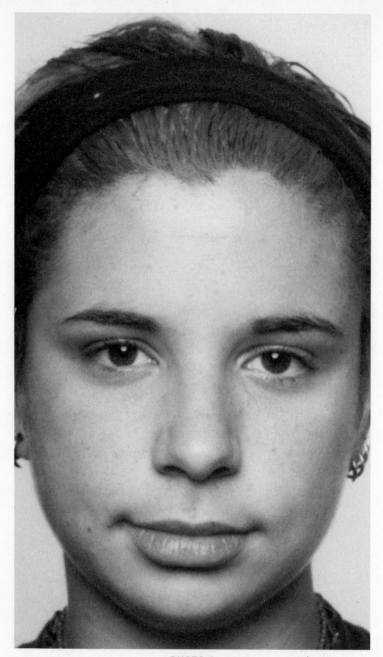

PHOTO 4

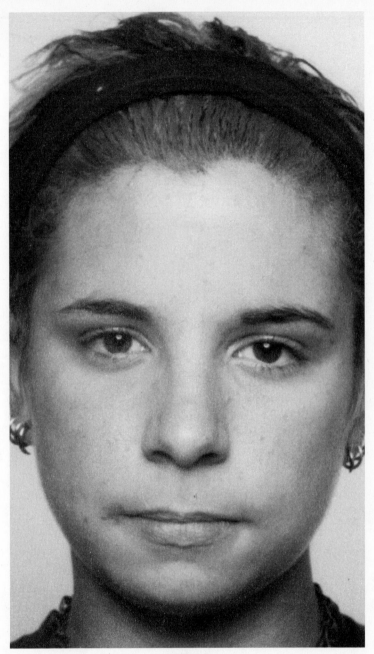

PHOTO 5

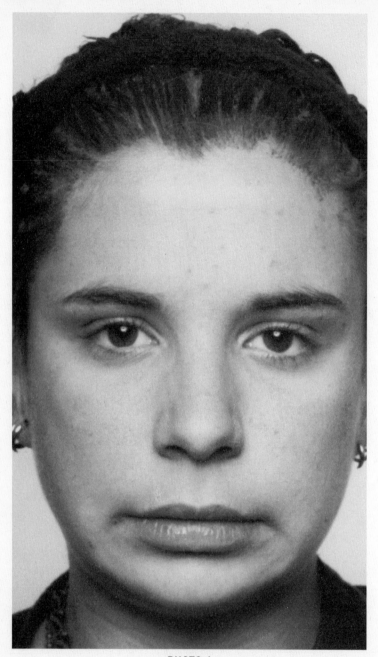

PHOTO 6

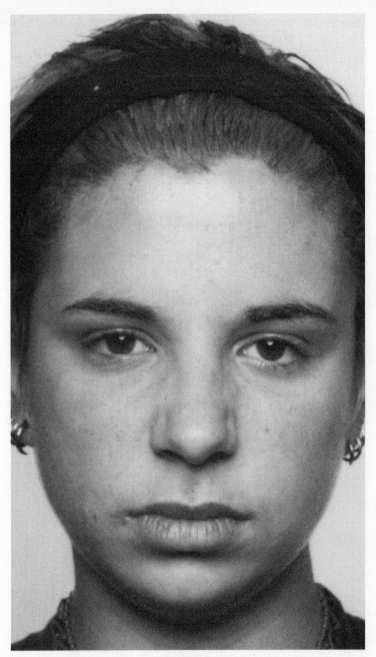

PHOTO 7

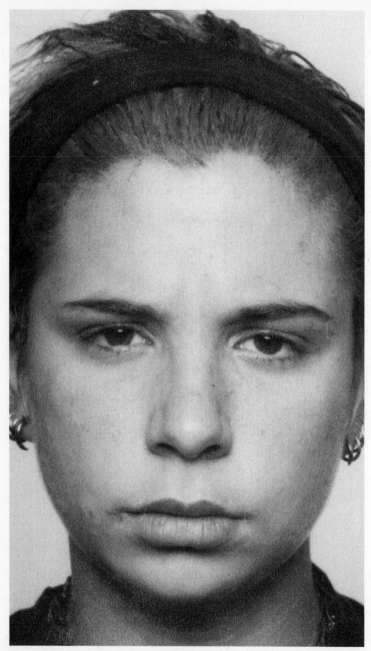

PHOTO 8

PHOTO 9

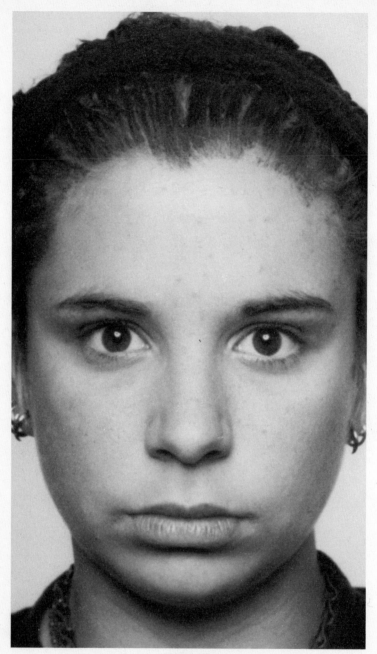

PHOTO 10

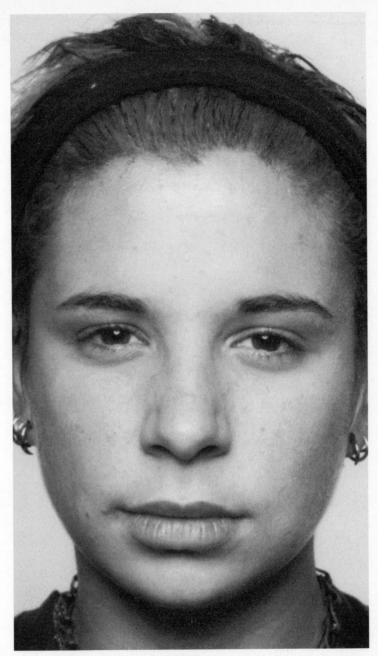

PHOTO 11

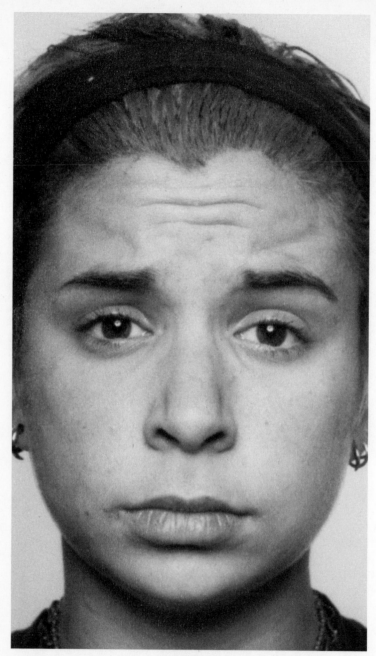

PHOTO 12

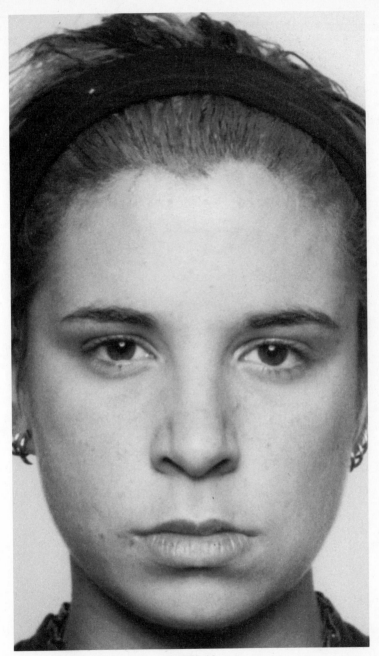

PHOTO 13

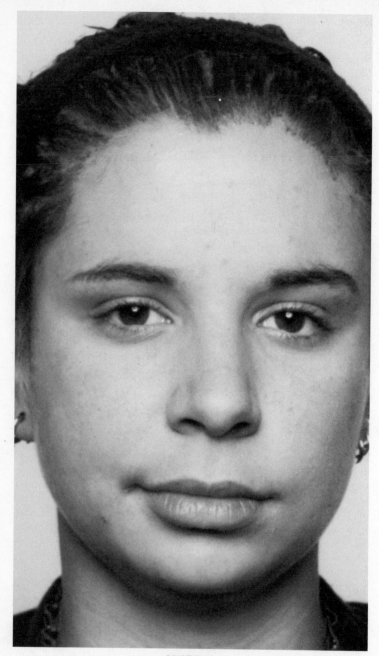

PHOTO 14

Recognizing the Expressions—The Answers

Photo 1

Slight sadness. If you thought of any related word, such as "blue" or "dejected" or "depressed," that would also be correct. The expression is shown in the drooping upper eyelids. Tired or sleepy could also be correct, not because it is a related word but because the drooping eyelids she shows can occur in tiredness as well as sadness; when the upper eyelids begin to droop in tiredness, you might, however, see the eyes lose their focus, and an occasional yawn or shaking of the head. More about sadness signs in chapter 5.

Photo 2

Disgust. Again, a related word would be acceptable, but not one in the anger family, such as annoyed or irritated. The clue is in the slight contraction of the muscle that wrinkles the nose and narrows the eyes. Chapter 8 explains more about how to distinguish anger from disgust.

Photo 3

Slight sadness, again, this time expressed in the lips with the slight pulling down of the lip corners. Compare the position of the lips in this picture with the position in photo 1, in which the lips are relaxed. Sadness can be expressed through the lips, the eyelids, or both, as described in chapter 5.

Photo 4

Slight enjoyment; any word in that set of words—pleased, OK, feels good— would be correct. Compare the lips in this picture with the relaxed lips in photo 1. Chapter 9 describes the appearance of enjoyment.

Photo 5

Highly controlled or very slight anger (annoyance)—or determination. You can't be certain when the only clue is a slight pressing and narrowing of the lips. You don't want to miss this clue, even though it is ambiguous, because if you spotted it in real life, you probably would be able to figure out whether it is an anger sign or determination based on when it was shown or what was being said by you or that person. This can be one of the earliest signs of anger, alerting you before matters get irreversible; sometimes this sign occurs before the other person recognizes that he or she is becoming angry. More about anger signs in chapter 6.

Photo 6

Slight or highly controlled fear. The most common mistake is to interpret this as a sign of disgust. The clue to fear is the slightly stretched lips. Sometimes when a person is describing or thinking about a time when he or she was afraid, but not actually feeling it in the moment, the person will show this subtle fear expression. Fear is discussed in chapter 7.

Photo 7

Disgust again, this time shown not in the eyes or nose but in the slightly raised upper lip. Disdain could also describe this expression. Disgust is discussed at further length in chapter 8.

Photo 8

Upset, unhappy, miserable, perplexed . . . These are all possibilities, all of which refer to the anger theme of having an obstacle in the path of a goal. It might even be highly controlled anger. The lowered brows and tensed lower eyelids signal anger. More about this and how to tell which one it is in chapter 6.

Photo 9

A masked expression of anger. The person looks happy because of her smiling lips, but the eyebrows don't fit an enjoyable emotion. This could either be an attempt to mask anger (the emotion shown in the eyebrows) with a happy smile, a blend of anger and enjoyment, or amusement about being perplexed or confounded. The eyebrows in this picture are the same as those shown in photo 8, but the movement is a little stronger. More on anger in chapter 6.

Photo 10

Fear or surprise—or just rapt attention. It's hard to be certain when the clue is limited to just the raised upper eyelids. If it is fear or surprise, it would be either slightly felt or highly controlled stronger feelings. Fear and surprise are explained in chapter 7.

Photo 11

Controlled anger, very slight annoyance just beginning, or having trouble focusing on something (literally or figuratively). When the clue is the tensed eyelids, the context could help in identifying the correct understanding of the person's emotion. More on anger in chapter 6.

Photo 12

Worry, apprehension, or controlled fear. This configuration in the eyebrows is one of the most reliable signs of these feelings. Chapter 7 shows how this differs from the registration of surprise in the eyebrows.

Photo 13

Controlled anger or annoyance. The clue is the jaw, which is moved forward. The lower eyelids are also slightly tensed. Again, chapter 6 describes the full range of anger expressions.

Photo 14

Contempt, smug, or disdainful. The tightening of one lip corner signals this set of related emotions. More about contempt and how it differs from disgust in chapter 8.

Don't worry about how many you missed. Most people who look at these photographs briefly do not get more than five correct. Even when people get to look longer, most don't get more than ten correct. They are hard—because they are partial, slight, and sometimes involve two emotions merging into a blend. It should get easier to recognize these emotions once you have read the explanations of how each emotion is registered in the face and see many more photographs of subtle expressions that will help you become more aware of these facial signals.

Remember at the opening of this chapter I explained that there were three types of subtle expressions—partial, slight, and micro expressions? It's important to keep in mind that if you are able to pick up partial or slight emotional expressions like the ones in this test, or a micro expression that flashes briefly across the face, you don't know why the expression has been shown in this manner. There are several possibilities:

Slight expression	• Beginning of an emotion • Weak emotion • Diminished emotion • Failed attempt to conceal an emotion
Partial expression	• Weak emotion • Diminished emotion • Failed attempt to conceal an emotion
Micro expression	• Deliberate suppression of an emotion • Unconscious suppression of an emotion

With so many possibilities, it might seem that you won't be able to use this information effectively. But consciously recognizing what emotion a person is feeling is a big step in improving communication. In some cases, based on the context and a partial or slight expression, you may be able to tell that another person's emotion is just beginning; your reaction during the person's refractory period, which I discuss in chapter 3, can make a difference. Sometimes, in fact, you may know how a person is feeling before he or she knows, especially if the signal is a micro expression that resulted from suppression. You may also be able to recognize that there is a chance a person is trying to diminish or conceal her expressions, and that may influence your response to what he or she is saying or doing. As you become more familiar with each emotion family described in chapters 5 through 9, and practice identifying slight and partial expressions, you will find that this powerful information can be applied to your friendships, your workplace, and your family life.

To order a CD for practicing the recognition of all the subtle expressions shown in this book, go to emotionsrevealed.com. That Web site also offers another CD for learning how to recognize very brief micro expressions.

Notes

1: Emotions Across Cultures

1. Ekman, P. & Friesen, W.V. 1969. "The repertoire of nonverbal behavior: Categories, origins, usage, and coding." *Semiotica,* 1: 49–98. Ekman, P. & Friesen, W.V. 1974. "Nonverbal behavior and psychopathology." In R.J. Friedman & M.N. Katz (eds.), *The Psychology of Depression: Contemporary Theory and Research.* Washington, D.C.: J. Winston. See pages 203–32.
2. I am in debt to Carrol Emmons who wrote to each of us and suggested that we meet because of our overlapping interests.
3. Ekman, P., Sorenson, E.R. & Friesen, W.V. 1969. "Pan-cultural elements in facial displays of emotions." *Science,* 164 (3875): 86–88.
4. Izard, C. 1971. *The Face of Emotion.* New York: Appleton-Century-Crofts.
5. Birdwhistell, R.L. 1970. *Kinesics and Context.* Philadelphia: University of Pennsylvania Press.
6. I first described display rules in a *Semiotica* article with Wallace V. Friesen, "The repertoire of nonverbal behavior," 1969. A less elaborate version of this idea can be found in the writings of Otto Klineberg and others who preceded me, although I did not know that at the time I wrote. Kleinberg, O. 1940. *Social Psychology.* New York: Holt.
7. Ekman, P. 1972. "Universals and cultural differences in facial expressions of emotion." In J. Cole (ed.), *Nebraska Symposium on Motivation, 1971.* Lincoln, Neb.: University of Nebraska Press. See pages 207–83.
8. Johnson, H.G., Ekman, P. & Friesen, W.V. 1975. "Communicative body movements: American emblems." *Semiotica,* 15 (4): 335–53.
9. Joining me were my colleague Wally Friesen, my then wife, Diana Russell, and Neville Hoffman and his wife. During my first trip to New Guinea in 1967, Neville was just finishing his two-year term as the Australian doctor who worked at a hospital in the district station, where villagers would come if

they were very sick. He was well liked and well known. He and his wife also knew Pidgin very well.

10. Ekman, P., Friesen, W. V., O'Sullivan, M., Chan, A., Diacoyanni-Tarlatzis, I., Heider, K., Krause, R., LeCompte, W. A., Pitcairn, T., Ricci-Bitti, P. E., Scherer, K. R., Tomita, M. & Tzavaras, A. 1987. "Universals and cultural differences in the judgments of facial expressions of emotion." *Journal of Personality and Social Psychology,* 53: 712–17. Ekman, P. 1999. "Facial expressions." In T. Dalgleish & T. Power (eds.), *The Handbook of Cognition and Emotion.* Sussex, U.K.: John Wiley & Sons. See pages 301–20.

11. Karl was then married to the former roommate (Eleanor Rosch) of my then wife, Diana, and had heard through his wife, from my wife, about what I claimed to have found.

12. Ekman, "Universals and cultural differences in facial expressions of emotion."

13. Wierzbicka, A. 1999. *Emotions Across Languages and Cultures: Diversity and Universals.* Paris: Cambridge University Press.

14. Thompson, J. 1941. "Development of facial expression of emotion in blind and seeing children." *Archives of Psychology,* 37. Fulcher, J. S. 1942. "'Voluntary' facial expression in blind and seeing children." *Archives of Psychology,* 38. Eibl-Eibesfeldt, I. 1970. *Ethology, the Biology of Behavior.* New York: Holt, Reinhart and Winston. Galati, D., Scherer, K. R. & Ricci-Bitti, P. E. 1997. "Voluntary facial expression of emotion: Comparing congenitally blind with normally sighted encoders." *Journal of Personality and Social Psychology,* 73: 1363–79.

15. Ekman, P. & Friesen, W. V. 1978. *Facial Action Coding System: A Technique for the Measurement of Facial Movement.* Palo Alto, Calif.: Consulting Psychologists Press. An electronic second edition was published in 2002. Ekman, P. & Rosenberg, E. L. 1997. *What the Face Reveals: Basic and Applied Studies of Spontaneous Expression Using the Facial Action Coding System (FACS).* New York: Oxford University Press. Cohn, J. F., Zlochower, A., Lein, J. & Kanade, T. 1999. "Automated face analysis by feature point tracking has high concurrent validity with manual FACS coding." *Psychophysiology,* 36: 35–43. Bartlett, M. S., Viola, P. A., Sejnowski, T. J., Golomb, B. A., Larsen, J., Hager, J. C. & Ekman, P. 1996. "Classifying facial action." In D. Touretzky, M. Mozer, & M. Hasselmo (eds.), *Advances in Neural Information Processing Systems 8.* Cambridge, Mass.: MIT Press. See pages 823–29.

16. See a number of articles and books for further information: Levenson, R. W., Ekman, P., Heider, K. & Friesen, W. V. 1992. "Emotion and autonomic nervous system activity in the Minangkabau of West Sumatra." *Journal of Personality and Social Psychology,* 62: 972–88. Levenson, R. W., Carstensen, L. L., Friesen, W. V. & Ekman, P. 1991. "Emotion, physiology, and expression in old age." *Psychology and Aging,* 6: 28–35. Levenson, R. W., Ekman, P. & Friesen, W. V. 1990. "Voluntary facial action generates emotion-specific autonomic nervous system activity." *Psychophysiology,* 27: 363–84. Ekman, P., Levenson, R. W. & Friesen, W. V. 1983. "Autonomic nervous system

activity distinguishes between emotions." *Science*, 221: 1208–10. Ekman, P. & Davidson, R. 1994. *The Nature of Emotion: Fundamental Questions.* New York: Oxford University Press. Ekman, P. & Davidson, R. J. 1993. "Voluntary smiling changes regional brain activity." *Psychological Science*, 4: 342–45. Davidson, R. J., Ekman, P., Saron, C., Senulis, J. & Friesen, W. V. 1990. "Emotional expression and brain physiology I: Approach/withdrawal and cerebral asymmetry." *Journal of Personality and Social Psychology*, 58: 330–41. Ekman, P., Davidson, R. J. & Friesen, W. V. 1990. "Emotional expression and brain physiology II: The Duchenne smile." *Journal of Personality and Social Psychology*, 58: 342–53.

17. Ekman, P. 1985. *Telling Lies: Clues to Deceit in the Marketplace, Marriage, and Politics.* New York: W. W. Norton. A third edition was published by W. W. Norton in 2002. Ecoff, N. L., Ekman, P., Mage, J. J. & Frank, M. G. 2000. "Lie detection and language loss." *Nature*, 405: 139. Frank, M. G. & Ekman, P. (submitted). "Appearing truthful generalizes across different deception situations." Bugental, D. B., Shennum, W., Frank, M. & Ekman, P. 2000. "'True Lies': Children's abuse history and power attributions as influences on deception detection." In V. Manusov & J. H. Harvey (eds.), *Attribution, Communication Behavior, and Close Relationships.* Cambridge: Cambridge University Press. See pages 248–65. Ekman, P., O'Sullivan, M. & Frank, M. 1999. "A few can catch a liar." *Psychological Science*, 10: 263–66. Ekman, P. 1997. "Lying and Deception." In N. L. Stein, P. A. Ornstein, B. Tversky, & C. Brainerd (eds.), *Memory for Everyday and Emotional Events.* Hillsdale, N.J.: Lawrence Erlbaum Associates. See pages 333–47. Frank, M. G. & Ekman, P. 1997. "The ability to detect deceit generalizes across different types of high-stake lies." *Journal of Personality and Social Psychology*, 72: 1429–39.

18. The participants at this meeting were: Richard Davidson, Paul Ekman, Owen Flannagen, Daniel Goleman, Mark Greenberg, Thupten Jinpa, Matthieu Ricard, Jeanne Tsai, Francisco Varela, and B. Alan Wallace.

19. Thanks to the Mind Life Foundation for inviting me to participate in this meeting, especially to Adam Engle, Richard Davidson, and Dan Goleman.

20. LeDoux, J. E. 1996. *The Emotional Brain: The Mysterious Underpinnings of Emotional Life.* New York: Simon and Schuster. Pankssepp, J. 1998. *The Foundations of Human and Animal Emotions.* New York: Oxford University Press. Damasio, A. R. 1994. *Descartes' Error: Emotion, Reason and the Human Brain.* New York: Putnam. Rolls, E. T. 1999. *The Brain and Emotion.* New York: Oxford University Press.

2: When Do We Become Emotional?

1. Unlike psychologists in other fields, those who study emotion recognize the importance of automatic processes, although a few emotion theorists still cling to the notion that we consciously decide when we will become emotional.

2. Goldie, P. 2000. *The Emotions.* Oxford: Oxford University Press. See page 47.

3. Boucher, J. D. & Brandt, M. E. 1981. "Judgment of emotion: American and Malay antecedents." *Journal of Cross-Cultural Psychology*, 12: 272–83.

4. Scherer, K. R., Wallbott, H. G. & Summerfield, A. B. (eds.) 1986. *Experiencing Emotion: A Cross-cultural Study*. Cambridge: Cambridge University Press.

5. Richardson, P. J. & Boyd, R. 2002. "Culture is part of human biology: Why the superorganic concept serves the human sciences badly." In M. Goodman & A. S. Morrat (eds.), *Probing Human Origins*. Cambridge, Mass: American Academy of Arts and Sciences.

6. Ekman, P. & Friesen, W. V. 1975. *Unmasking the Face: A Guide to Recognizing Emotions from Facial Clues*. Upper Saddle River, N.J.: Prentice Hall.

7. Lazarus, R. 1991. *Emotion and Adaptation*. New York: Oxford.

8. This phrase is Magda Arnold's. Arnold, M. (ed.). 1970. *Feelings and Emotions*. New York: Academic Press. See chapter 12.

9. Levenson, R. W., Ekman, P., Heider, K. & Friesen, W. V. 1992. "Emotion and autonomic nervous system activity in the Minangkabau of West Sumatra." *Journal of Personality and Social Psychology*, 62: 972–88. Levenson, R. W., Carstensen, L. L., Friesen, W. V. & Ekman, P. 1991. "Emotion, physiology, and expression in old age." *Psychology and Aging*, 6: 28–35. Levenson, R. W., Ekman, P. & Friesen, W. V. 1990. "Voluntary facial action generates emotion-specific autonomic nervous system activity." *Psychophysiology*, 27: 363–84. Ekman, P., Levenson, R. W. & Friesen, W. V. 1983. "Autonomic nervous system activity distinguishes between emotions." *Science,* 221: 1208–10. Ax, A. F. 1953. "The physiological differentiation between fear and anger in humans." *Psychosomatic Medicine,* 15: 433–42.

10. Frijda, Lazarus, and Scherer all agree with this view. See Scherer, K. R., Schoor, A. & Johnstone, T. 2001. *Appraisal Processes in Emotion*. New York: Oxford University Press.

11. Ohman, A. 1993. "Fear and anxiety as emotional phemonena: Clinical phenomenology, evolutionary perspectives, and information processing." In M. Lewis & J. Haviland (eds.), *The Handbook of Emotions*. New York: The Guilford Press. See pages 511–36.

12. Note that not all scientists accept Ohman's interpretation of his findings. For a good review of the counter interpretations, see Mineka, S. & Cook, M. 1993. "Mechanisms involved in the observational conditioning of fear." *Journal of Experimental Psychology,* 122: 3–38.

13. Darwin, C. 1998. *The Expression of the Emotions in Man and Animals*. 3rd edition. New York: Oxford University Press. See page 43.

14. I am grateful to Toobey and Cosmides's writings about emotion for emphasizing this point. Cosmides, L. & Tooby, J. 2000. "Evolutionary psychology and the emotions." In M. Lewis and J. M. Haviland-Jones (eds.), *The Handbook of Emotions*. 2nd edition. New York: The Guilford Press. See pages 91–115.

15. Magda Arnold's concept of "affective memory" and how it operates is very similar, but she did not emphasize, as I do, that some of what is stored is given not learned.

16. Mayr, E. 1974. "Behavior programs and evolutionary strategies." *American Scientist*, 62: 650–59.

17. Frijda, N. H. 1986. *The Emotions*. Cambridge: Cambridge University Press. See page 277.

18. I am indebted to Phil Shaver for reminding me that Tom Scheff has treated this matter extensively in his book. Scheff, T. 1979. *Catharsis in Healing, Ritual, and Drama*. Berkeley, Calif.: University of California Press.

19. I am grateful to Nico Frijda for reminding me of this.

20. Ekman, P. & Friesen, W. V. 1978. *Facial Action Coding System: A Technique for the Measurement of Facial Movement*. Palo Alto, Calif.: Consulting Psychologists Press.

21. Levenson et al., "Emotion and autonomic nervous system activity in the Minangkabau of West Sumatra." Levenson et al., "Emotion, physiology, and expression in old age." Levenson, Ekman & Friesen, "Voluntary facial action generates emotion-specific autonomic nervous system activity." Ekman, Levenson & Friesen, "Autonomic nervous system activity distinguishes between emotions."

22. Ekman, P. & Davidson, R. 1994. *The Nature of Emotion: Fundamental Questions*. New York: Oxford University Press. For more detailed discussion, see the following articles: Ekman, P. & Davidson, R. J. 1993. "Voluntary smiling changes regional brain activity." *Psychological Science*, 4: 342–45. Davidson, R. J., Ekman, P., Saron, C., Senulis, J. & Friesen, W. V. 1990. "Emotional expression and brain physiology I: Approach/withdrawal and cerebral asymmetry." *Journal of Personality and Social Psychology*, 58: 330–41. Ekman, P., Davidson, R. J. & Friesen, W. V. (1990). "Emotional expression and brain physiology II: The Duchenne smile." *Journal of Personality and Social Psychology*, 58: 342–53.

3: Changing What We Become Emotional About

1. I am grateful to Peter Goldie for drawing my attention to this example described by David Hume.

2. My thinking on this issue was sharpened by the discussion of my ideas at a meeting with His Holiness, the Dalai Lama about destructive emotions in March 2000. See the recent book by Daniel Goleman about this meeting. 2003. *Destructive Emotions: How Can We Overcome Them?*. New York: Bantam Books. I am especially grateful to Alan Wallace for the problems he raised about my earlier formulation.

3. LeDoux, J. E. 1996. *The Emotional Brain: The Mysterious Underpinnings of Emotional Life*. New York: Simon and Schuster. See page 204.

4. Ibid. See page 146.

5. LeDoux notes that Donald Hebb first introduced this term in his book *The Organization of Behavior*. 1949. New York: John Wiley & Sons.

6. Davidson, R. J. Forthcoming. "Affective style, psychopathology and resilience: Brain mechanisms and plasticity." *American Psychologist*.

7. Ekman, P. & Davidson, R. (eds.). 1994. *The Nature of Emotion: Fundamental Questions.* New York: Oxford University Press.

8. Lazarus, R. 1991. *Emotion and Adaptation.* New York: Oxford University Press. Gross, J. J. 1998. "Antecedent- and response-focused emotion regulation: Divergent consequences for experience, expression and physiology." *Journal of Personality and Social Psychology,* 74: 224–37. Gross, J. J. 1998. "The emerging field of emotion regulation: An integrative review." *Review of General Psychology,* 2: 271–99.

9. For further discussion of this technique, see Gross, "The emerging field of emotion regulation."

10. Segal, Z. V., Williams, J. M. G. & Teasdale, J. D. 2002. *Mindfulness-based Cognitive Therapy for Depression: A New Approach to Preventing Relapse.* New York: The Guilford Press.

11. For a number of different views on mood and emotion, see chapter 2 in Ekman, P. and Davidson, R. J. (eds.). 1994. *The Nature of Emotion.*

12. I thank Jenny Beers for suggesting this to me.

4: Behaving Emotionally

1. I am indebted here to Peter Goldie's discussion of this topic in his book *The Emotions.* 2000. New York: Oxford University Press. See page 113.

2. Ekman, P. 1985. *Telling Lies: Clues to Deceit in the Marketplace, Marriage, and Politics.* New York: W. W. Norton. The third edition was published by W. W. Norton in 2002.

3. Gottman J. M. & Levenson R. W. 1999. "How stable is marital interaction over time?" *Family Processes,* 38: 159–65.

4. For a discussion of Othello's error in the context of suspecting a lie, see my book *Telling Lies.*

5. Scherer, K., Johnstone, T. & Klasmeyer G. Forthcoming. "Vocal Expression of Emotion." In R. Davidson, H. Goldsmith & K. R. Scherer (eds.), *Handbook of Affective Science.* New York: Oxford University Press.

6. Ekman, P., O'Sullivan, M. & Frank, M. 1999. "A few can catch a liar." *Psychological Science,* 10: 263–66. Ekman, P. & O'Sullivan, M. 1991. "Who can catch a liar?" *American Psychologist,* 46: 913–20.

7. Banse, R. & Scherer, K. R. 1996. "Acoustic profiles in vocal emotion expression." *Journal of Personality and Social Psychology,* 70: 614–36.

8. Frijda's description of the actions that characterize each emotion includes what I have said and quite a bit more. I believe it is only these rudimentary, initial postural moves that are inbuilt, automatic, and universal.

9. Levenson, R. W., Ekman, P., Heider, K. & Friesen, W. V. 1992. "Emotion and autonomic nervous system activity in the Minangkabau of West Sumatra." *Journal of Personality and Social Psychology,* 62: 972–88. Levenson, R. W., Carstensen, L. L., Friesen, W. V. & Ekman, P. 1991. "Emotion, physiology, and expression in old age." *Psychology and Aging,* 6: 28–35. Levenson, R. W., Ekman, P. & Friesen, W. V. 1990. "Voluntary facial action generates emotion-

specific autonomic nervous system activity." *Psychophysiology,* 27: 363–84. Ekman, P., Levenson, R. W. & Friesen, W. V. 1983. "Autonomic nervous system activity distinguishes between emotions." *Science,* 221: 1208–10.

10. Stein, N. L., Ornstein, P. A., Tversky, B. & Brainerd, C. (eds.). 1997. *Memory for Everyday and Emotional Events.* Mahwah, N.J.: Lawrence Erlbaum Associates.

11. Davidson, R. J., Jackson, D. C. & Kalin, N. H. 2000. "Emotion, plasticity, context and regulations. Perspectives from affective neuroscience." *Psychological Bulletin,* 126: 890–906.

12. Gross describes front-end regulation, but he is not focusing on this involuntary, near-instantaneous regulation that Davidson proposes. Instead he is looking at more deliberately imposed attempts to reinterpret what is occurring. Gross, J. J. 1998. "Antecedent- and response-focused emotion regulation: Divergent consequences for experience, expression and physiology." *Journal of Personality and Social Psychology,* 74: 224–37. Gross, J. J. 1998. "The emerging field of emotion regulation: An integrative review." *Review of General Psychology,* 2: 271–99.

13. Greenberg, M. T. & Snell, J. L. 1997. "Brain development and emotional development: The role of teaching in organizing the frontal lobe." In P. Salovey & D. J. Sluyter (eds.), *Emotional Development and Emotional Intelligence.* New York: Basic Books.

14. Zajonc, R. B. 2001. "Emotion." In D. T. Gilbert, S. T. Fisk, & G. Lindzey. (eds.), *The Handbook of Social Psychology.* Vol. 1. 4th edition. Boston: McGraw-Hill. See pages 591–632.

15. It is more popular today to use connectionist models. I don't disagree with those formulations, but they are more difficult to understand, and for my purposes here I believe the computer metaphor of a program and instructions is more useful.

16. Mayr, E. 1974. "Behavior programs and evolutionary strategies." *American Scientist,* 62: 650–59.

17. I do not believe this is all apparent in the first day of life, but agree with the findings of Linda Camras and Harriet Oster that these emerge gradually as the infant develops. Camras, L., Oster, H., Campos, J., Miyake, K. & Bradshaw, D. 1992. "Japanese and American infants' responses to arm restraint." *Developmental Psychology,* 28: 578–82. Also, Rosenstein, D. & Oster, H. 1988. "Differential facial responses to four basic tastes in newborns." *Child Development,* 59: 1555–68.

18. Heim, C., Newport, D. J., Heit, S., Graham, Y. P., Wilcox, M., Bonsall, R., Miller, A. H. & Nemeroff, C. B. 2000. "Pituitary-adrenal and autonomic responses to stress in women after sexual and physical abuses in childhood." *Journal of the American Medical Association,* 284: 592–97.

19. Wallace, A. 1993. *Tibetan Buddhism, from the Ground Up.* Boston: Wisdom Publications. See page 103.

20. Ibid. See page 132.

21. Nigro, G. & Neisser, U. 1983. "Point of view in personal memories." *Cognitive Psychology,* 15: 467–82.

22. Langer, E. 2002. "Well-Being, Mindfulness versus Positive Evaluation." In C. R. Snyder & S. J. Lopez (eds.), *The Handbook of Positive Psychology*. New York: Oxford University Press.
23. Wyner, H. Unpublished. "The Defining Characteristics of the Healthy Human Mind."
24. I am grateful to Dan Goleman for suggesting this terminology to make clear my thinking about this.
25. Goldie, *The Emotions*. See page 65.
26. Schooler, J. W. 2001. "Discovering memories of abuse in light of meta-awareness." *Journal of Aggression, Maltreatment and Trauma*, 4: 105–36.

5: Sadness and Agony

1. We used the word *distress* instead of *agony*, but subsequent research suggested that distress covers more than agony; there is a fear element as well. Ekman, P. & Friesen, W. V. 1975. *Unmasking the Face: A Guide to Recognizing Emotions from Facial Clues*. Upper Saddle River, N.J: Prentice Hall.
2. Rynearson, E. K. 1981. "Suicide internalized: An existential sequestrum." *American Journal of Psychiatry*, 138: 84–87.
3. Vingershoets, A. J. J. M., Cornelius, R. R., Van Heck, G. L. & Becht, M. C. 2000. "Adult crying: A model and review of the literature." *Review of General Psychology*, 4: 354.
4. Ekman, P., Matsumoto, D. & Friesen, W. V. 1997. "Facial expression in affective disorders." In P. Ekman & E. L. Rosenberg (eds.), *What the Face Reveals: Basic and Applied Studies of Spontaneous Expression Using the Facial Action Coding System (FACS)*. New York: Oxford University Press. My first research grant supported my studies of patients with mental disorders, but at that time I had no way to measure facial behavior and so focused simply on body movements. The results I described here were obtained twenty years later, after we had developed the Facial Action Coding System described in chapter 1. In the mid-1960s, influenced by Silvan Tomkins, and with the funding to do cross-cultural research, I left the study of psychiatric patients to focus on emotions themselves, rather than emotional disorders. When I turned away from studying mental patients, we had neither the tools nor the basic knowledge about emotion to do research on severely disturbed patients. Fortunately, a number of investigators, using our Facial Action Coding System and other tools for measuring patients' facial and vocal expressions, are now doing such work; a number of examples are reported in *What the Face Reveals*.

6: Anger

1. Sternberg, C. R., & Campos, J. J. 1990. "The development of anger expressions in infancy." In N. L. Stein, B. Leventhal, & T. Trabasso (eds.), *Psychological and Biological Approaches to Emotions*. Hillsdale, N.J.: Lawrence Erlbaum Associates. See pages 247–82.

2. Berkowitz, L. 1969. "The frustration-aggression hypothesis revisited." In L. Berkowitz (ed.), *Roots of Aggression*. New York: Atherton Press. See pages 1–28.

3. My daughter Eve asked His Holiness, the Dalai Lama why we get angry with those we love, and he offered this explanation.

4. For an interesting discussion of the costs from an evolutionary viewpoint, see McGuire, M. & Troisi, A. 1990. "Anger: An evolutionary view." In R. Plutchik & H. Kellerman (eds.), *Emotion, Psychopathology and Psychotherapy*. New York: Academic Press.

5. Joseph Campos, University of California, Berkeley, and Mark Greenberg, Pennsylvania State University. 2000. Personal communication.

6. Holden, C. 2000. "The violence of the lambs." *Science,* 289: 580–81.

7. Konner, M. 2001. *The Tangled Wing: Biological Constraints on the Human Spirit.* 2nd edition. New York: Henry Holt. See chapter 9.

8. For a discussion of the role of genetic inheritance and environment in aggressive behavior, see Plomin, R., Nitz, K. & Rowe, D. C. 1990. "Behavioral genetics and aggressive behavior in childhood." In M. Lewis & S. Miller (eds.), *Handbook of Developmental Psychopathology*. New York: Plenum. Also see Miles, D. R. & Carey, G. 1997. "Genetic and environmental architecture of human aggression." *Journal of Personality and Social Psychology,* 72: 207–17.

9. Dalai Lama. Personal communication, 2001. See also Goleman, D. 2003. *Destructive Emotions: How Can We Overcome Them?.* New York: Bantam Books.

10. Tavris, C. 1989. *Anger: The Misunderstood Emotion.* New York: Touchstone Books.

11. Ibid. See pages 125–27.

12. McGuire and Troisi, "Anger."

13. Lemerise, E. & Dodge, K. 2000. "The development of anger and hostile interactions." In M. Lewis & J. Haviland-Jones (eds.), *Handbook of Emotions.* 2nd edition. New York: The Guilford Press. See pages 594–606.

14. McGuire and Troisi, "Anger."

15. Gottman, J. M. & Levenson, R. W. 1999. "How stable is marital interaction over time?" *Family Processes,* 38: 159–65.

16. Lazarus, R. 1991. *Emotion and Adaptation.* New York: Oxford University Press.

17. Goleman, *Destructive Emotions.*

18. See Izard, C. 1972. *Patterns of Emotions.* San Diego, Calif.: Academic Press. On depression and anger, see Harmon-Jones, E. "Individual differences in anterior brain activity and anger: Examining the roles of attitude toward anger and depression." Under review.

19. Harmon-Jones, "Individual differences."

20. Chesney, M. A., Ekman, P., Friesen, W. V., Black, G. W. & Hecker, M. H. L. 1990. "Type A behavior pattern: Facial behavior and speech components." *Psychosomatic Medicine,* 53: 307–19.

21. Rosenberg, E. L., Ekman, P., Jiang, W., Babyak, M., Coleman, R. E., Han-

son, M., O'Connor, C., Waugh, R. & Blumenthal, J.A. 2001. "Linkages between facial expressions of emotion in transient myocardial ischemia." *Emotion,* 1: 107–15. Rosenberg, E.L., Ekman, P. & Blumenthal, J.A. 1998. "Facial expression and the affective component of cynical hostility." *Health Psychology,* 17: 376–80.

22. Barefoot, J.C., Dahlstrom, W.G. & Williams, R.B. 1983. "Hostility, CHD incidence, and total mortality: A 25-year follow-up study of 255 physicians." *Psychosomatic Medicine,* 45: 59–63. Williams, R.B., Haney, L.T., Lee, K.L., Kong, Y., Blumenthal, J. & Whalen, R. 1980. "Type A behavior, hostility, and coronary atherosclerosis." *Psychosomatic Medicine,* 42: 539–49. Ironson, B., Taylor, C.B., Boltwood, M., Bartzokis, T., Dennis, C., Chesney, M., Spitzer, S. & Segall, G.M. 1992. "Effects of anger on left ventricular ejection fraction in coronary artery disease." *American Journal of Cardiology,* 70: 281–85. Mittleman, M.A., Maclure, M., Sherwood, J.B., Mulry, R.P., Tofler, G.H., Jacobs, S.C., Friedman, R., Benson, H. & Muller, J.E. 1995. "Triggering of acute myocardial onset by episodes: Determinants of myocardial infarction onset study investigators." *Circulation,* 92: 1720–25. Rosenberg, "Linkages."

23. Ekman, P. 1979. "About brows: Emotional and conversational signals." In M. von Cranach, K. Foppa, W. Lepenies, & D. Ploog (eds.), *Human Ethology.* New York: Cambridge University Press. See pages 169–248.

24. See Helena Cronin's excellent book, *The Ant and the Peacock: Altruism and Sexual Selection from Darwin to Today.* 1991. New York: Cambridge University Press.

25. Correctional Service of Canada report, as cited by Gayla Swihart, John Yuille, & Stephen Porter in *The Role of State-Dependent Memory in "Red-Outs."*

26. Laura Helmuth's report of the findings of University of New Hampshire sociologist Murray Straus in Helmuth, L. 2000. "Has America's tide of violence receded for good?" *Science,* 289: 585.

27. Davidson, R.J., Putnam, K.M. & Larson, C.L. 2000. "Dysfunction in the neural circuitry of emotion regulation—a possible prelude to violence." *Science,* 289: 591–94.

28. Raine, A. 1970. "Antisocial behavior in psychophysiology: A biosocial perceptual and a prefrontal dysfunction hypothesis." In D.M. Stoff, J. Breiling, & J.D. Maser (eds.), *The Handbook of Antisocial Behavior.* New York: John Wiley & Sons. See pages 289–303.

29. See Michael Rutter's discussion of findings by other investigators on adolescent-limited and adolescent-onset delinquency in the introduction to his *Genetics of Criminal and Antisocial Behavior.* 1996. New York: John Wiley & Sons.

30. American Psychiatric Association. 1994. "Intermittent explosive disorder." In *Diagnostic and Statistical Manual of Mental Disorders: DSM-IV.* Washington, D.C.: American Psychiatric Association. See pages 627–30.

31. For overviews on many of these issues, see the special section in the July 28, 2000, *Science* magazine [289 (28): 569–94]. Also for a good compilation of

different approaches to antisocial behavior, see Stoff, D. M., Breiling, J. & Maser, J. D. 1997. *The Handbook of Antisocial Behavior.* New York: John Wiley & Sons.

32. See Peter Goldie's interesting paper, "Compassion: A natural moral emotion." Forthcoming. In *Deutsche Zeitschrift fur Philosophie.*

7: Surprise and Fear

1. Ekman, P., Friesen, W. V. & Simons, R. C. 1985. "Is the startle reaction an emotion?" *Journal of Personality and Social Psychology,* 49(5): 1416–26.

2. Levenson, R. W., Ekman, P., Heider, K. & Friesen, W. V. 1992. "Emotion and autonomic nervous system activity in the Minangkabau of West Sumatra." *Journal of Personality and Social Psychology,* 62: 972–88. Levenson, R. W., Carstensen, L. L., Friesen, W. V. & Ekman, P. 1991. "Emotion, physiology, and expression in old age." *Psychology and Aging,* 6: 28–35. Levenson, R. W., Ekman, P. & Friesen, W. V. 1990. "Voluntary facial action generates emotion-specific autonomic nervous system activity." *Psychophysiology,* 27: 363–84. Ekman, P., Levenson, R. W. & Friesen, W. V. 1983. "Autonomic nervous system activity distinguishes between emotions." *Science,* 221: 1208–10.

3. This would be predicted by psychologist Leonard Berkowitz's theory, in which he maintains that the aversive events can result in either anger or fear, depending upon situational influences, prior learning, and inherited dispositions. Berkowitz, L. 1999. "Disgust: The body and soul emotion." In T. Dalglish & M. J. Power (eds.), *Handbook of Cognition and Emotion.* Chichester, U.K.: John Wiley & Sons. See pages 429–46.

4. I rely here on Rhudy and Meagher's study of fear and anxiety, although I am imposing my own terminology in describing their findings, and the findings of others they report. Rhudy, J. L. & Meagher, M. W. 2000. "Fear and anxiety: Divergent effects on human pain thresholds." *Pain,* 84: 65–75.

5. Ibid.

6. Schmidt, L. A. & Fox, N. A. 1999. "Conceptual, biological and behavioral distinctions among different categories of shy children." In L. A. Schmidt & J. Sculkin (eds.), *Extreme Fear, Shyness, and Social Phobia: Origins, Biological Mechanisms, and Clinical Outcomes.* New York: Oxford University Press. See pages 47–66.

7. Ibid.

8. Kagan, J. 1999. "The concept of behavioral inhibition." In ibid. See pages 3–13.

9. Crozier, W. R. 1999. "Individual differences in childhood shyness: Distinguishing fearful and self-conscious shyness." Schmidt & Fox, "Conceptual, biological and behavioral distinctions." See pages 14–29 and 47–66.

10. I draw heavily here on Ohman's very interesting chapter. Ohman, A. 2000. "Fear and anxiety: Evolutionary, cognitive, and clinical perspectives." In M. Lewis & J. Haviland-Jones (eds.), *The Handbook of Emotions.* 2nd edition. New York: The Guilford Press. See pages 573–93.

11. See my discussion in Ekman, P. 1985. *Telling Lies*. New York: W.W. Norton. The third edition was published by W.W. Norton in 2001.

8: Disgust and Contempt

1. Ekman, P. & Friesen, W.V. 1975. *Unmasking the Face: A Guide to Recognizing Emotions from Facial Clues*. Upper Saddle River, N.J.: Prentice Hall. See pages 66–67.
2. As quoted by Miller, W.I. 1997. *The Anatomy of Disgust*. Cambridge, Mass.: Harvard University Press. See page 97.
3. Ibid. See page 22.
4. Ibid. See page 118.
5. Rozin, P., Haidt, J. & McCauley, C.R. 1999. "Disgust: The body and soul emotion." In T. Dalglish & M.J. Power (eds.), *Handbook of Cognition and Emotion*. Chichester, U.K.: John Wiley & Sons. See page 435.
6. The percentages don't add up to 100 percent because there were some unclassified responses.
7. Gottman, J.M. & Levenson, R.W. 1999. "How stable is marital interaction over time?" *Family Processes*, 38: 159–65. Gottman, J., Woodin, E. & Levenson, R. 2001. "Facial expressions during marital conflict." *Journal of Family Communication*, 1: 37–57.
8. Miller, *The Anatomy of Disgust*. See pages 133–34.
9. Ibid. See pages 137–38.
10. Nussbaum, M.C. 2000. "Secret sewers of vice: Disgust, bodies and the law." In S. Bandes (ed.), *The Passions of Law*. New York: New York University Press. See pages 19–62.
11. Ibid. See page 44.
12. Ibid. See page 47.
13. Ibid.
14. Levenson, R.W. & Reuf, A.M. 1997. "Physiological aspects of emotional knowledge and rapport." In W.J. Icles (ed.), *Empathic Accuracy*. New York: The Guilford Press. See pages 44–47.
15. Ekman, P. & Friesen, W.V. 1975. *Unmasking the Face*. See page 67.
16. Miller, *The Anatomy of Disgust*. See page 207.
17. Ibid. See page 221.
18. Phillips, M.L., Senior, C., Fahy, T. & David, A.S. 1998. "Disgust—the forgotten emotion of psychiatry." *British Journal of Psychology*, 172: 373–75.

9: Enjoyable Emotions

1. Buell, H. (ed.). 1999. *Moments*. New York: Black Dog and Leventhal. See page 108.
2. See, for example, Synder, C.R. & Lopez, S.J. (eds.). 2002. *The Handbook of Positive Psychology*. New York: Oxford University Press. For a critique of this work, see R. Lazarus. Forthcoming. "Does the positivity movement have legs?" *Psychological Inquiry*.

3. Fredrickson, B. L. & Branigan, C. 2001. "Positive emotions." In T. J. Mayne & G. A. Bonanno (eds.), *Emotions: Current Issues and Future Directions*. New York: The Guilford Press. See pages 123–51.

4. For discussion of humor, see Ruch. W. & Ekman, P. 2001. "The expressive pattern of laughter." In A. W. Kaszniak (ed.), *Emotion, Qualia, and Consciousness*. Tokyo: Word Scientific Publisher. See pages 426–43. Also see Bachorowski, J. & Owren, M. J. 2001. "Not all laughs are alike: Voiced but not voiced laughter readily elicits positive affect." *Psychological Science*, 12: 252–57.

5. Ekman, P. 1992. "An argument for basic emotions." *Cognition and Emotion*, 6: 169–200.

6. Keltner, D. & Haidt, J. Forthcoming. "Approaching awe, a moral, aesthetic, and spiritual emotion." *Cognition and Emotion*.

7. Thanks to Paul Kaufman, who noted I had left out this emotion.

8. I consulted another Italian expert on emotion, Pio Ricci Bitti, who confirms that *fiero* is probably the best word for what I am describing, although he mentions an alternative word, *appagato*. I chose fiero because the sound of it seems to fit better with the experience. But the word itself doesn't matter; what matters is to specify another different type of enjoyment.

9. Lewis, M. 2000. "Self-conscious emotions." In M. Lewis & J. Haviland-Jones (eds.), *The Handbook of Emotions*. 2nd edition. New York: The Guilford Press.

10. Rosten, L. 1968. *The Joys of Yiddish*. New York: Pocket Books. See page 257.

11. Ibid.

12. Haidt, J. 2000. "The positive emotion of elevation." *Prevention and Treatment*, 3.

13. Lazarus, R. & Lazarus, B. N. 2001. "The emotion of gratitude." Paper presented at a meeting of the American Psychological Association, San Francisco, Calif.

14. Smith, R. H., Turner, T. J., Garonzik, R., Leach, C. W., Vuch-Druskat, V. & Weston, C. M. 1996. "Envy and *Schadenfreude*." *Personality and Social Psychology Bulletin*, 22: 158–68, Brigham, N. L., Kelso, K. A., Jackson, M. A. & Smith, R. H. 1997. "The roles of invidious comparison and deservingness in sympathy and *Schadenfreude*." *Basic and Applied Social Psychology*, 19: 363–80.

15. Thanks to Jenny Beer for bringing this to my attention.

16. For a very interesting treatment of love, see Solomon, R. C. 1988. *About Love*. New York: Simon & Schuster. For a recent review of research on romantic love, which considers it to be an emotion, see Hatfield, E. & Rapson, R. J. 2000. "Love and attachment processes." In Lewis and Haviland-Jones, *The Handbook of Emotions*.

17. See the following articles: Diener, E. 2000. "Subjective well-being: The science of happiness and a proposal for a national index." *American Psychologist*, 55: 34–43; Myer, D. G. 2000. "The funds, friends, and faith of happy people." *American Psychologist*, 55: 56–67.

18. For review of this and related research, see Averill, J. R. & More, T. A. 2000.

"Happiness." In Lewis and Haviland-Jones, *The Handbook of Emotions.* See pages 663–76.

19. Ibid.

20. Peterson, C. 2000. "The future of optimism." *American Psychologist,* 55: 44–55.

21. For a recent review and new findings, see Danner, D. D., Snowdon, D. A. & Friesen, W. V. 2001. "Positive emotions in early life and longevity: Findings from the nun study." *Journal of Personality and Social Psychology,* 80: 804–13.

22. Peterson, "The future of optimism."

23. Ibid. See page 49.

24. Ekman, P. 1992. "An argument for basic emotions." *Cognition and Emotion,* 6: 169–200.

25. Frank, M. G., Ekman, P. & Friesen, W. V. 1993. "Behavioral markers and recognizability of the smile of enjoyment." *Journal of Personality and Social Psychology,* 64: 83–93. Frank, M. G. & Ekman, P. 1993. "Not all smiles are created equal: The differentiation between enjoyment and non-enjoyment smiles." *Humor,* 6: 9–26.

26. Duchenne de Boulogne, G. B. 1990. *The Mechanism of Human Facial Expression.* Translated and edited by A. Cuthbertson. New York: Cambridge University Press. (Original publication 1862.)

27. Ibid. See page 72.

28. Ekman, P., Roper, G. & Hager, J. C. 1980. "Deliberate facial movement." *Child Development,* 51: 886–91.

29. Darwin, C. 1998. *The Expression of the Emotions in Man and Animals.* 3rd edition. New York: Oxford University Press.

30. Ekman, P. & Friesen, W. V. 1982. "Felt, false and miserable smiles." *Journal of Nonverbal Behavior,* 6(4): 238–52.

31. Fox, N. A. & Davidson, R. J. 1987. "Electroencephalogram asymmetry in response to the approach of a stranger and maternal separation in 10-month-old children." *Developmental Psychology,* 23: 233–40.

32. John Gottman, University of Washington, Seattle. 2000. Personal communication.

33. Keltner, D. & Bonanno, G. A. 1997. "A study of laughter and dissociation: Distinct correlates of laughter and smiling during bereavement." *Journal of Personality and Social Psychology,* 4: 687–702.

34. Harker, L. & Keltner, D. 2001. "Expressions of positive emotion in women's college yearbook pictures and their relationship to personality and life outcome across adulthood." *Journal of Personality and Social Psychology,* 80: 112–24.

35. Konow, James D. & Earley, Joseph E., as reported in *The New York Times,* May 19, 2001, page 17.

36. Ekman, P., Davidson, R. J. & Friesen, W. V. 1990. "Emotional expression and brain physiology II: The Duchenne smile." *Journal of Personality and Social Psychology,* 58: 342–53.

37. Ekman, P. 1985. *Telling Lies: Clues to Deceit in the Marketplace, Marriage, and Politics.* New York: W. W. Norton. See page 153.

Conclusion: Living with Emotion

1. For other work on what I have called emotional profiles, see Hemenover, S. H. Forthcoming. "Individual differences in mood course and mood change: Studies in affective chronometry." *Journal of Personality and Social Psychology;* and Davidson, R. J. 1998. "Affective style and affective disorders." *Cognition and Emotion,* 12: 307–30.

2. For work on shame, see Scheff, T. 2000. "Shame and the social bond." *Sociological Theory,* 18: 84–98; also Smith, R. 2002. "The role of public exposure in moral and nonmoral shame and guilt." *Journal of Personality and Social Psychology,* 83(1): 138–59. On embarrassment, see Rowland, S. & Miller, I. 1992. "The nature and severity of self-reported embarrassing circumstances." *Personality and Social Psychology Bulletin,* 18(2): 190–98.

3. Keltner, D. 1995. "Signs of appeasement: Evidence for the distinct displays of embarrassment, amusement, and shame." *Journal of Personality and Social Psychology,* 68: 441–54. See my chapter challenging these findings in Ekman, P. 1997. "Conclusion: What we have learned by measuring facial behavior." In P. Ekman & E. L. Rosenberg (eds.), *What the Face Reveals.* New York: Oxford University Press. See pages 469–95.

4. To learn more about envy, see Salovey, P. (ed.). 1991. *The Psychology of Jealousy and Envy.* New York: The Guilford Press. Also see chapter 10 in the fascinating book by Ben Ze'ev, A. 2000. *The Subtlety of Emotions.* Cambridge, Mass.: MIT Press.

5. Davidson, R. J., Scherer, K. R. & Goldsmith, H. H. 2003. *Handbook of Affective Sciences.* New York: Oxford University Press.

Afterword

1. Goleman, D. 2003. *Destructive Emotions: How Can We Overcome Them?* New York: Bantam Books.

2. There has been virtually no research as yet on this matter. I base what I have said on talking to people who, from my personal experience, have impulse awareness. They report that it is not always possible for them.

3. I talked with Richard J. Davidson, a professor at the University of Wisconsin, and with His Holiness the Dalai Lama.

4. Bennett-Goleman, T. & the Dalai Lama. 2002. *Emotional Alchemy: How the Mind Can Heal the Heart.* New York: Three Rivers Press. Wallace, A. & Quirolo, L. (eds.). 2001. *Buddhism with an Attitude.* Ithaca, N.Y.: Snow Lion Publications. Kabat-Zinn, J. 1995. *Wherever You Go There You Are: Mindfulness Meditation in Everyday Life.* New York: Hyperion.

5. Ekman, P. 1985. *Telling Lies: Clues to Deceit in the Marketplace, Marriage, and Politics.* New York: W. W. Norton. The third edition was published by W. W. Norton in 2002.

6. Ekman, P. In preparation. *Reading Faces.* Princeton, N.J.: Educational Testing Service.

Appendix: Reading Faces—The Test

1. Bugental, D. B., Shennum, W., Frank, M. & Ekman, P. 2000. " 'True Lies': Children's abuse history and power attributions as influences on deception detection." In V. Manusov & J. H. Harvey (eds.), *Attribution, Communication Behavior, and Close Relationships*. Cambridge: Cambridge University Press. See pages 248–65.

2. Ekman, P., O'Sullivan, M. & Frank, M. 1999. "A few can catch a liar." *Psychological Science,* 10: 263–66. Ekman, P. & O'Sullivan, M. 1991. "Who can catch a liar?" *American Psychologist,* 46: 913–20.

Illustration Credits

Page 11: From *The Face of Man: Expressions of Universal Emotions in a New Guinea Village.* Copyright © 1980 Paul Ekman.

Page 12: From *The Face of Man: Expressions of Universal Emotions in a New Guinea Village.* Copyright © 1980 Paul Ekman.

Page 83: Bettye Shirley at press conference. Copyright © 1974 Associated Press. Reprinted by permission of AP/Wide World Photos.

Page 89: Refugee camp in Tuzla, Bosnia. Copyright © 1995 Luc Delahaye/Magnum Photos. Reprinted by permission.

Page 99: From *The Face of Man: Expressions of Universal Emotions in a New Guinea Village.* Copyright © 1980 Paul Ekman.

Page 111: Canadian demonstrators become violent. Copyright © Corbis/Bettman. Reprinted by permission.

Page 116: Maxine Kenny being restrained in courtroom. Copyright © 1998 Jay Racz/The Press-Enterprise. Reprinted by permission.

Page 137: From *The Face of Man: Expressions of Universal Emotions in a New Guinea Village.* Copyright © 1980 Paul Ekman.

Page 149: The fall. Copyright © 1979 Louis Liotta/*New York Post.* Reprinted by permission.

Page 152: Bus accident in Surabaya, East Java. Copyright © 1996 Jawa Pos Daily. Reprinted by permission.

Page 162: Accident at the roller derby. Copyright © 1973 Gene Kappock/*New York Daily News.* Reprinted by permission.

Page 163: Jack Ruby shoots Kennedy assassin Lee Harvey Oswald. Copyright © 1963 Robert H. Jackson/*Dallas Times-Herald.* Reprinted by permission.

Page 173: From *The Face of Man: Expressions of Universal Emotions in a New Guinea Village.* Copyright © 1980 Paul Ekman.

Page 191: Stirm family reunion. Copyright © 1973 Slava Veder/Associated Press. Reprinted by permission of AP/Wide World Photos.

Index

admiration, 195
Advanced Research Projects Agency (ARPA), 2
affect-about-affect, 69–70
affect programs, 65–66, 67–68, 69, 70, 71
affective style, 47–48, 81
aggressiveness, 130
agony, 82–109, 151, 158
  medications for, 87–88
  mood with, 159
  of strangers, 133
Allen, Woody, 103–4
Allport, Gordon, 174
amusement, 59, 148, 193, 198, 199, 200, 210
  with children, 202
  in grief, 85
  physical action with, 61
  smiles in, 204
Anatomy of Disgust, The (Miller), 175
ancestral past, 27, 29
Anga (people), 6
anger, xvi, xvii, 15, 109, 110–47, 158, 184, 190, 198
  acting on, 115
  and agony, 87
  bodily changes in, 26
  constructive, 122–23
  following contempt, 182
  control of, 118, 119, 138, 139, 141, 142
  cycle of, 111
  in depression, 93
  and disgust, 186, 187

in emotional disorders, 203
enjoying, 125
in husband/wife example, 54, 55, 68–69
experience of, 213
facial expression, 9*f,* 10, 12*f,* 58, 125
and fear, 154, 163, 164
function of, 42
getting out, 120
in grief, 84–85
and irritability, 50
love and, 201
managing, 121, 122, 123
message from, 124–25
and mood, 159
physical action with, 61
physiological changes in, 63
provocation, 119
recognizing in others, 135–42, 137*f,* 138*f,* 139*f,* 140*f,* 141*f*
recognizing in ourselves, 133–35
in refractory period, 40–41
response to, 143–47
signals, 56–57
subtle signs of, 138–42
surprise merges into, 148
useful/adaptive, 123–24
anger episodes, log of, 48
anger response system, 71–72, 114, 115
  individual differences in, 214
anger signs
  using information from, 142–47
anger theme, 46, 110–12
  learned, 25–26, 27, 40

angina, 127
anguish, xvi, xvii, 61, 143, 194
anhedonia, 203
annoyance, 115, 139, 182
anticipation, 79–80, 87, 157, 201
Antisocial Personality Disorder, 132
antisocial violence, 132–33
anxiety, 159
anxious moods, 159, 160
appraisal, 192, 216
    see also automatic appraisal
appraisal awareness, 74
apprehensive mood, 50
Aristotle, 53
assuming appearance of emotion, 35–37
attentiveness, xv, 75–81, 96, 115, 144, 218
    in anger, 120, 121
auditory pleasures, 192
automatic appraisal, 13, 48, 62, 65, 69
    affect programs, 68
    awareness of, 74
    modifying/canceling, 74
automatic appraising mechanisms
    (autoappraisers), 21, 22, 27, 29–30,
    31, 32, 35, 37, 38, 40
    sensitivity to triggers, 23–24, 25
automatic processing, 30–31
autonomic nervous system (ANS), 20, 36,
    63, 65, 66, 67, 215
awareness xvi, 21, 37, 65, 73, 74, 120,
    216, 218
awe, 194n, 195, 210

Bateson, Gregory, 2, 3
behavior, emotional, 13, 16, 19, 52–81,
    216
    in anger, 112
    controlling, 53–54, 77, 81
    destructive, 72
    learned and innate, 62, 71
    moderating, 53, 54, 77
    new, 70–71
    regretting, 53, 79–90
    regulation of, 63–65
behavior therapy, 49
behavioral science, 3n, 4
bipolar depression, 94
Birdwhistell, Ray, 2, 3–4, 6
birth of child, 201
bittersweet experiences, 105
blend(s), 69, 70, 105
    contempt/enjoyment, 186
    disgust/anger, 185–86
    in smiles, 211–12
blood flow to hands/legs, 20, 26, 63, 158

blood pressure, 68, 69, 127, 135
blue mood, 50, 93, 159
Blumenthal, James, 127
blushing, 63, 217
bodily changes, 15, 26
    in fear, 20, 21, 153–54, 161
    in sadness, 94–95
bodily movement, responses involving,
    71
Boucher, Jerry, 22–23
brain, vital events stored in, 23–24
brain activity, 132, 156
brain changes, 15, 20, 21, 96
brain-imaging techniques, 18
brain injuries, 67
brain mechanisms of emotion, 16, 65–66
Brannigan, Christine, 192
Brazil, 3, 5
Buddhists, 15–16, 74, 180n

Calder, Andrew, 204
Campos, Joe, 114
Capriati, Jennifer, 195–96, 196f
cardiac activity, 63, 68
Carrey, Jim, 103–4
cell assembly, 43–45
changing/changes
    difficulty of, 218
    inescapable, 65
    what we become emotional about, 22,
    33, 38–51
cheeks
    in disgust and contempt, 186
    in sadness, 98, 106
    in smile, 206, 207, 208
children, 201–2, 219
    anger in, 114, 120
    and disgust, 174, 175
chin
    in fear and surprise, 162, 163
chin boss, 98, 99
choice
    about acting on emotion, 73, 74
    to control anger, 119
    in emotional behavior, 53, 80
Clinton, William, 92, 104, 141
cognitive empathy, 180
comfort, need for, 104, 106
comforting, 89, 90
compassion, 180
compassionate empathy, 180
concentration, 138, 139, 140, 142
conscious mind, 30, 31, 32
consciousness, 73, 74–75, 96
    of bodily feelings, 76

contempt, xvi, 151, 180–83, 190
  disdainful mood and, 50
  emotional disorders with, 182–83
  facial expression, 58, 170
  in hatred, 113
  in love, 202
  physical action with, 61
  recognizing in others, 183–86
  recognizing in ourselves, 183
contentment, 193, 199, 200, 202, 204
core disgust, 175, 176
core relational themes, 24
coronary artery disease, 126–28
Cronin, Helena, 130, 131
crow's-feet wrinkles, 183, 208
crying, 92, 98
cultural anthropology, 3–4
cultural differences
  in disgust, 174, 176
  regarding gratitude, 198
  in reaction to suffering, 179–80
  regarding subjective well-being, 202–3
  in triggers, 23
culture, 1–16, 91

Dalai Lama, 15–16, 32n, 53n, 74, 118,
  122, 180n
danger, 19–20, 155–56
Dani (people), 12–13
Darwin, Charles, 2, 3, 14, 28, 29, 100,
  136, 138, 195, 206, 217n
Dashiel, John, 8
David, A. S., 182
Davidson, Richard, 36, 64
death
  of child, 82–83, 95, 117, 119
  of family member, 119
  of loved one, 86–87
dehumanization, 178–79
density, 47
  and moods, 50, 51
depression, 88, 93–94, 125
  medications for, 87
  in sadness-agony, 129, 159
despair, xvii, 42, 99
destructive emotions, xv, 15, 32n
diary, emotion, 80
Diener, Ed, 202
disappointment, 111–12, 201
disdainful mood, xvii, 15, 33, 148, 151,
  172–80, 181–82, 190
  bodily changes in, 26
  and disdainful mood, 50
  emotional disorders with, 182–83

facial expression, 10, 12f, 58
fascination with, 175
with fear, 154
function of, 42
in hatred, 113
learned, 176
love and, 201, 202
physical action with, 61
recognizing in others, 183–86
recognizing in ourselves, 183
in smiles, 211–12
"Disgust—The Forgotten Emotion of
  Psychiatry" (Phillips, Senior, Fahy,
  and David), 182
displaced anger, 125
display rules, 4
Dole, Bob, 92
DSM-IV, 133
Duchenne de Boulogne, G. B., 204–6
Duchenne smile, 205f, 207–8, 207f, 212
duration of emotional response
  individual differences in, 214, 215

eating disorders, 183
ecstasy/bliss, 195, 199, 201, 204
Eibl-Eibesfeldt, Irenäus, 6
elevation, 198, 199, 200, 204
embarrassment, xvi, 137, 198, 217
emotion alert database, 29–30, 42, 43, 44,
  45, 66
  open, 44, 66, 176
emotion episode(s), xv, 216
  memory of, 20–21, 22
  reexperiencing past, 33–34
emotion structures, moods and, 51
emotional attachment, 113
emotional attitude, 113
emotional disorders, 92, 93, 125, 203
  with anger, 129, 130, 131, 132
  with disgust and contempt, 182–83
  with fear, 159–60
  with sadness and agony, 129
emotional empathy, 180
emotional profile, 215, 216
emotions, xiii, xv, xvi, 13
  beginning of, xiv, xvii, 21
  concealing, 68, 143
  controlled/controlling, 42, 52–53, 143
  at core of life, 42, 50
  across cultures, 1–16
  defining characteristics of, 216–17
  distinguishing from moods, 50–51
  inappropriate, 17–18, 21, 22, 29, 31,
    39, 41
  linking of second with first, 69–70

override knowledge, 38–39
rapid sequences, 69
when we become emotional, xiv–xv,
17–37
see also enjoyable emotions; experience
of emotions
empathy, 34–35, 37, 95, 96, 180
emphasis sign, 165–66
enjoyable emotions, 190–212
absence of, 203
motivate our lives, 199–200
not experienced, 197
enjoyment, xvi, 98, 99, 151, 190, 200
of anger, 125
and contempt, 186
facial expression, 9f, 11f
of fear, 158, 159
physical action with, 61
pursuit of, 200
recognizing in others, 204–12
of sadness, 97
smile signifying, 36, 212
envy, xvi, 217
euphoric/high mood, 50
evolution, 14, 25, 27, 43, 51, 55, 61, 65,
67, 88, 131, 176, 216, 217, 219
in emotional responses, 26–27
fear in, 27–28, 153–54
purpose of, 19, 20
exasperation, 112
excitement, 42, 193, 195, 199, 200, 201,
202, 210
and euphoric mood, 50
excessive, 203
and fiero, 196
smiles in, 204
expectations, 63, 65
experience of emotions, xvi–xvii, 216
differences in, 213–18
and emotional response, 28, 29, 30
reliving, 128–29
expression, emotional. *See* facial expressions
*Expression of the Emotions in Man and
Animals, The* (Darwin), 28, 100
extraversion, 203
eye muscle in smile, 205–7, 208, 211
eyebrows
in anger, 129, 134, 135, 137, 138, 139,
140, 146
in disgust and contempt, 185, 186
in fear and surprise, 161, 162, 163,
165–66, 167, 168
in sadness, 97–98, 100, 101, 102,
103–4, 105, 106
in smile, 206, 207, 208

eyelids
in anger, 129, 135, 139–40
in disgust and contempt, 184, 185–86
in fear and surprise, 160, 161, 162, 163,
164, 165, 167, 168
in sadness, 98, 102, 103, 106
in smile, 206, 211
eyes
glaring, 135, 136, 137
in surprise and fear, 164, 165, 167

face. *See* facial expressions
Facial Action Coding System (FACS),
14–15, 36, 126
facial expressions, xiv, xv–xvi, 14, 36, 53,
54, 55, 58, 67, 71, 126, 253
agony, 88
in anger, 120, 134–35, 138
atlas of, 14
changing appearance, 204–6
concealing, 220, 240
constructive, 53
cross-cultural studies of, 1–16
in depression, 94
duration of, 143
in enjoyable emotions, 193
erasing, 68
extreme, 151
in fear, 20, 157, 160–61
innate and universal, 2–4, 5–8, 10–14
interfering with, 62
interpreting, 8–9, 76
measuring, 2, 6, 14, 35–36
messages in, 91
number of, 14
producing emotional sensations,
36–37
reading: test, 219–40
regulating, 220
sadness, 88, 95–96, 97–106
signalling disgust, 184
as signals, 58–59, 60, 61
signs of surprise and fear in, 164–68,
164f, 165f, 166f, 167f, 168f
socially learned and culturally different,
2, 4, 5, 11, 12
subtle, 76, 218, 220
suppression of, 90–91
type A/B personality, 126
universality of, 2–4, 5–8, 10–14, 26,
36
wrong, 17
facial movements. *See* facial expressions
facial muscles. *See* facial expressions
Fahy, Tom, 182

false expression, 15
family relationships, 201–2
fear, xvi, xvii, 9, 15, 44, 152–60, 190
  and anger, 113, 125
  and apprehensive mood, 50
  bodily changes in, 26
  coping with, 156, 157
  core of, in pain, 158
  differs with threat, 156
  in emotional disorders, 203
  excitement and, 193
  facial expression, 9*f,* 10, 11, 20, 58
  factors in, 156–57
  function of, 42
  in grief, 85
  learned, 42–43
  loss of support theme for, 25
  moods/disorders/personalities, 159–60
  physical action with, 61, 62
  in physical threat, 110, 111
  physiological changes in, 63
  prepared by evolution for, 27–28
  recognizing in others, 162–68
  recognizing in ourselves, 160–62
  in refractory period, 40
  and relief, 194
  and sadness, 105
  sensations of, 20
  signs of, in face, 164–68, 164*f,* 165*f,*
    166*f,* 167*f,* 168*f*
  sources of, 57–58
  surprise merges into, 148
  trigger, 24
  and wonder, 194
fear affect program, 71
fear responses, learned, 70
fear themes, 28, 44
fed-up disgust, 177
fiero, 196–97, 199, 200, 201, 202, 203
  smiles in, 204
Fodor, Jerry, 39*n*
Fore people, 6–8
Frank, Mark, 204
Fredrickson, Barbara, 192
freeze or flee, 154, 156
Friesen, Wally, 5, 6, 14, 24, 35–36, 84, 126
Frijda, Nico, 30, 44*n,* 86*n*
frustration, 110, 112, 125
full expression, 220
functional Magnetic Resonance Imaging
  (fMRI), 18
fury, 151

Gajdusek, Carleton, 5, 6, 10
generating emotional experience, 37

genetic factors, 94, 117, 133
gesture, 2
glare, 126, 127*f,* 140, 163
Goffman, Erving, 90
Goldie, Peter, 22, 74
Gottman, John, 56, 121, 177, 180, 182,
  188
gratitude, 198, 199, 200, 201, 204
grief, 84–85, 86, 86*n,* 87, 99
grin-and-bear-it smile, 104, 210–11
guilt, xvi, 217
gustatory pleasures, 192

habits, 62, 81
Haidt, Jonathan, 194–95, 198
Hall, Edward, 2, 3
hand movements, 1–2
happiness, 59, 190, 202
  facial expression, 10, 58
  personality traits in, 203
hatred, xvi, 113, 118
heart attack, 127, 128
heart disease, risk for, 128, 159
heart rate, 20, 26, 63, 68, 69
  in anger, 25, 127, 135
  in fear, 158
Heider, Karl, 12–13, 150*n*
help, call for, 88, 89, 91, 113
hesitant smile, 209–10, 209*f*
hostile personality, 41, 159
hostility, 125–26, 128
hot triggers, 32, 34, 51
  anger, 112
  identifying, 75, 218
  weakening, 54, 71, 75
hubris, 197*n*
hunger drive, xvii
husband/wife interaction
  contempt in, 181
  disgust in, 177

imagination, 33–34
impulse awareness, 74
impulse to help, 89
impulse to hurt, 114–15
impulsive violence, 131–32
individual differences in emotional
  experience, 68, 213–18
infants, anger in, 110, 114
information
  access to, 77, 79
  contradictory, 40
  encapsulated, 39*n*
  inaccessible, 38–39
  incorporating new, 40–41

using, 106–9, 218, 220
using: anger, 142–47
using: disgust and contempt, 187–89
using: smiles, 212
using: surprise and fear, 169–71
initial emotional charge, 47
instrumental violence, 132
intensity, 117, 220
    in contempt, 181–82
    in fear, 156, 157, 165, 169
    in smiles, 204
    wrong, 17
interest, 193
indifference
    causing anger, 110–11, 112, 113, 125
Intermittent Explosive Disorder (IED),
    133
interpersonal disgust, 175, 176
intimacy, 125, 177–78
irritable mood, 49, 50, 51, 80
    and anger, 123, 125, 159
ischemia, 126–27, 128
Izard, Carrol, 3, 4

Japan/Japanese, 3, 4, 5, 12, 13, 176
jaw
    in anger, 135, 136, 140
    in fear and surprise, 161, 168
jealousy, xvi, 217
joy, 87, 92, 190

Kagan, Jerome, 159
Keltner, Dacher, 194–95, 217
Kenny, Don, 115, 117, 119
Kenny, Maxine, 115–19, 116f, 133, 136,
    140, 142
knowledge
    cannot override emotions, 38–39
Konner, Melvin, 114
kvell, 197

Langer, Ellen, 73
language, 13, 35
laws, disgust in, 178–79
Lazarus, Bernice, 198
Lazarus, Richard, 24, 29, 122, 198
leakage, 15
learning, 26
    from mistakes, 54
    regulation of emotions based on, 64
    see also species-constant learning
Leavelle, J. R., 163–64, 163f
LeDoux, Joseph, 42–43, 44, 51
Levenson, Robert, 33, 36, 56, 63, 177, 213
Lewis, Michael, 197n

Liotta, Lou, 148
lips
    in anger, 129, 135, 136, 137, 138,
        140–42, 146
    in disgust and contempt, 183, 184, 185,
        186
    in fear and surprise, 161, 163, 168
    in sadness, 98, 99, 104
    in smile, 207, 208, 211, 212
    in terror or fear, 162
living with emotion, 213–18
loss, 87
    experiencing, 97
    meaning of, 86, 88
    sadness and agony in, 23, 24, 83, 84,
        87–88
love, xvi, 201–2
lying, 15

McGuire, Michael, 112
Malaysia, 22–23
mania, 203
manic-depression, 94
Mayr, Ernst, 66
Mead, Margaret, 2, 3, 4, 6
medications, 87–88, 94
meditation, 49, 76n
melancholic personality, 93, 159
memory/memories, 20–21, 22, 37, 63
    in anger experience, 134
    of danger, 160
    in grief, 85
    retrieval of relevant, 65
    of sadness, 95
    as trigger, 32–33
    types of, 73–74
mental disorders, xvi, 30, 191
mental illness, 132
meta-consciousness, 74–75
micro expression, 15, 220, 239–40
Miller, William, 175, 176, 177–78, 181
Minangkabau (people), 36
mindfulness, 73
miserable smile, 210–11
mixed smiles, 211–12
mood(s), 69, 76, 81, 113, 193n
    emotions differ from, 50–51
    emotions in/and, xvii, 92–93, 125, 129,
        159
    related to disgust and contempt, 182
    related to enjoyable emotions, 202
moral judgment
    regarding disgust, 178, 179
morally repugnant behavior
    in disgust, 175, 176, 183

mourners
    conversing with deceased, 86–87
mourning, 84, 85, 87, 88
mouth
    in fear and surprise, 168
    in sadness, 104–5
muscle of difficulty, 138
muscles, 6, 151
    control over, 62, 71
    in facial movements, 26, 35–36
    see also facial muscles
Muskie, Edmund, 92

naches, 197, 199, 200, 202, 203, 204
nasolabial furrow, 106
natural selection, 26, 27, 28, 29, 30
near-miss car accident example, 19–21,
    40, 44–45, 71
negative emotions, xvii, 58–59, 158, 192
    contempt, 182
    using, 189
Neisser, Ulric, 73–74
nervous system, 44
    see also autonomic nervous system
    (ANS)
neurochemistry, changes in, 65*n*
New Guinea, 5, 6–8, 9–11, 13, 24, 83,
    85–86, 135–36, 137, 150*n*, 154, 172
    boy with sad expression, 99*f*, 100–1
Nigro, Georgia, 73–74
Nixon, Richard, 211, 211*f*
norm violations, 35, 37
nose
    in disgust and contempt, 183, 184, 185,
    186
Nussbaum, Martha, 178–79

obsessive compulsive disorder, 182
O'Connell, Charlie, 162, 162*f*
olfactory pleasures, 192
Ohman, Arne, 27–28, 153
optimism, 203
oral contamination theme, 175, 176, 183
oribicularis oculi muscle, 205–6, 211
Osgood, Charles, 2
O'Sullivan, Maureen, 175
Oswald, Lee Harvey, 163–64, 163*f*
Othello's error, 57, 169
other people
    call for help from, 88
    instructing us about what to be
        emotional about, 35, 37
    in meaning of loss, 86
    observing emotional feelings of, 76, 81
    recognizing anger in, 135–42

    recognizing disgust and contempt in,
        183–86
    recognizing enjoyment in, 204–12
    recognizing sadness in, 97–106
outrage, 178–79

pain, 153
    core of fear, 158
panic, 156, 158
panic attacks, 156, 157, 160
partial expression, 101, 220, 239–40
pathological anxiety, 160
paths for generating emotions, 19, 31–37
perplexity, 100, 138, 139, 140, 142
personality, 41, 70, 132
personality trait(s)
    in anger, 125–26, 127–28
    emotion control to, 92, 93
    and enjoyable emotions, 203
    hostility, 127–28
Peterson, Christopher, 203
Phillips, Mary L., 182
phobias, 159, 182–83
physical action, 61–62, 67, 68
physiological changes, 13, 15, 36, 37,
    68–69
    awareness of, 76
    with fear, 158
    producing visible signs, 62–63
    in response to facial movements, 96
    in sensory pleasures, 192
physiology of emotion, xiv
pleasure, 50, 85, 194
Poe, Edgar Allan, 37
Poggi, Isabella, 196
polite smile, 208, 212
positive emotions, xvii, 58, 153, 191
post-rationalizing, 22
posttraumatic stress disorder, (PTSD), 67,
    159–60
pout, 98, 104
premeditated violence, 131–32
preset actions/instructions, 63, 65, 219
pride, 196–97
psychoanalysis/psychoanalysts, 47, 65
psychology/psychologists, 4, 13, 30
psychotherapy/psychotherapists, 29, 42,
    48, 49, 87, 94
purchasing-power income, 202
Purloined Letter (Poe), 37

question-mark signal, 166

rage, 116, 117, 193
Reagan, Ronald, 210–11, 210*f*

reappraisal, 49, 75, 77, 79, 122
recovery time, 214
reevaluations, 69, 75
reexperiencing emotions, 34
referential expression, 129
reflective appraising, 24–25, 31–32, 37
reflective consciousness, 74
refractory period, 39–40
   attentiveness in, 81
   long, 39–41, 46, 47, 50, 53, 67, 69, 77,
      78, 79, 80, 145, 216, 240
   managing anger in, 122
rejection, 85
   and anger, 111, 112, 125
regulation, emotional, 63–64, 67
regulatory patterns, 64, 65, 67, 72
relationships, xiii, xvi, 201–2
   anger in, 116, 120, 121–22
   and sadness, 108, 109
   using information from expressions in,
      170–71, 187–89, 212
   and well-being, 203
relief, 59, 86, 87, 148, 193–94, 198, 199,
      200, 201, 202
   physical action with, 61
   physiological changes in, 63
   smiles in, 204
resentment, 112–13, 128, 198
respiration, 63, 68, 135, 195
responses/reactions, xv, 26–27, 29, 30–31,
      70
   changing, 17–18, 64
   controlling, 49
   event(s) and, 45–47
   individual differences in, 214–15
   involuntary, 51
   interrupting, 45
   learned, 44
   learning new, 176
   managing, xvi, 69
   signals triggering, 54
   speed and strength of, 48
   to suffering, 179–80
   unlearning, 71–72
restrained anger, 138, 138f
retribution, 130
reunions, 201
revenge, 112, 113, 119, 130
road rage, 46
romantic love, 201, 202
Rosenberg, Erika, 126–27
Rosten, Leo, 197
Rozin, Paul, 174, 175, 176, 177, 181
Ruby, Jack, 163, 163f, 164
Rynearson, Ted, 86

sadness, xvi, xvii, 8, 10, 11f, 15, 33,
      82–109, 143, 151, 158, 190
   blue mood and, 50
   bodily changes in, 26
   in emotional disorders, 203
   facial expression, 10, 11f, 15, 58
   function of, 42, 88
   loss trigger for, 23, 24
   medications for, 87–88
   and mood, 159
   physical action with, 61
   recognizing in others, 97–106
   recognizing in ourselves, 94–97
   of stranger(s), 133
sadness/anguish reaction, trigger for,
      32
sadness expression
   components of, 101–6, 101f, 103f,
      104f, 105f, 106f
   response to, 106–9
sadness signals, 56
   as cry for help, 113
schadenfreude, 199, 204
Schechner, Richard, 194
Scherer, Klaus, 23, 60
Schooler, Jonathan, 74–75
Scott, David Lynn, III, 115–16, 117, 118,
      119
Scott, Sophie, 204
script(s), 41–42, 45, 48, 49, 69, 76, 80
self-respect, 202–3
self-righteous anger, 112
Senior, Carl, 182
sensations, xvi, 75–76
   awareness of, 218
   angry, 133, 135
   with disgust and contempt, 182,
      183
   facial expressions producing,
      36–37
   in gratitude, 198
   pattern of, xv
   with sadness, 96–97
   with sensory pleasures, 192
   with wonder, 195
   in worry, 161–62
sensory pleasures, 42, 191–92, 198, 199,
      200, 203
   with children, 202
   physical action with, 61
   in sexual relations, 201
   smiles in, 204
sex, xvii, 158, 177, 201
Shakespeare, William, 57
shame, xvi, 217

Shirley, Bettye, 82–83, 83*f,* 84, 85, 87, 90,
    94, 95, 96, 97–98, 100, 103, 106,
    107, 160
shyness, 159
sights, enjoyable, 191, 192
signals, xv–xvi, 20, 54–61, 65, 217
    ability to recognize, 219
    of anger, 125
    enjoyable emotions, 204
    facial experience as, xv–xvi, 58–59, 60,
        61, 65
    gratitude, 198
    sensory pleasures, 192
    strength of, 215
    suppressing, 56
    universals in, 66–67
skin temperatures, 26, 63, 68
slight expression, 220, 239–40
smells, 173, 191–92
smiles/smiling, 94, 204–12, 205*f,* 207*f,*
    208*f,* 209*f,* 210*f,* 211*f,* 212*f*
    research on, 36–37
    in sadness, 98–99, 104, 105
social disgust, 176, 178
social phobias, 182–83
social smile, 206*n*
Sorenson, Richard, 10
Sorsby, Claudia, 194*n*
sounds of emotion, 84
    disgust, 173
    pleasurable, 191, 192
species-constant learning, 25, 26, 27
speed of emotional onset, 214, 215
startle reaction, 151, 163–64, 210
Stirm family, 190, 191*f,* 200–1
Stone Age cultures, 5–6, 24, 86
stonewalling, 56, 62, 121, 177
strength of emotional experiences, 58,
    214
    contempt, 181–82
    individual differences in, 214, 215
subjective well-being, 202–3
suffering, 89, 90, 95
    reaction to, 91–92, 179–80
sulking, 112
Surabaya truck photo, 151–52, 154, 160,
    162, 164
surprise, xvi, 10, 11, 58, 148–52, 198
    fixed, limited duration, 150–51
    physical action with, 61
    and sadness, 105
    signs of, in face, 164–68, 164*f,* 165*f,*
        166*f,* 167*f,* 168*f*
sweating, 20, 26, 63
symbolic gestures, 4

tactile pleasures, 61, 192
talking about past emotional experiences,
    34, 37, 128–29
tastes, 173, 174, 191, 192
Tavris, Carol, 119–20
tears, 92, 95
teasing (example), 45–49, 51
temperament, 64, 91
temperate person, 53
terror, 155, 157, 158, 161, 163, 164
    controlled, 165
    excitement and, 193
terror expression, 162
test (reading faces), xvi, 76, 219–40
themes, 24–26, 27, 28–29, 32, 81, 216
    anger, 110–12
    disgust, 174, 175, 176
    enjoyable emotions, 190, 201, 202
    evolution in, 26–27
    evolved, 38, 46
    fear, 152
    how acquired, 25–26
    are indelible, 43
    learned or inherited, 25–27, 29
    learning in, 29
    sadness, 97
    sensory pleasures, 192
    see also universal themes; variations
thoughts/thinking, 28, 55, 63, 198
threat of harm, 157–58
    and anger, 110–11, 112, 125
    in fear, 24, 152–53
    immediate/impending, 156, 157, 169
timing of fear, 156, 157
Tomkins, Silvan, xvii, 2–3, 6, 7, 59, 65,
    69, 70, 158, 192, 193, 200
touch, 191, 192, 204
triggers, xiv–xv, 17, 18, 30, 32, 75, 81,
    215, 218
    anger, 112, 213
    autoappraisers sensitivity to, 23–28
    behavioral patterns learned for dealing
        with, 67
    connection to cell assembly, 43–45
    cooling off, 34
    culture-specific/individual specific, 18
    disgust, 174, 175–76
    erasing, 42
    fear, 28–29, 152–53
    individual, 25
    learned, 29, 38, 43, 44, 46, 153, 192
    learned early in life, 29, 47
    learning new, 176
    moods and, 51
    resemblance to original situation, 46–47

sensory pleasures, 192
shared, 18
universal/individual-specific, 22, 23, 24
unlearned, 152–53
weakening, 45–51, 53, 78, 80
see also hot triggers
Troisi, Alfonso, 112
Tuzla refugees, 88–89, 89*f*, 92, 94, 98–99, 106, 107
Type A/B personality, 126, 140
types
in emotions, 58

unconditional stimulus, 27–28
United States, 3, 5, 22–23
universal themes. *See* themes
universals, 214
in disgust, 174
in emotion signals, 66–67
in facial expressions, 2–4, 5–8, 10–14, 26, 36
individual differences around, 213
triggers, 22, 23, 24
upsetting emotions, 191, 203
upward contempt, 188, 189

variations, 216
anger, 112
disgust, 176
enjoyable emotions, 202
fear, 152
learned, 29, 44, 153
sadness, 97
sensory pleasures, 192
unlearning, 43
Veder, Sal, 190
verbal abuse, 118, 129–30
violence, xvi, 71–72, 119, 129–33, 151
adaptive value in, 131

with anger, 159
capacity for, 114–15
causes of, 133
justified, 130–31
useful purpose of, 118
visual pleasures, 192
vital events, 29, 45–47
autoappraisers scanning for, 23–24
evolution and, 19–21
vocal expressions/voice, 36–37, 71
anger in, 120
control of, 68
emotion signals in, xv–xvi, 59–61, 65
enjoyable emotions, 193, 204
sadness and agony in, 88

Waal, Frans de, 175*n*
Wallace, B. Alan, 73
well-being, smiling in, 207
Western culture, 23, 92
Western facial expressions, 4
will to survive, xvii
Wilson, E. O., 28*n*
Wilson, Margaret Bush, 210, 210*f*
withdrawal, 90, 121, 177
witnessing someone else's emotional reaction, 34–35
wonder/wonderment, 61, 194–95, 199, 200, 201
smiles in, 204
Woodin, Erica, 177
words, 13–14, 83–84, 190–91, 199
worry, 158, 164, 168
sensations in, 161–62
sign of, 166, 169
Wyner, Henry, 74

Zajonc, Robert, 65
zygomatic major muscle, 205

About the Author

PAUL EKMAN, PH.D., is a professor of psychology in the Department of Psychiatry at the University of California Medical School, San Francisco. He has received many honors, most notably the Distinguished Scientific Contribution Award of the American Psychological Association in 1991, and an honorary doctor of humane letters from the University of Chicago in 1994. In a recent study of the most influential psychologists of the twentieth century, Ekman was listed among the top one hundred.

Ekman's interests have focused on nonverbal behavior and communication, specifically the expression and physiology of emotion as well as interpersonal deception. In the 1970s, Ekman and psychologist Wally Friesen developed a tool for measuring expressions in the face—the Facial Action Coding System—which is currently used by hundreds of scientists around the world. The author or editor of thirteen previous books, including *Telling Lies,* he is a frequent consultant on emotional expression to government agencies, such as the FBI, the CIA, and the ATF, to lawyers, judges, and police, and to corporations, including the animation studios Pixar and Industrial Light and Magic. He lives in Oakland, California.